ETA's Terrorist Campaign

This book analyses the rise and decline of the Basque terrorist group *Euskadi ta Askatasuna* (ETA, Basque Homeland and Freedom). ETA declared a unilateral ceasefire in November 2011, bringing to a close a campaign of political violence that started in the late 1960s. By the beginning of the twenty-first century, the overwhelming majority of secession supporters agreed that an independent Basque homeland would be realised through 'ballots' and not 'bullets'.

Providing an inter-disciplinary overview of radical Basque nationalism that pays special attention to the drivers for ETA's decline, defeat and disbandment, this book includes chapters by historians, political scientists and sociologists who offer three important theoretical and empirical contributions to the literature on nationhood and security studies. First, the book reassesses the military conflict that opposed ETA and the Spanish state, by paying special attention to tactical and strategic considerations as well as to the counter-terrorist policy itself. Second, it provides an original interpretation of the politics of fear which surrounded the process of victimisation, as well as assessing the extent to which the issue of violence led to the polarisation of citizens. Third, the authors examine the historical narratives and rituals that contributed to the production and reproduction of identity binaries and memories of war.

Arguing that the defeat of ETA must be contextualised within the strategic evolution of Basque nationalism, the declining resonance of the radical message and the effectiveness of the Spanish counter-terrorist effort, this book is essential reading for students and scholars working in the areas of European politics, nationalism and terrorism studies.

Rafael Leonisio is Postdoctoral Researcher at the University of the Basque Country, Spain.

Fernando Molina is tenured Research Fellow at the University of the Basque Country, Spain.

Diego Muro is Assistant Professor at the Institut Barcelona d'Estudis Internacionals (IBEI), Spain.

Routledge Studies in Extremism and Democracy

Series editors: Roger Eatwell
University of Bath
and
Matthew Goodwin
University of Kent.

Founding series editors: Roger Eatwell
University of Bath
and
Cas Mudde
University of Antwerp-UFSIA.

This new series encompasses academic studies within the broad fields of 'extremism' and 'democracy'. These topics have traditionally been considered largely in isolation by academics. A key focus of the series, therefore, is the (inter-)*relation* between extremism and democracy. Works will seek to answer questions such as to what extent 'extremist' groups pose a major threat to democratic parties, or how democracy can respond to extremism without undermining its own democratic credentials.

The books encompass two strands:

Routledge Studies in Extremism and Democracy includes books with an introductory and broad focus which are aimed at students and teachers. These books will be available in hardback and paperback. Titles include:

Understanding Terrorism in America
From the Klan to al Qaeda
Christopher Hewitt

Fascism and the Extreme Right
Roger Eatwell

Racist Extremism in Central and Eastern Europe
Edited by Cas Mudde

Political Parties and Terrorist Groups (2nd Edition)
Leonard Weinberg, Ami Pedahzur and Arie Perliger

The New Extremism in 21st Century Britain
Edited by Roger Eatwell and Matthew Goodwin

New British Fascism
Rise of the British National Party
Matthew Goodwin

The End of Terrorism?
Leonard Weinberg

Mapping the Extreme Right in Contemporary Europe
From Local to Transnational
Edited by Andrea Mammone, Emmanuel Godin and Brian Jenkins

Varieties of Right-Wing Extremism in Europe
Edited by Andrea Mammone, Emmanuel Godin and Brian Jenkins

Right-Wing Radicalism Today
Perspectives from Europe and the US
Edited by Sabine von Mering and
Timothy Wyman McCarty

Revolt on the Right
Explaining support for the radical right
in Britain
Robert Ford and Matthew Goodwin

Routledge Research in Extremism and Democracy offers a forum for innovative new research intended for a more specialist readership. These books will be in hardback only. Titles include:

ETA's Terrorist Campaign

From violence to politics, 1968–2015

**Edited by
Rafael Leonisio,
Fernando Molina
and Diego Muro**

Routledge
Taylor & Francis Group

LONDON AND NEW YORK

First published 2017
by Routledge
2 Park Square, Milton Park, Abingdon, Oxon OX14 4RN

and by Routledge
711 Third Avenue, New York, NY 10017

Routledge is an imprint of the Taylor & Francis Group, an informa business

British Library Cataloguing in Publication Data
A catalogue record for this book is available from the British Library

Library of Congress Cataloging in Publication Data
Names: Leonisio, Rafael, editor. | Molina Aparicio, Fernando, editor. | Muro, Diego, editor.
Title: ETA's terrorist campaign : from violence to politics, 1968–2015 / edited by Rafael Leonisio, Fernando Molina and Diego Muro.
Description: Abingdon, Oxon ; New York, NY : Routledge, 2017. | Series: Routledge studies in extremism and democracy
Identifiers: LCCN 2016009834| ISBN 9781138100145 (hardback) | ISBN 9781315657806 (e-book)
Subjects: LCSH: ETA (Organization)–History. | Terrorism–Spain–History. | Paâis Vasco (Spain)–History–Autonomy and independence movements. | Spain–Politics and government–1975–1982. | Spain–Politics and government–1982–
Classification: LCC HV6433.S72 E85625 2017 | DDC 363.3250946–dc23
LC record available at https://lccn.loc.gov/2016009834

ISBN: 978-1-138-10014-5 (hbk)
ISBN: 978-1-315-65780-6 (ebk)

Typeset in Times New Roman
by Wearset Ltd, Boldon, Tyne and Wear

Contents

Plates

Figures

Tables

Contributors

Martin Alonso is an independent researcher. He has a PhD in Political Science and a degree in Sociology, Philosophy and Psychology. He has focused his interest on the analysis of nationalist discourses, the rhetoric of identity and its relationship to political violence. Currently he is working on an essay about the pro-independence process in Catalonia.

Javier Argomaniz is Lecturer at the Handa Centre for the Study of Terrorism and Political Violence (HCSTPV), where he has published widely on state, non-state and civilian responses to political violence. His work has been published in *Terrorism and Political Violence, Studies in Conflict and Terrorism, Cooperation and Conflict, Intelligence and National Security* and a number of other peer-reviewed journals.

Francisco J. Caspistegui is Professor of Contemporary History at the University of Navarre and member of the Scientific Committee of the Carlism Museum. He has developed his research and teaching on twentieth-century history, with Carlism and Navarre as objects of special interest. He has also paid attention to the history of sport and the history of historiography.

Jesús Casquete is Professor of History of Political Theory at the University of the Basque Country. He has been invited researcher at several German institutions supported by the Foundation Alexander Humboldt. He is the author of several books, including *En el nombre de Euskal Herria. La religión política del nacionalismo vasco radical* (2009), *Políticas de la muerte* (2009, edited with Rafael Cruz) and *Diccionario ilustrado de símbolos del nacionalismo vasco* (2012, co-edited). He has published articles in the journals *Mobilization, Totalitarian Movements and Political Religions, Social Movement Studies*, and *Politics, Religion and Ideology*.

Luis Castells has been a full Professor of Contemporary History at the University of the Basque Country since 1993. In recent years his research has been focused on the question of memory and violence in the Spanish transition, and the process of nation-building in contemporary Spain. He is also a member of the scientific committee of the Research Project History and

Memory of Terrorism in the Basque Country, funded by the Victims of Terrorism Memorial located in Vitoria, Spain.

Gaizka Fernández holds a doctorate in History from the University of the Basque Country. He is a high school teacher at the Instituto de Educación Secundaria Ataulfo Argenta. His lines of research have centred on the study of terrorist violence and Basque nationalism. He has published four books and several articles in academic journals.

Javier Gómez is head of the Fernando Buesa Foundation Documentation Centre. He has a PhD in History (University of the Basque Country, UPV-EHU). He was Postdoctoral Fellow at the Centro de Investigação e Estudos de Sociologia (CIES-Instituto Universitário de Lisboa). His main research interests are collective memory, projects of nationalization, terrorism and political violence.

Óscar Jaime-Jiménez is tenured Professor in Political Science at the Public University of Navarre. He has also been a visiting researcher at Oxford University. He was Executive Adviser to the Spanish National Police Director General (2004–2012). He has been mainly working in several aspects related to anti-terrorist police response and the influence of political transitions on police organisations.

Rafael Leonisio is a postdoctoral researcher at the University of the Basque Country, Spain. His main areas of research are political parties, electoral behaviour and comparative politics. His work has been published in *Regional and Federal Studies*, *Revista Española de Investigaciones Sociológicas* and *Revista de Estudios Políticos*.

Raúl López holds a doctorate in History from the University of the Basque Country. He is the author of several books and journal articles about contemporary social movements and political violence in the Basque Country, Spain's transition to democracy, and Basque nationalism and socialism in the twentieth century. He has held visiting positions at the Queen's University of Belfast and at the University of Newcastle.

Fernando Molina is tenured Research Fellow in Contemporary History at the University of the Basque Country (Spain). His main research interests are nationalism and political violence, state nationalisation, biography and social economy. He has published a number of English and Spanish articles on these issues in journals such as *Ayer*, *Historia y Política*, *Journal of Contemporary History*, *Nations and Nationalism* or *European History Quarterly*, and collective books.

Diego Muro is Assistant Professor at the Institut Barcelona d'Estudis Internacionals (IBEI) and Research Associate at the Barcelona Centre for International Affairs (CIDOB). His main research interests are comparative politics, ethnic and nationalist conflict, and terrorism and counter-terrorism.

His work has been published in *Ethnic and Racial Studies*, *Ethnicities*, *Nations and Nationalism*, *South European Society aand Politics*, *Studies in Conflict and Terrorism* and *West European Politics*.

José Antonio Pérez is a research fellow at the University of the Basque Country. His main research interests are Social History in Francoist Spain and political violence in the contemporary Basque Country. He is a member of the Governing Board of the Valentin de Foronda University Institute of Social History. He is also the principal investigator of the Research Project 'History and Memory of Terrorism in the Basque Country', funded by the Victims of Terrorism Memorial located in Vitoria, Spain.

Antonio Rivera is full Professor of Contemporary History and main researcher of the Research Project 'Political Violence, Memory and Identity in the Basque Country'. He is also a member of the Scientific Committee of the Research Project 'History and Memory of Terrorism in the Basque Country', funded by the Victims of Terrorism Memorial located in Vitoria, Spain.

Acknowledgements

It is often said that editing a book is a challenging task. This was not the case for us. Our – perhaps unique – experience was that all our contributors met their deadlines and were happy to revise their pieces when we made comments and suggestions. We salute the authors' professionalism and dedication to this collective endeavour and are very grateful for their hard work and good temper. The only setback was that the son of Javier Gómez refused to come into this world at the time when he was expected. For reminding us all of what is important in life, we dedicate this book to little Diego.

We would also like to thank Routledge for keeping us on our toes and for providing professional guidance. We are grateful to Craig Fowlie for his early support of the project and Emma Chappell for her patience while waiting for the final typescript. We need to thank the photographic archives of the city of Bilbao, La Gaceta del Norte and El Correo for their kind permission to use the pictures reproduced in this volume. We are particularly grateful to Raúl López, Lourdes Ortega and Mauricio Martín for their assistance in this matter.

This book could have not been completed without the financial support of various institutions. Diego Muro acknowledges help from the 'Ways Out' project (CSO2012–35061) funded by the Spanish Ministry of Economy and Competitiveness (MINECO). Fernando Molina was aided by the Research Group on Basque Political and Social History (IT-708–13) funded by the Basque government as well as the MINECO-funded project (HAR2014–51956-P), and Rafael Leonisio thanks the Euskobarometro team and the Consolidated Research Group (IT-610–3) funded by the Basque government (2013–2018).

A final note of thanks goes to our families for graciously coping with life with three scholars. Without them, none of this would make sense.

Rafael Leonisio, Fernando Molina and Diego Muro
February 2016

Introduction

Rafael Leonisio, Fernando Molina and Diego Muro

The main goal of this book is to examine the rise and decline of the terrorist group *Euzkadi Ta Askatasuna* (ETA, Basque Homeland and Freedom). The Basque group was founded in 1959, and its campaign of political violence, extortion and threats lasted from 1968 until it finally declared a unilateral cessation of hostilities in 2011. In contrast to the copious literature on other violent ethno-nationalist campaigns (e.g. Northern Ireland, Kurdistan, Sri Lanka), much less has been published on the Basque terrorist campaign, although it resulted in 845 deaths. At the time of writing, ETA had not formally disbanded but few analysts believe that the group could restart its clandestine activities, mainly because of the absence of social support and the effectiveness of the counter-terrorist effort.

The defeat of ETA must be contextualised within the strategic evolution of Basque nationalism as a whole and the declining resonance of terrorism as the 'weapon of the weak'. By the beginning of the twenty-first century, the overwhelming majority of Basque secessionists had come to the conclusion that an independent state can be realised only through 'ballots', not 'bullets'. The lesson has also been learned by Catalan politicians and civil society organisations which actively pursued a peaceful secessionist agenda from 2010 onward. The loss of social support for the targeting of civilians caused a decline of social mobilisation in support of radical Basque nationalism and the eventual decline and defeat of ETA.

This book provides up-to-date scholarship on ETA in three key areas. First, by paying special attention to tactical and strategic considerations as well as to the counter-terrorist policy itself, it aims to deepen our understanding of the conflict between two actors with opposing and incompatible goals – ETA and the Spanish state. Second, the book offers an original and interdisciplinary understanding of the politics of fear that involved the process of victimisation as well as the polarisation of the citizenry around the divisive issue of violence. Third, the volume examines the historical narratives and rituals that contributed to the production and reproduction of identity oppositions and war memories. In order to deal with these areas of research systematically, the book has been organised into three thematic parts which contain similar numbers of chapters.

The volume provides an unusual equilibrium between historians, political scientists and sociologists with expertise on Basque politics and ETA. The overwhelming majority of these scholars have published their contributions in

Spanish and are not well known to an international audience; hence the need for this volume. Besides popularising the work of current experts on ETA for the global scholarly community, there is another reason for putting together this group of scholars, namely the need to move beyond parochial accounts of Basque violence. To date, much of the scholarly literature on ETA (both in Spain and abroad) has provided 'thick' historical overviews that have often treated the Basque case as something exceptional or even unique (see the Conclusion). It is the contention of the co-editors that terrorist campaigns may be best understood with the tools of historical and social research.

The contributors have been encouraged to provide comparative and theoretical approaches to the case under examination. Methodologically speaking, the first goal of this volume is to assess the end of ETA from a *comparative perspective*. The contributors have been asked to place their topic in a wider perspective and, when possible, provide a contrast with other European cases and contexts. The book will be of interest to Hispanists and scholars of ethnic studies but it is our hope that other comparativists will also see the value of incorporating the case of ETA into their analyses. The second goal is to provide a *theoretically informed* analysis of ETA's case. We feel that social and political phenomena are best understood when the tools of social research are systematically applied. For example, it is not possible to understand contemporary Basque politics without making reference to the economic modernisation of the nineteenth century, the 'negative nationalisation' of the autocracies of the twentieth century, the democratic transition and the opening up of political opportunity structures of the 1970s or the process of increasing interconnectedness that resulted from EU integration and globalisation. Similarly, the explanatory variables that account for the emergence of terrorism, the reproduction of violence and the effectiveness of security policies are also found in instances beyond the Basque case, as the next section explains.

Research questions

In addition to the comparative and theoretical agenda driving this volume, the contributors have been asked to engage with a series of ongoing debates in the academic literature on political violence and terrorism, which are of direct relevance to the understanding of our case study. These research questions deal with the importance of regime type in combating violent internal dissent, the effectiveness of terrorism in gaining policy concessions, the mechanisms by which terrorist groups come to an end and the consequences of terrorist campaigns. A brief summary of the relevance of the policy and the theoretical implications of these debates may be found below.

Are democracies more able to deal with terrorism than autocracies?

The relationship between regime type and incidents of political violence has been the subject of extensive research (Eubank and Weinberg 1994, 2001;

Endlers and Sandler 2006). The main finding is that democracy has been the most common target of terrorism. For example, William Eubank and Leonard Weinberg have argued that terrorist groups are more likely to be found in democratic than in non-democratic settings (Eubank and Weinberg 2001). Quan Li has confirmed an association between democracy and terrorist incidents, and Robert Pape has argued that democracies have been the main target of suicide terrorists (Li 2005; Pape 2005). A first explanation for this positive effect is that terrorists take advantage of the freedom of expression and assembly to form clandestine organisations under the noses of the authorities. A second explanation for acts of international terrorism against democracies could be that they arise when executives of these states interfere in other countries' affairs through military intervention or occupation (Chenoweth 2013, 355). The motivations of terrorist groups which target citizens of democracies may not be the destruction of a system of liberties or the 'democratic rules of the game' but a fight against domestic or foreign domination and for the right to self-determination. In other words, the ultimate goal of terrorists is not normally the annihilation of a state but gaining policy concessions from it.

In contrast to the authors who find that stable democracy and terrorism go together, a few authors have argued that terrorism is also prevalent in autocracies (Aksoy *et al.* 2012). Despite their apparent strength, autocracies are intrinsically weak regimes because of their lack of inclusiveness and inability to provide a peaceful and conventional channel for resolving political conflicts. The presence of a disaffected population that is systematically excluded from political institutions may fuel the popularity of radical groups that resort to violence. This interpretation of dictatorships as a root cause of terrorism was a vital part of the Bush administration's post-9/11 national security programme, which promoted democracy in Afghanistan and Iraq as a tool of counter-terrorism (Gottlieb 2010, 236; Dalacoura 2011).

The relationship between regime type and violence in the Basque case is unusual. ETA was founded under the Franco dictatorship (1939–1975) owing to the absence of opportunities for political participation, which confirms the view that autocracies are unable to channel political conflict and incorporate disenfranchised groups. The clandestine group also survived the process of democratic transition in the late 1970s and fought against the pluralistic regime for more than three decades. This is in line with research which supports the idea that transitioning regimes and new democracies with internally inconsistent institutions are more likely to experience domestic terrorism than advanced democracies and authoritarian regimes (Chenoweth 2013, 356). As will be shown later in this book, the democratic transition was the most intense period of terrorist activity for ETA. The most puzzling question is: How did ETA manage to fight a fully democratic state for so long? All in all, ETA fought a dictatorship for seven years and a democracy for 36. In terms of deaths, about 5 per cent of victims were killed during the Francoist regime (1939–1975) but the overwhelming majority of victims (95 per cent) lost their lives under democracy (1976–2011). Indeed, the Basque case is useful because it provides an idea of 'why' terrorism survives in democratic and non-democratic settings and also of 'how' democratic governments may combat terrorism.

The ability of democracies to fight terrorism depends on the level of economic development and the quality of democracy. Wealthy, advanced democracies generally do not suffer from high levels of chronic terrorism unless they interfere in other countries' affairs through military intervention or occupation, in which case they become prominent targets of transnational groups. However, democracies with low levels of legitimacy, poor standards of human rights, intermediate levels of political and economic development, and unresolved conflict among ethnic or political groups experience the most terrorism (Chenoweth 2013, 256). An obvious consequence of both high per capita income and years of democracy is the availability of resources at the hands of security agencies, which may explain performance variation across countries. Democracies also have more constraints than autocracies when fighting terrorism. For a liberal democracy, fighting terrorism is not straightforward because it is not just a matter of efficacy; it is also a matter of rights and values. In defending itself against terrorism, a liberal democracy is not just protecting the physical security of its citizens but it is also defending the integrity of the political system in which these individuals participate. While an authoritarian government must simply find the most efficacious way to fight terrorism, a liberal democracy must find methods that are effective but do not undermine civil liberties, the rule of law and patterns of democratic governance. The danger for democracies is to accept an inevitable trade-off between security and liberty and to implement a counter-terrorist policy that diminishes democracy more than do the acts of terrorism themselves (Crenshaw 2010, 2).

To sum up, the evidence linking democracy and terrorism is robust but it is not consistent across time and space. Not all democracies are equally prone to terrorism; nor are they correspondingly able to combat terrorism. Unsurprisingly, advanced democracies with high levels of economic development are better prepared to fight domestic and international terrorism than are new and poor democracies. Regardless of their age or quality however, all liberal democracies face the challenge of devising counter-terrorist policies that are both efficient and respectful of the system of liberties. And when democracies affected by terrorism fail to strike a balance between security and liberty, terrorists confirm that indiscriminant violence is a useful instrument of coercion.

Does terrorism 'work' in liberal societies?

Terrorist groups use political violence because it helps them obtain some of their goals. If it did not produce any of the intended results, why would so many organisations continue to use terrorism throughout the world? One challenge faced, when trying to answer the question 'Does Terrorism Work?', is the problem of identifying clearly when clandestine groups have been fully 'effective' and when they have been only moderately 'successful'. This and other contentions divide the camp between those who maintain that terrorism is an effective tool to achieve political objectives and those who argue that it is not (Merari and Elad 1986; Dershowitz 2002; Pape 2003; Kydd and Walter 2006).

Alan Dershowitz figures prominently as someone who has pointed out that terrorists have succeeded in furthering their political goals. In his 2002 bestseller *Why Terrorism Works*, he lists a series of terrorist actions where the perpetrators not only went unpunished but were rewarded for their crimes. From the 1960s onward, terrorist acts resulted in increased publicity and freedom for the terrorists because states, the media, and ultimately the citizens gave in. For Dershowitz, the prime example of this involved the Palestinians. Despite launching a campaign of highjacking and blowing up aeroplanes in the late 1960s, Palestinian terrorism gained legitimacy from heads of state throughout the world. According to Dershowitz, 'the international community responded to [Palestinian] terrorism between 1968 and 2001 by consistently rewarding and legitimizing it, rather than punishing and condemning it' (Dershowitz 2002, 85).

Other authors besides Dershowitz stress the efficacy of terrorist violence. David Lake (2002, 20) has argued that it is a 'rational and strategic' tactic because it enables the perpetrators to achieve superior bargaining positions. Likewise, Robert Pape maintains that 'suicide terrorism has been rising largely because terrorists have learned that it pays' (2003, 343). Similarly, Andrew Kydd and Barbara Walter (2006, 49) have argued that 'extremist organizations such as Al-Qaeda, Hamas and the Tamil Tigers engage in terrorism because it frequently delivers the desired response'. These scholars, who point to the efficacy of indiscriminate violence, often subscribe to a rationalist understanding of terrorism as a winning tactic for the aggrieved to redress their grievances by coercing governments into making concessions. This strategic approach to violence is based on bargaining theory, which emphasises how terrorism helps challengers gain concessions by lending credibility to their threats. However, the work of Lake, Pape or Kydd and Walter has also been criticised because they give disproportionate attention to a few successful examples (from Palestine, Sri Lanka and Turkey) and because their strategies for measuring 'success' are at best dubious. Measuring the 'political returns' of violence is complicated by the fact that government concessions take multiple forms and this introduces an element of subjectivity into databases and coding strategies.

Not all scholars agree that terrorism succeeds in producing desirable effects for its perpetrators. A second set of scholars, for example, does not go so far as to say that terrorism simply 'does not work'. They are quick to admit that, from the militant's perspective, it is clear that terrorism is tactically successful in harming civilians, instilling fear and capturing the attention of an audience. At the same time, the indiscriminate use of violence by clandestine groups often increases the popularity of the perpetrators, terrorises victims, and forces governments to overreact. However, they are much more critical about the position that the strategic use of terrorism and indiscriminant targeting of civilians is a useful instrument of coercion that can force executives to make substantial policy concessions. They also doubt that terrorism is 'rational' given that less costly strategies such as campaigns of nonviolent resistance are twice as effective as their violent counterparts (Chenoweth and Stephan 2011).

The work of Max Abrahms explains 'Why Terrorism Does Not Work'. He argues that 'terrorist groups rarely achieve their policy objectives', and 'terrorist success rates are actually extremely low' (Abrahms 2006, 43–44). The focus of his work is on terrorists' capacity to secure their strategic or ultimate goals. He concedes that terrorism is effective in obtaining tactical goals such as producing fear and harm but that it is ineffective politically. Such strategic inefficacy is inherent in the tactic of targeting civilians, although he acknowledges that strategic incentives alone do not necessarily explain terrorists' actions (Abrahms 2012).

Other learned scholars doubt that terrorism results in political success. Thomas Schelling (1991, 20) argued that 'Terrorism almost never appears to accomplish anything politically significant' and David Rapoport (2001, 54) confirmed that, 'by their own standards, terrorists rarely succeed'. Again, in the words of Peter Neumann and M.L.R. Smith, 'campaigns of terrorism – shocking and brutal as they may seem – rarely succeed in achieving their stated objectives' (Neumann and Smith 2008, 100). More recently, empirical studies have confirmed that only a handful of terrorist groups in modern history have managed to accomplish their political aims (Abrahms 2006, 2013; Jones and Libicki 2008; Cronin 2009; Fortna 2015). Contrary to the view of academics who adopt bargaining theory, the empirical evidence seems to suggest that terrorism is highly correlated with political failure.

To recapitulate, there is a broad, emergent school of work which suggests that terrorism is effective (e.g. Dershowitz, Pape, Walter, Kydd, Gould, Berrebi, Klor, Merari, Elad); but there is another cohort, (exemplified by Abrahms, Rapoport, Neumann, Smith, Chenoweth, Stephan, Cronin), in whose judgement terrorism does not work. In relation to our case study, ETA is an example of a terrorist group that used violence to harm civilians, instil fear and provoke an overreaction from the government, but failed to obtain any of its long-term strategic objectives, particularly the constitution of an independent socialist state for the alleged Basque homeland. Currently it is under Spanish and French sovereignty. And yet this is not to say that the violent campaign did not have any impact on ethnic solidarities and nationalist ideologies. ETA created a wartime social environment that formulated a stereotypical perception of the 'self' and the 'other', which was just as incisive at embedding Basque sentiments of belonging in individuals and groups as alternative processes of identification, socialisation and nationalist mobilisation. Ultimately, the violent confrontation reinforced the cohesion of the national community and created committed activists who willingly took up arms in an intoxicating cycle of violence (Muro 2008, 196).

When do terrorist groups end?

The third research topic covered in this volume is the decline and disappearance of terrorist groups. A substantial body of research on terrorism and political violence focuses on 'root causes' and how individuals engage in political violence in the first place. However, in the fight against terrorism, the most pertinent studies are those which investigate how terrorism ends (Crenshaw 1991; Wilkinson 1999; Gvineria 2009). During the past decade, observers from a myriad different fields, including criminology, armed conflict, electoral studies and labour trends, have called for a rectification of this lack of research into how individuals disengage from clandestine organisations.

Several contributions on this issue have focused on the idea of 'duration'. On average, it is possible to argue that modern terrorist groups do not last very long. According to research by David Rapoport (1992), the average duration of groups in 90 per cent of the cases is no more than one year. This finding may appear counter-intuitive, especially if we bear in mind the media attention that a handful of cases get (from the IRA and ETA to Al Qaeda or Daesh). In addition to the short life span of groups, terrorists are not very lethal. According to the Global Terrorism Database (GTD), the majority of terrorist incidents (52 per cent) between 1970 and 2007 did not produce any casualties. About 20 per cent of the cases produced a single victim and 14 per cent of the attacks produced between two and ten victims. The number of attacks that caused over 25 deaths is less than 3 per cent. This is a very low percentage given the universe of cases collected by the GTD ($n=82,910$) and proves the fact that only a small number of groups have the appetite (or perhaps the ability) to kill large numbers of people.

Besides longevity and lethality, scholars have studied the decline and demise of terrorist campaigns. It is worth drawing attention to the book *How Terrorism Ends* by Audrey Kurth Cronin (2009). Cronin begins her book by explaining how terrorist campaigns may be understood as a 'triad' of interaction between three actors: the group, the government and the audience. She identifies six common patterns that have contributed to the ultimate demise of terrorist organisations: (1) the capture or killing of a group's leader (decapitation); (2) entry of the group into a legitimate political process (negotiation); (3) achievement of group aims (success); (4) group implosion or loss of public support (failure); (5) defeat and elimination through brute force (repression); and (6) transition from terrorism into other forms of violence (reorientation). Each of these pathways is analysed in detail and Cronin provides examples of how different cases followed one or several of these pathways, as they are not necessarily mutually exclusive and combinations are possible. ETA is listed as a group that lost popular support (failure) prior to the decay caused by a counter-terrorist effort that effectively used surveillance technology and infiltrations to weaken the underground organisation.

Another book worth mentioning is *How Terrorist Groups End* (2008) by Seth Jones and Martin Libicki, two political scientists at the RAND Corporation. The authors argue that all terrorist groups eventually disappear but the question they want to answer is: 'How do they end?' Jones and Libicki examine the demise of 648 terrorist groups between 1968 and 2006 and offer a series of policy recommendations firmly rooted in their findings. Their dataset reveals five causal mechanisms by which terrorist groups come to an end: (1) politics; (2) policing; (3) military force; (4) splintering; or (5) victory. Of the cases examined, 43 per cent ended their campaigns after joining the political process or a negotiated settlement, and 40 per cent ended as the result of police and intelligence efforts. By contrast, only 7 per cent of groups were defeated by military force and 10 per cent disappeared after obtaining victory in the form of significant policy concessions. With regard to policy recommendations, Jones and Libicki argue that negotiations are a viable alternative to violence when the terrorists' goals are well defined. The narrower the goals of a terrorist organisation, the more likely it can achieve them through a political solution. At the same time, the authors argue that military tools are useful against insurgencies but are less effective when targeting terrorist groups. Considering the 'war on terror' against Al Qaeda and its franchises, their report suggested a rethink of counter-terrorism strategies based on the use of police and intelligence efforts and relying on military force only to counter insurgent activity.

Finally, it is important to point out that domestic terrorism has progressively declined in advanced democracies. Unlike the 1960s and 1970s, when most Western democracies had one or several groups operating within their borders, indigenous political violence has practically vanished. True, the phenomenon of lone wolves and self-starters is a real threat to industrial democracies but the number of attacks (and victims) has declined in the past 50 years. In fact, it may be argued that terrorism affects Western countries much less than it affects non-Western ones. According to data from the National Consortium for the Study of Terrorism and Responses to Terrorism (START), the number of terrorist attacks increased worldwide between 2000 and 2014. However, the violence was not distributed equally across countries. In 2014, for example, only five countries – Iraq, Afghanistan, Pakistan, Nigeria and Syria – accounted for more than 80 per cent of all terrorist deaths.

What are the consequences of violence?

The fourth and final research question deals with the effects of terrorism. On the one hand, it is possible to identify a series of authors who have examined the causal relationship between political violence and changes in political, economic and social spheres. On the other hand, there are authors who have centred their attention on the ideational and psychological repercussions of terrorism.

The field of terrorism has traditionally neglected a series of topics that include the political and economic consequences of violence (Krueger 2007). Scholars have started to fill the research gap on the impact of violence upon public affairs, particularly with regard to the impact of terrorism upon political preferences and election outcomes. For example, recent research has proved that societies affected by terrorism experience a shift in public opinion towards more conservative preferences (Criado 2015). Working with an experimental design, Merolla and Zechmeister (2009) have found that citizens tend to prefer strong leaderships when they are challenged by a terrorist threat. On the basis of a different methodology, in this case a national survey conducted shortly after the 9/11 attacks, Davis and Silver (2004) concluded that the greater the sense of intimidation, the lower the public's support for civil liberties. Furthermore, Hetherington and

Suhay (2011) found that the threat of terrorism provides incentives for aggressive and restrictive policies that may threaten civil liberties.

Research on the electoral consequences of violence for both the incumbent and party systems has not produced fully consistent results. For example, both Gassanberg *et al.* (2008) and Kibris (2011) have concluded that terrorism erodes the political standing of the incumbent party. By contrast, Hetherington and Nelson (2003) have shown that in the case of the USA there has been an increase in public approval ratings for the President following terrorist incidents. Landau *et al.* (2004) have also found that in the aftermath of the 9/11 terrorist attacks support for President Bush increased. As for electoral politics, terrorism has been shown to benefit the share of votes for right-wing parties (Berrebi and Klor 2008; Kibris 2011). In the case of Spain, the electoral consequences of terrorism were examined for the 11 March 2004 Al Qaeda-inspired attacks which left 193 casualties and produced an unexpected electoral result that punished the incumbent (Bali 2007; García 2012) as well as the consequences of ETA's violent campaign (Criado 2011; De la Calle and Sánchez-Cuenca 2013).

With regard to the economic consequences of violence, Krueger (2007) has stated that scholars disagree over the impact of terrorism upon modern economies. Whereas some academics argue that the effect tends to be small, there are scholars who claim that the magnitude of loss is considerable. There is evidence that terrorism has a negative effect on GDP growth and a positive effect on public spending to cover additional security needs (Hobjin 2002; Gupta *et al.* 2004) Among those who argued that the economic effects are large, we could include the work of Abadie and Gardeazabal (2003), who proved that the Basque region suffered approximately a 10 per cent decline in GDP due to ETA's political violence from the late 1970s onward. In addition, some scholars have argued that ETA pressured Basque entrepreneurs and liberal professionals to finance its activities. Between 1978 and 2008, ETA extracted €115 million from small and medium-sized businessmen after threatening them with kidnappings-for-ransom and extortion activities (the so-called 'revolutionary tax'). Buesa and Baumert (2013) show that the revolutionary tax extorted from this part of the population was one of the main sources of income for ETA from the 1970s onward. Besides personal and material damage, terrorist activity also induces a change in the risk perception of economic agents, leading to a permanent reduction in investment, consumption of goods and tax revenues (Salvadori 2015). In other contexts, scholars have examined the moderate impact of violence upon house prices in Northern Ireland (Besley and Mueller 2012), the effects of terrorist attacks on companies' stock values (Karolyi and Martell 2006) or how an increase in the perception of the risk of terrorism following 9/11 led to vacancies in tall office buildings (Abadie and Dermisi 2008).

Terrorism scholars have mainly focused on perpetrators of violence but victims have rarely been considered. Much remains to be done with regard to the study of victims of terrorism, particularly in its definitional and methodological aspects (Alonso 2012; Argomaniz and Lynch 2015). However, research on the social effects of violence has started to concentrate on those who have been most directly affected by indiscriminant violence: the victims themselves (Le Vine 1997; Sinclair and Antonius 2013; Lynch and Argomaniz 2015). Recent contributions have dealt with the experience of victimhood and the specific policies public institutions could adopt to deal with the physical and psychological consequences (Argomaniz and Lynch 2015; Danieli *et al.* 2005). Other works have focused on the political impact which associations of victims of terrorism can make and have introduced the concept of 'healing through action', a process by which psychologically resilient victims become politically active and demand institutional reform in order to bring closure (Muro 2015).

With regard to the ideational consequences of terrorism, it is worth emphasising the impact of political violence upon the reproduction of master narratives. Terrorism represents a specific form of 'communication' (Schmid 2004; Tuman 2010) and usually fosters a total narrative that defines and shapes reality according to the identity of the perpetrators (e.g. the Basque case in Wieviorka 1997). In terrorist practice 'events become metaphors, as part of a narrative process and metonyms for a theory' (Apter 1997, 12). An interesting body of interdisciplinary research founded on social psychology, sociology and political philosophy has been done by Alonso (2009, 2010), intertwining the practice of political violence with the making of 'rhetorical devices' (Alonso 2011) and discursive structures that favour the social and political reproduction of terrorism. The background of this research comes from classical works like Staub (1989), Apter (1997) or Beck (1999), all of which show how 'violence begets discourse and discourse begets violence. It is discourse that transforms triggering events into sustained political violence' (Apter 1997, 18). Consequently, terrorism interacts with public opinion, exchanging languages and story lines with the media (Hewitt 1990; Buragohain 2005; Lewis 2005; De Nelson 2008; Tuman 2010; Matusitz 2013), and promoting 'master narratives' and metanarratives directed to legitimise its political project (Jackson 2005; Hodges and Nilep 2007; Hodges 2011; Schmid 2013).

Content of the book

The book is divided into three parts of similar length. The first part focuses on the actors – ETA and the Spanish state – that opposed each other for 43 years. The second part focuses on the politics of fear and the effects of political violence on victims and public opinion. The third and final part focuses on historical narratives and memories that made violence possible.

Part I devotes two chapters to ETA and two chapters to the Spanish state. Chapter 1 by Gaizka Fernández provides a historical overview of ETA from its origins in the late 1950s to the Spanish transition to democracy in the 1970s. The emergence of terrorism is explained by a combination of external factors (dictatorial context, passive attitude of the PNV, example of anti-colonial movements, etc.) as well as internal factors (war rhetoric, the ideological and organisational evolution of ETA, the emotional state of its militants, etc.). In Chapter 2, Diego Muro examines the violent secessionist campaign between 1975 and 2011, and argues that ETA unilaterally ended its terrorist campaign after failing for 43 years to achieve its strategic goal of creating an independent socialist state for the Basque homeland. The chapter emphasises two explanatory variables – the efficiency of counter-terrorist policy and the loss of social support – in bringing about the demise of the group. Chapter 3 by Jose Antonio Pérez continues to examine the dyadic relationship and centres its attention on the impact of both paramilitary groups and the police upon the Spanish process of democratisation. Pérez argues that ETA was responsible for the majority of victims but the actions of other terrorist organisations and abuses by the police allowed radical Basque nationalism to argue that there was a 'conflict between two warring factions'. In Chapter 4, Óscar Jaime-Jiménez addresses the security response to terrorism and provides an accurate description of the emergence of a political consensus against ETA. The Spanish police forces became increasingly efficient over time and benefited from collaboration with France, the increasing social pressure against violence, the materialisation of a state policy by the hegemonic political parties and the war against terror after 2001.

Part II focuses on the politics of fear and victimisation. In Chapter 5, Jesús Casquete examines the making and unmaking of the so-called Basque Movement of National Liberation, which he describes as an 'uncivil community'. More specifically, he studies the political liturgy and recurring demonstrations of the radical Basque movement concerning ETA, which he considers to be a political religion. In Chapter 6, Javier Gómez examines the effects of killing on the elimination of political dissent and the creation of categories of 'perpetrators' and 'victims'. He also analyses the radical Basque 'social milieu' as an effective background for the practice of violence by ETA activists (providing them with accomplices and safe havens) and the making of a territory of terror, a French (external) and rural (internal) place where perpetrators gathered and took refuge. In Chapter 7, Javier Argomaniz deals with the victims of terrorism, a subject that, as we have noted earlier, has not received the attention it deserves. The chapter delivers a concise comparative analysis of the social practices of victims of terrorism in Spain and the United Kingdom. It examines the divergent political contexts of the victimisation process, the contrasting frameworks of support and the political standing of victims' associations within these two societies. In Chapter 8, Rafael Leoniosio and Raúl López consider the role of Basque public opinion and behaviour towards ETA's terrorism. The authors examine an original dataset of deadly attacks, protest demonstrations and social response.

Part III concerns issues of narratives and memory. In Chapter 9, Martin Alonso and Fernando Molina provide an analysis of the master narrative forged in the public space and the academy that accounts for the terrorism of ETA. In their view, politicians, journalists, intellectuals, historians and social scientists manufactured a 'historical epic' of political violence using romantic and historicist arguments through story lines such as the 'Basque problem', the 'Basque question' or the 'Basque conflict'. In Chapter 10, Luis Castells and Antonio Rivera examine the aftermath of ETA and war memories in the public sphere. They argue that those who supported the use of strategic violence, along with moderate Basque nationalists who controlled the Basque regional executive, aimed to blur the category of victims of terrorism. They show how the politics of memory used by the Basque government is currently founded on an 'integrative memory' aiming to blur the line between perpetrators and victims and to equate their collective sufferings, highlighting the image of the collective victimisation of Basques. Finally, in Chapter 11, Francisco J. Caspistegui analyses Basque politics and how political violence has been examined by international academics and popular culture. His chapter tracks the defining elements of the dominant image of Basques in the academic literature and in fiction, and their impact on attitudes towards the Basque question.

To recapitulate, the book provides a multidisciplinary approach to the study of ETA. The contributors are well-known experts on the Basque case who have aimed at providing an up-to-date account of their research with comparative and theoretical dimensions. In short, the main goal of the book is to contribute to current debates in both terrorism and Basque studies, and to offer reflective and nuanced answers to existing controversies in the fields of terrorism and political violence: (1) Are democracies more able to deal with terrorism than autocracies? (2) Does terrorism 'work' in liberal societies? (3) When do terrorist groups end? and (4) What are the consequences of political violence? Finally, the book examines three facets of ETA's violence – the dyadic relationship between ETA and the Spanish state, the politics of fear, and narratives and memory – and confirms the significance, appeal and interest of Basque terrorism for an international readership.

Bibliography

Abadie, Alberto and Javier Gardeazabal (2003) 'The economic cost of conflict: A case study of the Basque Country'. *American Economic Review* 93: 113–132.

Abadie, Alberto and Dermisi, Sofia (2008) 'Is terrorism eroding economics in central business districts? Lesson from the office real estate market in downtown Chicago'. *Journal of Urban Economics* 64: 451–463.

Abrahms, Max (2006) 'Why terrorism does not work'. *International Security* 31: 42–78.

Abrahms, Max (2012) 'The political effectiveness of terrorism revisited'. *Comparative Political Studies* 45: 366–393.

Aksoy Deniz, David B. Carter and Joseph Wright (2012) 'Terrorism in dictatorships'. *The Journal of Politics* 74: 810–826.

Alonso, Martín (2009) 'El Síndrome de Al-Andalus: relatos de expoliación y violencia política'. In *Comunidades de Muerte*, ed. Jesús Casquete, 19–54. Barcelona: Anthropos.

Alonso, Martín (2010) 'Estructuras retóricas de la violencia política'. In *Violencia política. Historia, memoria y víctimas*, eds Antonio Rivera and Carlos Carnicero, 118–148. Madrid: Maia.

Alonso, Martín (2011) 'Collective identity as a rhetorical device'. *Synthesis Philosophica* 51: 7–24.

Alonso, Martin (ed.) (2012) *El lugar de la memoria. La huella del mal como pedagogía democrática*. Bilbao: Bakeaz.

Apter, David E. (1997) 'Political violence in analytical perspective'. In *The Legitimization of Violence*, ed. David E. Apter, 1–32. New York: New York University Press.

Argomaniz, Javier and Orla Lynch (eds) (2015) *International Perspectives on Terrorist Victimisation. An International Approach*. Basingstoke: Palgrave.

Bali, Valentina (2007) 'Terror and elections: Lessons from Spain'. *Electoral Studies* 26: 669–687.

Beck, Aaron T. (1999) *Prisoners of Hate. The Cognitive Basis of Anger, Hostility, and Violence*. New York: HarperCollins.

Berrebi, Claude and Esteban F. Klor (2008) 'Are voters sensitive to terrorism? Direct evidence from the Israeli electorate'. *American Political Science Review* 102: 279: 301.

Besley, Timothy and Hannes Mueller (2012) 'Estimating the peace dividend: The impact of violence on house prices in Northern Ireland'. *American Economic Review* 102: 810–833.

Buesa, Mikel and Thomas Baumert (2013) 'Untangling ETA's finance: An in-depth analysis of the Basque terrorist's economic network and the money it handles'. *Defence and Peace Economics* 24: 317–338.

Buragohain, Monmi (2005) *Studying Media and Terrorism: An Analysis of Mass Communication Literature from 1970 through 2005*. Master's thesis, California State University, Fresno.

Chenoweth, Erica (2013) 'Terrorism and democracy'. *Annual Review of Political Science* 16: 355–378.

Chenoweth, Erica and Maria J. Stephan (2011) *Why Civil Resistance Works: The Strategic Logic of Nonviolent Conflict*. New York: Columbia Press.

Crenshaw, Martha (1991) 'How terrorism declines'. *Terrorism and Political Violence* 3: 69–87.

Crenshaw, Martha (2010) *The Consequences of Counterterrorism*. New York: Russell Sage Foundation.

Criado, Henar (2011) 'Bullets and votes: Public opinion and terrorist strategies'. *Journal of Peace Research* 48: 497–508.

Criado, Henar (2015) 'What makes terrorism salient? Terrorist strategies, political competition, and public opinion'. *Terrorism and Political Violence*, doi: 10.1080/09546553.2015.1008628.

Cronin, Audrey K. (2009) *How Terrorism Ends. Understanding the Decline and Demise of Terrorist Campaigns*. Princeton, NJ: Princeton University Press.

Dalacoura Katerina (2011) *Islamist Terrorism and Democracy in the Middle East*. Cambridge: Cambridge University Press.

Danieli, Yael, Daniel Brom and Joe Sils (eds) (2005) *The Trauma of Terrorism. Sharing Knowledge and Shared Care*. New York: Routledge.

Davis, Darren W. and Brian D. Silver (2004) 'Civil liberties vs. security: Public opinion in the context of the terrorist attacks on America'. *American Journal of Political Science* 48: 28–46.

De la Calle, Luis and Ignacio Sánchez-Cuenca (2013) 'Killing and voting in the Basque Country: An exploration of the electoral link between ETA and its political branch'. *Terrorism and Political Violence* 25: 94–112.

De Nelson, Sonia Ambrosio (2008) 'Understanding the press imaging of "terrorist": A pragmatic visit to the Frankfurt School'. *International Communication Gazette* 70: 325–337.

Enders, Walter and Todd Sandler (2006) *The Political Economy of Terrorism*. New York: Cambridge University Press.

Eubank, William L. and Leonard Weinberg (1994) 'Does democracy encourage terrorism?' *Terrorism and Political Violence* 6: 417–463.

Eubank, William L. and Leonard Weinberg (2001) 'Terrorism and democracy: Perpetrators and victims'. *Terrorism and Political Violence* 13: 155–164.

Fortna, Virginia (2015) 'Do terrorists win? Rebels' use of terrorism and civil war outcomes'. *International Organization* 69: 519–164.

García, José (2012) 'Re-examining the evidence on the electoral impact of terrorist attacks: The Spanish election of 2004'. *Electoral Studies* 31: 96–106.

Gassanberg, Martin, Richard Jong-A-Pin and Jochen O. Mierau (2008) 'Terrorism and electoral accountability: One strike, you're out'. *Economics Letters* 100: 126–129.

Gottlieb, Stuart (ed.) (2010) *Debating Terrorism and Counterterrorism: Conflicting Perspectives on Causes, Contexts and Responses.* Washington, DC: CQ Press.

Gupta, Sanjeev, Benedict Clements, Rina Bhattacharya and Shamit Chakravarti (2004) 'Fiscal consequences of armed conflict and terrorism in low and middle income countries'. *European Journal of Political Economy* 20: 403–421.

Gvineria, Gaga (2009) 'How does terrorism end?' In *Social Science for Counterterrorism: Putting the Pieces Together*, eds Paul K. Davis and Kim Cragin, 257–298. Santa Monica: RAND.

Hetherington, Marc J. and Michael Nelson (2003) 'Anatomy of a rally effect: George W. Bush and the war on terrorism'. *PS: Political Science and Politics* 36: 37–42.

Hetherington, Marc J. and Elizabeth Suhay (2011) 'Authoritarianism, threat, and Americans' support for the war on terror'. *American Journal of Political Science* 55: 546–560.

Hewitt, Christopher (1990) 'Terrorism and public opinion: A five country comparison'. *Terrorism and Political Violence* 22: 145–170.

Hobjin, Bart (2002) 'What will homeland security cost?' *Federal Reserve Bank of New York Economic Policy Review* 8: 21–33.

Hodges, Adam (2011) *The 'War on Terror' Narrative: Discourse and Intertextuality in the Construction and Contestation of Sociopolitical Reality.* New York: Oxford University Press.

Hodges, Adam and Chad Nilep (eds) (2007) *Discourse, War and Terrorism.* Amsterdam: John Benjamins.

Jackson, Richard (2005) *Writing the War on Terrorism: Language, Politics and Counter-Terrorism.* Manchester: Manchester University Press.

Jones, Seth G. and Martin C. Libicki (2008) *How Terrorist Groups End: Lessons for Countering al Qa'ida.* Santa Monica, CA: RAND.

Karolyi, George A. and Rodolfo Martell (2006) 'Terrorism and the stock market'. Available at SSRN: http://dx.doi.org/10.2139/ssrn.823465.

Kibris, Arzu (2011) 'Funerals and elections: The effects of terrorism on voting behavior in Turkey'. *Journal of Conflict Resolution* 55: 220–247.

Krueger, Alan B. (2007) *What Makes a Terrorist. Economics and the Roots of Terrorism.* Princeton, NJ: Princeton University Press.

Kydd, Andrew and Barbara F. Walter (2006) 'The strategies of terrorism'. *International Security* 31: 49–80.

Lake, David A. (2002) 'Rational extremism: Understanding terrorism in the twenty-first century'. *Dialogue-IO* 1: 15–29.

Landau, Mark J., Sheldon Solomon, Jeff Greenberg, Florette Cohen, Tom Pyszczynski, Jamie Arndt, Claude H. Miller, Daniel M. Ogilvie and Alison Cook (2004) 'Deliver us from evil: The effects of mortality salience and reminders of 9/11 on support for President George W. Bush'. *Personality and Social Psychology Bulletin* 30: 1136–1150.

Le Vine, Victor T. (1997) 'On the victims of terrorism and their innocence'. *Terrorism and Political Violence* 9: 55–62.

Lewis, Jeff (2005) *Language Wars: The Role of Media and Culture in Global Terror and Political Violence*. Chicago, IL: Chicago University Press.

Li, Quan (2005) 'Does democracy promote or reduce transnational terrorist incidents?' *Journal of Conflict Resolution* 49: 278–297.

Lynch, Orla and Javier Argomaniz (2015) *Victims of Terrorism. A Comparative and Interdisciplinary Study*. London: Routledge.

Matusitz, Jonathan (2013) *Terrorism and Communication: A Critical Introduction*. Thousand Oaks, CA: Sage.

Merari, Ariel and Shlomi Elad (1986) *The International Dimension of Palestinian Terrorism*. Boulder, CO: Westview Press.

Merolla, Jennifer L. and Elisabeth J. Zechmeister (2009) 'Terrorist threat, leadership and the vote: Evidence from three experiments'. *Political Behavior* 31: 575–601.

Muro, Diego (2008) *Ethnicity and Violence: The Case of Radical Basque Nationalism*. London and Abingdon: Routledge.

Muro, Diego (2015) 'Healing through action? The political mobilization of victims of Al Qaeda-inspired violence in Spain and the United Kingdom'. *Studies in Conflict & Terrorism*, doi: 10.1080/1057610X.2015.1005462.

Neumann, Peter R. and Michael L.R. Smith (2008) *The Strategy of Terrorism: How it Works, and Why it Fails*. London: Routledge.

Pape, Robert A. (2003) 'The strategic logic of suicide terrorism'. *American Political Science Review* 97: 243–361.

Pape, Robert (2005) *Dying to Win*. New York: Random House.

Rapoport, David C. (1992) 'Terrorism'. In *Routledge Encyclopedia of Government and Politics. Vol 2*, eds M.E. Hawkesworth and Maurice Kogan, 1061–1079. London: Routledge.

Rapoport, David C. (2001) 'The international world as some terrorists have seen it: A look at a century of memoirs'. In *Inside Terrorist Organisations*, ed. David C. Rapoport, 32–58. London: Frank Cass.

Salvadori, Luca (2015) 'Does tax enforcement counteract the negative effects of terrorism? A case study of the Basque Country'. *IEB Working Paper* 2015/09. Available at SSRN: http://ssrn.com/abstract=2580355.

Schelling, Thomas C. (1991) 'What purposes can international terrorism serve?' In *Violence, Terrorism, and Justice*, eds. Raymond Gillespie Frey and Christopher W. Morris, 18–32. New York: Cambridge University Press.

Schmid, Alex P. (2004) 'Frameworks for conceptualizing terrorism'. *Terrorism and Political Violence* 16: 197–221.

Schmid, Alex P. (2013) 'The literature on terrorism'. In *The Routledge Handbook of Terrorism Research*, ed. Alex P. Schmid, 457–474. London: Routledge.

Sinclair, Samuel Justin and Daniel Antonius (2013) *The Political Psychology of Terrorism Fears*. New York: Oxford University Press.

Staub, Ervin (1989) *The Roots of Evil. The Origins of Genocide and Other Group Violence*. Cambridge: Cambridge University Press.

Tuman, Joseph S. (2010) *Communicating Terror: The Rhetorical Dimensions of Terrorism*. Thousand Oaks, CA: Sage.

Wieviorka, Michel (1997) 'ETA and Basque political violence'. In *The Legitimization of Violence*, ed. David E. Apter, 292–349. Basingstoke: Macmillan/UNRISD.

Wilkinson, Paul (1999) 'Politics, diplomacy and peace processes: Pathways out of terrorism?' *Terrorism and Political Violence* 11: 66–82.

Part I
ETA and the Spanish state

1　The origins of ETA

Between Francoism and democracy, 1958–1981

Gaizka Fernández

Introduction

The civil milieu of *Euskadi ta Askatasuna* (ETA – Basque Country and Freedom) usually explains the origins of this terrorist organisation by appealing to the supposed existence of a secular, ethnic conflict between Basques and Spaniards, of which ETA would be the most recent expression. According to this point of view, an originally independent Basque nation was at some time in its history conquered by Spain, which converted it into a type of colony (Fernández 2015). Over the centuries the Basques supposedly resisted the oppression of the invaders, resorting to arms on occasion, as occurred during the two Carlist Wars (1833–1840 and 1872–1876), the Spanish Civil War (1936–1939) and the period of ETA's activity (1958–2011).

In fact, that secular, ethnic conflict never existed. It is no more than an 'imaginary war' (Elorza 1995, 49), on which ETA and its milieu, the so-called patriotic left (*izquierda abertzale*), have built their cosmovision. It is their particular version of the triadic structure of nationalist rhetoric (Levinger and Lytle 2001), which in this case derives from a combination of the tendentious view of history of Sabino Arana, founder of the Basque Nationalist Party (*Partido Nacionalista Vasco* – PNV), the influence of the Third World national liberation movements of the 1950s and 1960s, and the dictatorial context of Francoism from which ETA initially developed.

Another commonly used explanation for the birth of this organisation is the alleged 'genocide' that the Basque people suffered following the Spanish Civil War. There is no question that the victors carried out a harsh repression against the vanquished, but they did so throughout Spain and not only in the Basque Country. In total, the Francoist repression is calculated to have resulted in the killing of around 130,000 Spanish republicans after the conflict. There were between 1,600 and 1,800 victims in the Basque Country (the provinces of Biscay, Gipuzkoa and Araba) and between 2,200 and 2,500 in Navarre. This was a huge number of murders, but it was lower than those recorded in the provinces of Málaga (7,471), Badajoz (8,914) or Seville (12,507), where no terrorist groups on ETA's scale emerged. On the other hand, the absolute majority of mortal victims of the Francoist repression in the Basque Country and Navarre were singled out because they were militants of non-nationalist, left-wing parties and trade unions. For example, only 12 of the 194 people murdered in Araba were affiliated to the PNV. The rest were leftists (Gómez 2014).

Nor was the Franco dictatorship alien to the Basque Country and Navarre, since both regions contributed many volunteers who fought on the Francoist side in the Civil War. Repression was subsequently one of the regime's foundations, but it did not rest solely on that. It could also count on the blessing of a large part of the Catholic Church, the support of a high percentage of the bourgeoisie and the popular classes, and the backing of the right wing (including non-nationalist Basques). To this support must be added the passivity of the majority of society, which in the 1960s began to enjoy a certain degree of economic prosperity. In the words of the first military leader of ETA Xabier Zumalde (alias *El Cabra*) (2004, 423),

> [T]he people, with the exception of a few romantics, knew nothing – or did not want to know anything – about the so-called 'Basque problem'. They were more interested in buying a car SEAT 600, or at least a television, than getting into trouble.

The image of an unvanquished Basque Country standing up to Franco does not correspond to reality.

The purpose of this chapter is to go over the first stage of ETA's history. On the one hand, the organisation's origins are examined. These are situated in the context of Francoism, and the chapter analyses the extent to which the dictatorship had an influence on ETA's appearance. In addition, the causes that led this organisation to opt for terrorist violence are analysed. On the other hand, the chapter studies the different branches of ETA that emerged during the transition to democracy in Spain, a period when there were many more mortal victims than under the dictatorship itself.

The new generation of Basque nationalists

ETA above all resulted from a generational clash between the old nationalists in exile and the youths who had not fought in the Civil War but who wished to continue it in some way. The PNV and the Basque leftists had nourished the hope that the victory of Great Britain and the USA in the Second World War would result in the fall of Franco's dictatorship, and the alliance between Nazi Germany and fascist Italy. In order to incite the intervention of the Western democracies, the Basque government-in-exile of President José Antonio Aguirre and the trade unions organised general strikes in 1947 and 1951. In spite of substantial support for the strikes the final goal was not achieved. The Cold War saved the regime: in 1953 Franco signed an international agreement with the USA and a Concordat with the Vatican; two years later Spain was admitted to the United Nations. In 1960 Aguirre died and was replaced by Jesús María Leizaola, also from the PNV. From then onward the Basque government-in-exile played a merely token role. The new generation of nationalists began to accuse the older generation of apathy and ineffectiveness (De Pablo *et al.* 2001).

Inside the Basque Country, nationalism had been transmitted intergeneration-ally through channels like the clandestine press, propaganda, literature, music, ritual celebrations and places of memory. It was also transmitted orally in social networks like the family, circles of friends and their leisure-time rituals, associative life, the Basque-language cultural milieu and the Church (Pérez-Agote 1987; Gurrutxaga 1990). By such means and in a conjuncture that gave them credibility – the dictatorship – young people received the dogmas of Sabino Arana (racism, irredentism, independentism, hatred for anything that seemed Spanish, etc.), including the narrative of a secular, ethnic conflict (Jáuregui 1985). On the one hand, Francoism appeared to be consolidating itself; it maintained its centralism and prevented any traces of dissidence. Nationalist symbols were also prohibited. On the other hand, the Basque language, although not officially banned, continued to be marginalised and was in decline. Finally, during the 1950s and 1960s, Spain underwent a new process of industrialisation that resulted in the relocation of a significant section of the rural population to the big industrial centres (Madrid, Barcelona, etc.). Thousands of immigrants from the other parts of Spain arrived in the Basque Country in search of work. The population virtually tripled in three decades. This resulted in the re-emergence of a xenophobic rejection of immigrants, who were perceived as 'colonists' by some nationalists (Fernández and López 2012, 49–54).

In 1952 a small group of nationalist university students, some of whom had been militants in student organisations of the PNV, founded a magazine called *Ekin* (To Do), the name by which the group was subsequently known. The following year, during the foundational meeting of the new group, these young nationalists sealed their commitment to the homeland by solemnly swearing on an issue of the magazine *Gudari* (Warrior, Soldier), published by the nationalist battalions during the Civil War. This was more than a symbol: in the words of one of its leaders José Luis Álvarez Enparantza (*Txillardegi*) (1997, 177), the members of *Ekin* considered themselves 'to be soldiers and that organization, which did not even have a name, saw itself as the continuation of the Basque Army'. In spite of that combative spirit, their efforts were only dedicated to studying. Through their readings they managed to rediscover Basque nationalism. When the members of *Ekin* began to impart educational courses, they came into contact with the PNV's youth organisation, *Eusko Gaztedi* of the Interior (EGI – Basque Youth Force). In 1956, due to the ideological affinity between the two groups, *Ekin* became integrated into EGI. However, mutual suspicions, attempts by the PNV leadership to control the militants proceeding from *Ekin* and the party's internal problems resulted in a rapid deterioration in relations between the two, especially in Biscay. In 1958 the former members of *Ekin* broke with the PNV (Jáuregui 1985, 75–83).

The breakaway militants formed a group called ETA. It made itself known publicly in 1959 through a manifesto with a moderate content. In it the members of ETA declared that they were heirs to the trajectory of the Basque government.

ETA was defined as a patriotic, apolitical, secular and democratic organisation that defended the right to self-determination (De Pablo *et al.* 2001, 235). In spite of that declaration, ETA had adopted the most extremist version of Basque nationalism. In the words of Frederico Krutwig, who was later to become one of its most famous theoreticians, when he met them in person the first ETA members 'seemed to us to represent a tendency that was more retrograde than the PNV…. They had gone back to the most retrograde Aranism' (*Muga* 03/1980). However, ETA had made two significant changes to the principles of Sabino Arana. On the one hand, it declared itself to be secular; that is, it favoured a separation between religion and politics. On the other, although its militants did not abandon xenophobia, ETA distanced itself from the surname-based racism of Sabino Arana. The new criterion for ethnic exclusion was the language: a Basque was someone who spoke the Basque language. In fact only a minority of Basques did so, which is why an ideological criterion was later given preference: a Basque was a Basque nationalist (Fernández and López 2012, 54–73).

During the dictatorship the relationship between the PNV and ETA was a difficult one. The leaders of ETA accused the party of being an inefficient anachronism and later labelled it 'bourgeois', while the PNV responded by pointing to the 'fascist' or 'communist' character of the latter. According to Gurutz Jáuregui (1997, 75), ETA and the PNV were separated by 'the dialectic between pragmatism and intransigence, their positions with respect to violence, and ETA's inclination towards Marxism'. It should be added that the two groups were rivals competing to attract Basque nationalist supporters. In that sense, the PNV could only observe with concern how, as the 1960s progressed, ETA attracted a growing sector of Basque youth and, above all, how the organisation absorbed two splits from EGI in 1963 and 1972.

The evolution of the first ETA

Up until 1967 ETA was mainly involved in propaganda activities, but it was possible to discern a desire to go beyond this. From its foundation the organisation had a branch dedicated to action (later its military front). In December 1959 its activists planted explosives at the Civil Government of Araba, a police station in Bilbao and the newspaper *Alerta* in Santander. On 18 July 1961 the group burnt three Spanish flags in San Sebastián and tried to derail a train carrying Francoist veterans from Gipuzkoa, who were travelling to that city to commemorate the twenty-fifth anniversary of the Francoist rebellion (Jáuregui 1985, 75–83).

As a consequence of its initial actions, ETA experienced its first arrests. Some of the organisation's members escaped to France, where for decades, thanks to the unofficial tolerance of the government, ETA benefited from an authentic 'sanctuary' where its activists were barely troubled by the police. It was in the French Basque Country that its I Assembly was held in 1962, at which ETA defined itself as a Basque Revolutionary National Liberation Movement. Its goal was to create an independent nation-state, which would be monolingual (in Basque), secular and democratic. However, this was precisely when ETA started to undergo its ideological evolution (Jáuregui 1985, 139–147; Sullivan 1988, 47–48).

The first ETA had inherited from the PNV its rejection of Marxism in general and communism in particular. Nonetheless, the big workers' strikes that took place in May 1962 impressed the leaders of the organisation, who proposed the need to link nationalism with the workers' struggle. While for a large proportion of ETA members this approach was for instrumental reasons, others became passionately interested in labour issues. Outstanding among the latter, who were known as the labour current of ETA, was Patxi Iturrioz (*Larrínaga*). During the II Assembly, held in March 1963, ETA decided to participate in the workers' movement (Garmendia 1996, 96–122 and 344).

Vasconia, written by Frederico Krutwig and first published in 1963, had a considerable influence in ETA. On the one hand, it softened the organisation's distrust of Marxism. On the other, drawing inspiration from Mao Zedong and the national liberation movements of the Third World, Krutwig contributed the novel image of the Basque Country as a colony subjected to two imperialist powers: Spain and France. It was necessary to defeat these powers militarily through a national liberation war, in which the patriotic end justified the violent means (Krutwig 2006).

At ETA's III Assembly, held between April and May 1964, a report entitled 'The Insurrection in Euzkadi', written by Julen Madariaga and inspired by *Vasconia*, was approved. It proposed starting a guerrilla war to defeat the occupying armies and seize power. It was an unviable plan. There was no similarity between the modern, industrialised and prosperous Basque Country and the colonies of the Third World. Besides, while ETA members possessed a few weapons, they did not know how to use them and they lacked ammunition. Nonetheless, it was proof that a Third World current had appeared within the organisation (Jáuregui 1985, 225–237).

Shortly afterwards, the founders of ETA were expelled from the French Basque Country and lost control of the group, which passed to José Luis Zalbide, a referential figure in the Third Worldist current, and Patxi Iturrioz, leader of the workerist faction. Their imprint became clear at the IV Assembly (1965), at which the organisational apparatus was restructured into sections and there was also far-reaching strategic and ideological change. After accepting that Madariaga's project for guerrilla war was unviable, approval was given to a report by Zalbide which recognised ETA's limitations and opted for a model of 'revolutionary war' based on the action–reaction–action spiral. According to this strategy the organisation's violence would provoke police repression against the Basque population, which would result in the latter supporting the 'revolutionary war'. There was an indispensable condition for this to work: ETA's organisational structure would have to be capable of withstanding the reaction of the police (Hordago 1979, vol. III, 515). Xabier Zumalde was appointed head of the military front, which undertook the training of a group of youths.

A new political goal for ETA was also approved at the IV Assembly: building a socialist society. This marked the start of the stage of 'the two-sided coin', to use the expression by José María Garmendia (1996, 220–234), which involved 'the attempt to combine national liberation and social liberation'. The organisation had thrown open its doors to the influence of the numerous currents of Marxism. As a result, Patxi Iturrioz's workerist tendency sought to find a way of adapting nationalism to socialism (Sullivan 1988, 58–65).

One of the problems faced by the first ETA was lack of funds, which led the organisation to carry out a bank robbery in September 1965. It was a fiasco. José Luis Zalbide was arrested and other leaders had to flee from Spain. With the internal balance among the different tendencies upset, Iturrioz was left in charge of the Political Office, which was responsible for publishing *Zutik* (Arise), and he therefore became the chief leader of ETA. From this position he tried to force a workerist evolution onto the organisation. The coin had fallen with its Marxist face showing. On the ideological plane, Iturrioz attempted to replace 'bourgeois nationalism' with a 'workers' patriotism' that would defend workers' interests. It also rejected linguistically based ethno-nationalism, anti-Spanish sentiment and the supposed secular conflict between Basques and Spaniards contained in the nationalist narrative. Moreover, the workerists denounced xenophobic prejudices and proposed opening up the organisation to immigrants. On the strategic side, Iturrioz proposed subordinating the military front to the political leadership, the creation of a class front and giving the leading role to the workers' movement. This turn to the left infuriated Xabier Zumalde's military front, which split from ETA in 1966. On the other hand, the Third Worldist and ethno-nationalist currents, led by *Txillardegi*, orchestrated a campaign of defamation against Iturrioz and his supporters (Garmendia 1996, 259–310; Jáuregui 1985, 293–358).

The first part of ETA's V Assembly was held in December 1966, in which the brothers José Antonio and Javier (*Txabi*) Etxebarrieta played a prominent role. The workers' faction was expelled and its leaders were 'sentenced' to death by the new leadership of ETA (Uriarte 2005, 67). While the sentence was not carried out, a very real operation of harassment and persecution was directed against the breakaway group. This was the 'first crusade against non-nationalists', to use the expression by José María Garmendia (2006, 124–135). Not only did ETA take part in this, but other nationalist forces did as well. They feared Iturrioz might create an organisation that would take up the baton of the *Partido Socialista Obrero Español* (PSOE – Spanish Socialist Workers' Party), which had been the main left-wing formation in the Basque Country until the Civil War.

During the second part of the V Assembly (March 1967) the action-repression strategy was ratified and the organisation was structured into four fronts: political, economic, military and cultural. The meeting confirmed the supremacy of the Third Worldist tendency, which was highly influenced by Krutwig and led by a new generation of leaders like the Etxebarrieta brothers, José María Escubi and José Luis Unzueta (*Patxo*). ETA, which now called itself a Basque Socialist National Liberation Organisation, officially adopted revolutionary nationalism, which Unzueta himself has since defined as 'a combination between Aranist radicalism and a type of *sui generis* Marxist populism' (1988, 103). This synthesis gave birth to the concept of the 'Basque Working People', the new subject of the ETA narrative: the 'Basque proletariat with national class consciousness', which suffered from a double oppression (as a working class exploited by the bourgeoisie and as a nation occupied by Spain) and was to be liberated by means of 'armed struggle' (*Zutik* 44, 01/1967).

Txillardegi's ethno-nationalist tendency, which disagreed with the dominant Third Worldist line, abandoned ETA in April 1967. Its members turned their energies to producing the journal *Branka* (1966–1971), which became a lobby in favour of a nationalist front and the ideological purity of nationalism (Jáuregui 1985, 359–410).

ETA's violence

ETA had proposed to set the action–reaction strategy underway at its V Assembly. In mid-1967 some successful robberies were carried out, which provided the organisation with funds to arm itself and support its leaders economically. Numerous bombs were planted against symbols of the dictatorship, such as plaques commemorating the dead on the Francoist side in the Civil War. On 2 June 1968 the ETA leadership took a far-reaching decision: to assassinate the heads of the Politico-Social Brigade of Bilbao and San Sebastián. Its head in the San Sebastián was Superintendent Melitón Manzanas, whose assassination was to have been carried out by *Txabi* Etxebarrieta. He was unable to do so. On 7 June the stolen automobile in which Etxebarrieta and his comrade Iñaki Saraseta were travelling was stopped for a routine traffic check by the civil guardsman José Antonio Pardines. The agent found that the numbers in the documentation and on the car's chassis did not match. Sarasketa suggested they should disarm the guardsman, as he was alone. However, Etxebarrieta, probably under the influence of amphetamines, shot Pardines in the back. He was finished off on the ground with four shots. In their subsequent getaway, Etxebarrieta and Sarasketa were intercepted in Tolosa (Gipuzkoa) by agents of the Civil Guard. There was an exchange of gunfire and Etxebarrieta was killed. Sarasketa was arrested shortly afterwards. He was put on trial and sentenced to death, later commuted to life imprisonment, and remained in prison until 1977 (Garmendia 1996, 355–375).

ETA put out its own particular version of the events in which Etxebarrieta, instead of appearing as a murderer, was portrayed as a victim sacrificed by the Civil Guard (a police body that plays the symbolic role of antagonist or villain in the ant-Francoist imaginary). In this way, Etxebarrieta was placed on a level with the Argentinian Ernesto *Che* Guevara: he was a hero who had given his life for the homeland; that is, 'the First Martyr of the Revolution' (Hordago 1979, vol. VII, 484–488). A large part of the Basque population, which distrusted the official mass media, believed ETA.

The death of Etxebarrieta, its charismatic leader, had a profound impact on ETA's militants. As one of the latter, Eduardo Uriarte (2005, 90–91), recalls. 'we were consumed by the desire for vengeance, above all by the need to provide some type of answer to show that ETA was not finished'. That was the state of mind of the ETA leaders when they approved the resumption of the plan to assassinate the superintendents. Etxebarrieta's death functioned as a precipitating factor, but it was not the cause of ETA's opting to practise violence – unlike the rest of the anti-Francoist groups. The main motive for starting the terrorist spiral was the logic of the gang's leaders, who considered the circumstances of the time to be favourable (the massive attendance at Etxebarrieta's funeral) and took advantage of them for their own strategic ends. The authoritarian character of the dictatorship, police repression, the pain caused by Etxebarrieta's death, the narrative of a secular, ethnic conflict, the desire to emulate the Basque soldiers of the Civil War and their youth all conditioned the ETA leaders, but did not determine their actions. In deciding to kill they were making use of their free will.

On 2 August 1968 an ETA cell assassinated Superintendent Melitón Manzanas at his home in Irún (Gipuzkoa). Accused of being a professional torturer, his death was welcomed by the anti-Francoist opposition. From that point onward the action–repression–action spiral grew so quickly that there was no way of stopping it. The dictatorship answered the provocation with a brutal repression. The government issued a decree law on the repression of banditry and terrorism, and declared a state of exception in Gipuzkoa, which was extended to the rest of Spain following the outbreak of conflict in different universities. Over the following years there was a sharp increase in the number of people arrested in the Basque Country, many of whom had nothing to do with ETA: 434 in 1968, 1,953 in 1969 and 831 in 1970 (Castells 1984, 104). In addition, the police forces committed numerous excesses, such as maltreatment and torture, which earned them the hostility of the population (Casanellas 2014).

ETA continued its terrorist campaign. Eduardo Uriarte (2005, 94–103) admits that not only were they 'blinded by the previous routine, but they also felt they had to demonstrate that the organisation had not been dismantled, contrary to what the regime's mass media were announcing. During the Easter holidays of 1969 ETA planted 14 bombs. The prolongation of the campaign enabled the police to arrest the group's leadership in April. One of the leaders, Miguel Echevarría (*Makagüen*), managed to escape. During his getaway he killed the taxi-driver Fermín Monasterio Pérez (Garmendia 1996, 368–375; Alonso *et al.* 2010, 25–26).

The year 1970 was critical for ETA, as its internal contradictions came out into the open. Four tendencies emerged that confronted each other due both to internal rivalries and to a basic dilemma: Should it continue to be a terrorist organisation that fought against Spain or should it transform itself into a Leninist party? The latter position was held by the provisional leadership and by the Red Cells, a study group formed of exiles. On the other hand, the defenders of the anti-colonialist theses were grouped around Krutwig and Julen Madariaga. Finally, the military front, led by Juan José Etxabe (*Haundixe*), had started to operate on its own account (Garmendia 1996, 377–422).

The provisional leadership of ETA obtained approval for its theses at the VI Assembly (August 1970), although the consequences were disastrous for the organisation: ETA broke up. The bulk of the militants, who remained faithful to the leadership, became known as ETA VI. This group gradually abandoned nationalism and 'armed struggle'. The anti-colonialist faction and Etxabe's military front did not recognise the 'legality' of the VI Assembly and broke away to form ETA V, which defined itself as a Basque Revolutionary National Liberation Movement. The adjective 'socialist' had disappeared (Sullivan 1988, 105–109; Garmendia 1996, 422–462).

In spite of starting out from an advantageous position, ETA VI ended up losing the battle for possession of the historical acronym ETA. First, its attempt to free the leaders of the gang who were imprisoned was a total failure. Moreover, the latter publicly supported ETA V. Second, ETA V kidnapped Eugen Beihl, the consul of the German Federal Republic in San Sebastián; this was a propaganda victory at the international level. Third, the Francoist police arrested the leadership of ETA VI in March 1971. Finally, its ideological incoherence and internal disagreements resulted in a new split in ETA VI in July 1972 (Garmendia 1996, 462–492).

In any case, ETA V was not experiencing its finest hour. It was saved by the dictatorship itself. On 3 December 1970 a summary trial began in Burgos against 16 activists accused of the assassination of Superintendent Manzanas. The dictatorship's goal was to set an example with the trial, which is why it allowed the press to have access. Taking advantage of the situation and thanks to a pre-planned staging of their statements before the military court, the defendants and their lawyers denounced the dictatorship (Uriarte 2005, 115–135).

Three of the six defendants who were condemned to capital punishment received a double death sentence. The anti-Francoist forces orchestrated an enormous campaign of mobilisations to save their lives. Stoppages, strikes and demonstrations took place not only in Spain, where another state of siege was declared, but throughout Western Europe as well. The authorities found themselves overwhelmed. Franco, in what he thought was a show of strength, commuted the death penalties. But it was too late. The anti-Francoist opposition had moved closer to radical Basque nationalism, and the moderate nationalists themselves, in spite of their earlier reticence, were dazzled by ETA's aura.

The great split in ETA

In 1972 ETA merged with EGI-*Batasuna*, which was the most radicalised sector of the PNV's youth organisation, and was led by Iñaki Mujika Arregui (*Ezkerra*) (Sullivan 1988, 164–165). The new ETA, which was under the charismatic leadership of Eustaquio Mendizábal (Txiki), was defined by two characteristics. In the first place, its doctrinal framework was reduced to an extremist and dogmatic nationalism, since it feared any ideological debate that might result in a new 'non-nationalist' drift. Second, there was a sharp increase in ETA's terrorist attacks: two in 1970, 16 in 1971, 43 in 1972, 26 in 1973, 19 in 1974, 39 in 1975, 21 in 1976 and 68 in 1977. The high point of its campaign came in 1973 with the assassination of the President of the Spanish government, Admiral Luis Carrero

Blanco. ETA claimed two lives in 1968, one in 1969, another in 1972, six in 1973, 19 in 1974 and 14 in 1975. In total, the terrorists claimed the lives of 43 people during the dictatorship (López 2015). A large proportion of Basque citizens and the anti-Francoist opposition identified ETA's victims with Francoism, which is why there was understanding of its crimes, if not justification for them.

Bombs appeared to be politically more profitable than strikes. All ETA's members had to subordinate themselves to the dictates of the military front, which gave rise to serious internal disagreements that were aggravated by the death of Txikia in a gunfight in April 1973. The controversy over how to coordinate politics with violence re-emerged. In the first part of the VI Assembly, held in 1973, a new leadership was elected which was dominated by the military front (Hordago 1979, vol. XV, 106 and 118–120).

The workers' front of ETA was unable to take part in trade union struggles, as both police and workers identified it with terrorist actions. This made it vulnerable to the repression and unattractive as a means of protest. As a result, this faction was unable to compete with the trade unions. Many of its members considered that the workers' front had become no more than a recruiting office for the military. In spring 1974, facing the 'impossibility' of continuing to work within ETA, a sector of the workers' front in Gipuzkoa broke away from the organisation (*Sugarra* 1, 1975).

On 13 September 1974 ETA's military front, which was once again acting on its own account, planted a bomb in the Rolando cafeteria in Correo Street in Madrid, close to the head office of the body responsible for public order throughout Spain. Twelve people died in the explosion and around 70 were wounded. Although the attack had been aimed at the police, only the thirteenth mortal victim, who died from his wounds in January 1977, was a member of the police force. The dilemma over whether or not to claim responsibility for the attack accelerated a crisis that had been developing for some time. While the military front defended the need to claim responsibility for the massacre the rest of the Executive Committee was opposed, since this was considered to be counterproductive. Finally, the military front broke away to form its own organisation. In the final instance the split was due to disagreements over how to coordinate the exercise of violence and politics (Sullivan 1988, 187–188; Alonso *et al.* 2010, 40–47).

Led by José Miguel Beñaran (*Argala*), the military front was renamed ETA Militar (ETA-M). Foreseeing that a 'bourgeois democracy' was going to be established in Spain, ETA-M stated that it had renounced 'mass struggle' in order to dedicate itself exclusively to 'armed struggle' ('ETAren Agiria', 1974). Thus, by separating the two spheres, the ultranationalist parties would be safe from police repression and ETA-M itself would be free from any 'reformist' contamination that might proceed from the former. The group transformed itself into an efficient and hierarchised 'army', from which any trace of internal democracy disappeared. Its doctrine was reduced to the most intransigent and sectarian version of nationalism and to an unconditional commitment to terrorist violence (Sullivan 1988, 188–189; Domínguez 1998).

The majority of the members of ETA formed ETA Político-Militar (ETA-PM). Its radical nationalism was tempered by a dose of Marxism and it intended to continue combining mass struggle' with terrorism. In May 1975 ETA-PM signed an alliance with radical nationalist forces from Galicia and Catalonia with the aim of spreading armed struggle throughout Spain. However, the joint campaign was aborted by the work of a secret service agent infiltrated in ETA-PM, which made it possible for the police to effectively dismantle the gang's cells. Two of those arrested were executed by firing squad on 27 September 1975 together with three members of the *Frente Revolucionario Antifascista y Patriota* (FRAP – Antifascist Patriotic Revolutionary Front). Nor did ETA-PM's mass struggle produce positive results (Fernández 2013, 82–83).

This tactical failure forced the ideological leader of ETA-PM, Eduardo Moreno Bergaretxe (*Pertur*), to renew the group's structure and strategy (Amigo 1978). It was decided to create a Leninist-type party that would function as the vanguard of radical nationalism and take advantage of all the resorts of the future 'bourgeois democracy', including the ballot box. On the other hand, ETA-PM would remain as the party's subordinate armed wing. In addition, *Pertur* proposed that a new formation form an alliance with the extreme left, which was better prepared for political activity. In spite of *Pertur*'s mysterious disappearance in July 1976, which has still not been clarified, the plan he had designed was approved by ETA-PM at its VII Assembly (September 1976). *Euskal Iraultzarako Alderdia* (EIA – Party for the Basque Revolution) appeared at the end of 1976.

ETA during the transition

Following Francisco Franco's death in November 1975 and Juan Carlos I's ascent to the throne, a new scenario opened up in Spain. The most reformist sectors of the regime, led by the President of the government, Adolfo Suárez, committed themselves to recovering parliamentary democracy. Now, there were many actors opposed to the political change and some of them did so by resorting to arms. The transition was thus a complex and convulsive process involving a high level of political violence. During those years there were 336 victims of terrorism in the Basque Country and Navarre. The deaths of some of these victims were caused by organisations of the extreme right, which were suspected of having links with the more reactionary sectors of the state administration. These groups, of which the best known was the *Batallón Vasco-Español* (BVE – Spanish-Basque Battalion), murdered 32 people who were accused of being linked to ETA or the extreme left. However, the overwhelming majority of politically motivated murders were committed by the various branches of ETA: 17 victims in 1976, 11 in 1977, 66 in 1978, 80 in 1979, 96 in 1980, 32 in 1981 and 38 in 1982. The majority of them were policemen or civil guardsmen (López 2015).

The first elections were held in June 1977 and were won by Suárez's party, *Unión de Centro Democrático* (UCD – Union of the Democratic Centre). EIA stood as part of the *Euskadiko Ezkerra* (EE – Basque Left) coalition, which won

6.18 per cent of the votes in the Basque provinces. On the contrary, ETA-M called for a boycott. Its call went unheeded: abstention in the Basque Country (22.77 per cent) and Navarre (17.76 per cent) was similar to the Spanish average (21.17 per cent). This failure led ETA-M's leadership to reconsider its strategy. It first supported and then took control of *Herri Batasuna* (HB – Popular Unity), a coalition of four parties (LAIA, HASI, ESB and ANV) which ended up becoming the electoral wing of the terrorist gang. In the next elections in 1979, HB (15 per cent of the votes in the Basque Country) easily overtook EE (8 per cent). While the former entrenched itself in intransigence, the latter gradually adopted more moderate positions (Fernández and López 2012, 117–146).

The first Parliament drew up and approved the Spanish Constitution (1978), but first it dealt with the question of an amnesty for what were then termed 'political prisoners', which included those sentenced for violent crimes. This was a demand made by the opposition parties and was accepted by the government. The Amnesty Law was approved on 15 October 1977 in order to deactivate terrorism and achieve a definitive reconciliation between the 'two Spains', which is why the 'legal forgetting' covered both the crimes committed by ETA and other groups (66 murders) and those responsible for the Francoist repression. ETA's last prisoner, Francisco Aldanondo, left jail on 9 December (Fernández 2013, 125–128).

Now, in spite of the Amnesty Law, the different branches of ETA refused to stop carrying out political murders. ETA-M also refused to accept that the Basque Country should form an autonomous community within democratic Spain, which finally occurred following the approval of the Guernica Statute in 1979. For this group, the only solution to the territorial question was political independence, although this was not demanded by the majority of Basque citizens. ETA-M had placed itself in frontal opposition to the transition, but in spite of denying any legitimacy to the nascent democracy, which it denounced as a 'disguised dictatorship', the organisation made a strategic turn. Accepting that it was impossible to defeat the state militarily, ETA-M began a 'war of attrition', which lasted until the mid-1990s. This consisted in killing the greatest possible number of policemen and members of the armed forces, thus inciting their senior officers to revolt, in order to put pressure on the government to give into its demands. ETA-M was confident that in order to avoid an eventual *coup d'état*, Suárez's government would give into its demands (Domínguez 1998). Events did not work out that way and on 23 February 1981 an attempted *coup d'état* ended in failure.

On the other hand, the EE coalition and its nucleus EIA (the party led by Mario Onaindia, one of the ETA members tried at the Burgos trial) evolved towards increasingly pragmatic positions. This evolution led them to support the Autonomy Statute for the Basque Country and, indirectly, parliamentary democracy and the constitutional framework. In parallel, ETA-PM voluntarily withdrew into the background. Its role during the transition was limited (in theory at least) to defending the 'popular conquests' that might be wrested from the government by EIA and its allied organisations. This approach took concrete shape in armed propaganda in support of the line spelt out by the party and in 'sectorial intervention'. Following the model of extreme-left terrorism in Italy (*Brigate Rosse, Nuclei Armati Proletari*, etc.), the group set itself up as the guarantor of the 'conquests' of the Basque working class; that is, it would act in support of labour demands: 'Basque workers can and should have an organization willing to intervene when they are affected by the violence of capital from the state' (*Hautsi* 4, 21 July 1977). ETA-PM also supported the demands of other social and cultural groups: the anti-nuclear, 'anti-repressive', pro-amnesty, feminist and citizens' movements and the movement in support of the Basque language, among others. Its 'sectorial intervention' took the form of bomb attacks, kidnappings and 21 murders over the course of its history.

In the summer of 1979 ETA-PM began its first campaign against tourism by planting over a dozen timed bombs in different towns on the Mediterranean coast of Spain, the destination of millions of foreign tourists. The organisation gave advance warning of where and when the explosions would take place as it did not want to cause mortal victims, but two Belgian citizens were wounded on the beach at Marbella. The purpose of the operation was to force the government to concede a new general amnesty linked to the Autonomy Statute; in the short term, ETA-PM's goals were for the National Police to abandon the prison in Soria and for its prisoners to be transferred to jails in the Basque Country. Several leaders of EIA acted as mediators between ETA-PM and Suárez's executive, which was very concerned that the campaign should not affect a strategic economic sector. Thanks to EIA's mediation, ETA-PM obtained some of its demands. However, the government went back on its word and did the exact opposite of what had been agreed: it transferred some of ETA-PM's prisoners from Basauri prison in the Basque Country to the prison in Soria (*Hautsi* 18, September 1979). In spite of the fact that the terrorist group's leadership had already called an end to the campaign, one cell acting on its own account planted bombs at Barajas Airport and the Chamartín and Atocha railway stations (Madrid). Unlike what had happened on earlier occasions, the cell only gave warning of the imminent explosions to the Civil Government, which gave no credibility to the phone call. The explosions on 29 July 1979 ended the lives of seven people and wounded over 100. Those deaths gave rise to conflicts within the organisation itself and, for the first time in its history, EIA criticised ETA-PM in the mass media, calling for a 'public self-criticism', an order that the gang obeyed a few days later. ETA-PM deactivated the remaining bombs or provided maps of where they were planted to the police (Alonso *et al.* 2010, 221–226).

The Madrid massacre was unmistakable proof that although it had initially seemed possible to maintain a relationship between EIA and ETA-PM, the parliamentary logic and the logic of terrorism were incompatible in the long term. Moreover, many leaders of both EIA and ETA-PM had verified that armed struggle was not only useless, but also counterproductive to their political interests. When the group assassinated two militants of UCD at the end of 1980, those who favoured ending the violence seized the initiative. In February 1981, following a formal request from EIA and the unsuccessful *coup d'état*, ETA-PM declared an indefinite truce. Mario Onaindia and the parliamentarian Juan Mari Bandrés negotiated the disbanding of ETA-PM with the UCD government. Nonetheless, a sector of the organisation was opposed to laying down its arms and in early 1982 ETA-PM divided into two groups. One faction, ETA-PM VII Assembly, accepted disbandment, and its members, whether prisoners or 'exiles', were reintegrated into civil life thanks to the government (1982–1985). No political concessions were made, nor did ETA-PM surrender its arms. Nor was there any public repentance: for the victims of terrorism the process concluded with the impunity of the killers. In spite of all this, the end of this sector of ETA-PM was one of EIA's greatest political successes. The other faction of ETA-PM, the VIII Assembly, attempted to remain active. After murdering a member of the armed forces in 1983 it disappeared, and its remnants were absorbed by ETA-M. Two members of ETA-PM VIII Assembly were later to play prominent roles in the 'patriotic left': Arnaldo Otegi and Francisco Javier López Peña (*Thierry*).

ETA-M and ETA-PM were joined by a new terrorist organisation in September 1977: the *Comandos Autónomos Anticapitalistas* (CAA – Autonomous Anti-capitalist Cells), which were responsible for killing 32 people (López 2015). These were cells that functioned in a more or less independent manner. On the one hand, a large number of these cells shared a doctrinal basis that mixed radical Basque nationalism, anti-capitalism, decision-making based on assemblies and councils, anarchism, and a rejection of trade unions and political parties. In other words, their model was the Italian autonomous movement of the 1970s; hence their activity bore considerable resemblance to extreme-left terrorism. On the other hand, a second sector of the CAA, which proceeded from ETA-PM (1977), understood 'autonomy' to mean freedom of action and not a specific ideological position. This divergence, which together with police action was one of the reasons for its disappearance, explains why it was so difficult to trace a pattern in the over 100 terrorist attacks attributed to the CAA (Likiniano 1996).

The CAA had a particular impact on the business sector. For example, they persecuted the managers of Telefónica in the province of Gipuzkoa, whom they accused of collaborating in hypothetical police phone tapping. On the morning of 23 October 1980 a terrorist cell kidnapped Juan Manuel García Cordero, the representative of that company in Gipuzkoa. His corpse turned up some hours later. When claiming responsibility for the murder, the CAA threatened 'all of those who collaborate with the Police in controlling telephone and postal communications'. On 30 October the terrorists ended the life of Juan Carlos Fernández Aspiazu, an innkeeper who was responsible for Telefónica's public relations. In March 1982 two gunmen killed Enrique Cuesta Jiménez, who had succeeded García Cordero as the company's representative in Gipuzkoa. The national policeman Antonio Gómez García was wounded in this latter attack and died five days later (Alonso *et al.* 2010, 326–327, 330–331 and 390–394).

Another singular characteristic of the CAA were its attacks on Basque politicians from right-wing parties. But it was also the first branch of ETA to attack a party proceeding from the anti-Francoist opposition. On 27 October 1979 CAA murdered an affiliate of the PSOE and its trade union, Germán González López. On 23 February 1984 the terrorists killed the socialist senator Enrique Casas (Alonso *et al.* 2010, 244–245 and 468–470). One year later the CAA disappeared due to police action, lack of social support and internal disagreements.

Conclusion

Essential factors for understanding the genesis of terrorism in the Basque Country include: the dictatorship; its Spanish ultra-nationalism and centralism; the agonising sentiment caused by the decline of the Basque language and the arrival of thousands of immigrants; a literal reading of the narrative of a secular, ethnic conflict between Basques and Spaniards; hatred; the desire to avenge the Basque soldiers of the Spanish Civil War; the intergenerational clash; the desire to establish a distance from the PNV; and the Third Worldist mirage. These circumstances influenced the outlook of the ETA members. They did not, however, determine their activity: the ETA members were neither responding as automata to a concrete conjuncture, nor were they fulfilling an unavoidable destiny.

After ruling out other alternatives, the leadership of ETA opted for 'armed struggle', but it spent ten years immersed in debates and theorisations on guerrilla warfare. It is true that the logistical means were lacking during that decade; nor was there a firm resolve. The opposite occurred in 1968, first, when *Txabi* Etxebarrieta chose to shoot José Antonio Pardines from behind instead of disarming him, and later, when the leaders of ETA decided to reactivate the plan to assassinate the heads of the Politico-Social Brigade in Bilbao and San Sebastián in order to set in motion the action–reaction–action spiral. The ETA members made use of their free will in both cases.

The thesis of this chapter therefore fits the now classical arguments of Martha Crenshaw (2011). Like other organisations, ETA as a collective actor chose terrorism as a strategy to attain its goals. It is undeniable that this decision was taken under the influence of specific circumstances, but historical determinism, mere contextualisation and mono-causal theories must be ruled out. The leaders of the group opted for this type of violence freely and consciously after discarding other alternatives. The fact is that other courses of action were available, as shown by the peaceful trajectory of the rest of Basque nationalism and the anti-Francoist opposition.

Bibliography

Alonso, Rogelio, Florencio Domínguez and Marcos García (2010) *Vidas rotas. Historia de los hombres, mujeres y niños víctimas de ETA*. Madrid: Espasa.

Álvarez, José Luis (1997) *Euskal Herria en el horizonte*. Tafalla: Txalaparta.

Amigo, Ángel (1978) *Pertur. ETA 71–76*. San Sebastián: Hordago.

Casanellas, Pau (2014) *Morir matando. El franquismo ante la práctica armada, 1968–1977*. Madrid: Los Libros de la Catarata.

Castells, Miguel (1984) *Radiografía de un modelo represivo*. San Sebastián: Ediciones Vascas.

Crenshaw, Martha (2011) *Explaining Terrorism: Causes, Processes, and Consequences*. London: Routledge.

De Pablo, Santiago, Ludger Mees and José Antonio Rodríguez (2001) *El péndulo patriótico. Historia del Partido Nacionalista Vasco, II: 1936–1975*. Barcelona: Crítica.

Domínguez, Florencio (1998) *ETA: estrategia organizativa y actuaciones, 1978–1992*. Bilbao: UPV-EHU.

Elorza, Antonio (1995) *La religión política. 'El nacionalismo sabiniano' y otros ensayos sobre nacionalismo e integrismo*. San Sebastián: R&B.

Fernández, Gaizka (2013) *Héroes, heterodoxos y traidores. Historia de Euskadiko Ezkerra (1974–1994)*. Madrid: Tecnos.

Fernández, Gaizka (2015) 'Mitos que matan. La narrativa del conflicto vasco'. *Ayer* 98: 213–240.

Fernández, Gaizka and Raúl López (2012) *Sangre, votos, manifestaciones. ETA y el nacionalismo vasco radical (1958–2011)*. Madrid: Tecnos.

Garmendia, José María (1996) *Historia de ETA*. San Sebastián: Haranburu.

Garmendia, José María (2006) 'ETA: nacimiento, desarrollo y crisis (1959–1978)'. In *La historia de ETA*, ed. Antonio Elorza, 77–170. Madrid: Temas de Hoy.

Gómez, Javier (2014) *Matar, purgar, sanar. La represión franquista en Araba (1936–1945)*. Madrid: Tecnos.

Gurrutxaga, Ander (1990) *La refundación del nacionalismo vasco*. Bilbao: UPV-EHU.

Hordago, Equipo (1979–1981) *Documentos Y*. San Sebastián: Hordago, 18 volumes.

Jáuregui, Gurutz (1985) *Ideología y estrategia política de ETA. Análisis de su evolución entre 1959 y 1968*. Madrid: Siglo XXI.

Jáuregui, Gurutz (1997) *Entre la tragedia y la esperanza. Vasconia ante el nuevo milenio*. Barcelona: Ariel.

Krutwig, Federico (2006) *Vasconia*. Pamplona: Herritar Berri. First published 1963.

Levinger, Matthew and Paula F. Lytle (2001) 'Myth and mobilisation: The triadic structure of nationalist rhetoric'. *Nations and Nationalism* 7: 175–194.

Likiniano, Félix (1996) *Comandos Autónomos. Un anticapitalismo iconoclasta*. Bilbao: Felix Likiniano.

López, Raúl (2012) *Euskadi en duelo. La central nuclear de Lemóniz como símbolo de la Transición vasca*. Bilbao: Fundación Euskadi.

López, Raúl (2015) *Informe Foronda: los efectos del terrorismo en la sociedad vasca (1968–2010)*. Madrid: Los Libros de la Catarata.

Pérez-Agote, Alfonso (1987) *El nacionalismo vasco a la salida del Franquismo*. Madrid: CIS – Siglo XXI.

Sullivan, John (1988) *ETA and Basque Nationalism. The Fight for Euskadi, 1890–1986*. New York: Routledge.

Uriarte, Eduardo (2005) *Mirando atrás. Del proceso de Burgos a la amenaza permanente*. Barcelona: Ediciones B.

Zumalde, Xabier (2004) *Mi lucha clandestina en ETA. Memorias del primer jefe del Frente Militar (1965–1968)*. Arrigorriaga: Status ediciones.

2 ETA during democracy, 1975–2011

Diego Muro

Introduction

The Basque organisation ETA (*Euskadi ta Askatasuna*, Basque Homeland and Freedom) laid down its arms on 20 October, 2011. Having failed to achieve its strategic goal of creating an independent socialist state, this Basque terrorist group unilaterally decided to end its armed activity after 43 years of violent campaigning. This chapter provides an overview of ETA's secessionist campaign between 1975 and 2011, and emphasises two explanatory variables – the efficiency of counter-terrorist policy and the loss of social support – in bringing about its demise.

There are numerous accounts that provide an overview of ETA's tactics since 1959 (Garmendia 1996; Elorza 2000; Domínguez 1998; Sánchez-Cuenca 2001). Much of the research has focused on explaining why the group emerged under the Franco dictatorship (Jáuregui 1981; Unzueta 1988; Mees 2003), but other authors have tried to explain how an ethno-nationalist community legitimised ETA's violent campaign for territorial change (Zulaika 1988; Mata 1993; Muro 2008; Watson 2008; Fernández and López 2012). There has also been considerable analysis of the Spanish security response to this internal threat (Jaime-Jiménez 1998; Woodworth 2001; Reinares and Alonso 2007; Alonso 2010) as well as profiles of individual terrorists (Reinares 2001; Hamilton 2007). However, much less scholarly research has focused on the conditions that precipitated the decline of the organisation and the end of its terror campaign (Cid 2013; Whitfield 2014). To date, the most comprehensive accounts have been provided by journalists (Domínguez 2012; Escrivá 2012; Batista 2012; Aizpeoloa 2013; Azurmendi 2014). Needless to say, these descriptive accounts leave many questions unanswered and there is considerable room for more analytical and theoretically informed approaches.

The research questions driving this chapter are: Why did ETA declare a unilateral ceasefire in 2011? What are the causal factors that led the Basque group towards its end? Was ETA defeated or did it disband voluntarily? This chapter will explain that a combination of internal and external variables account for its demise. The main external cause was the counter-terrorist policy that eventually brought about the operational decline of the organisation and delegitimised it. The key components of that policy were the coordinated actions of the police and the courts, the international collaboration with France and the isolation of political parties that sympathised with ETA. The main internal cause was the gradual loss of social support and the realisation by the leaders of ETA that terrorism, defined as the deliberate creation and exploitation of fear through violence or the threat of violence in the pursuit of political change, was ineffective in gaining policy concessions.

The chapter is divided into five sections. After this introduction there is an overview of radical Basque nationalism and the ideology that transitioned from being a political-military movement waging a war of attrition and intimidation to a social-political movement that exclusively used peaceful means. The third section focuses on ETA during the first two decades of democracy and tries to account for the longevity of the terrorist group. It explains the resonance of the radical nationalist message and why ETA continued to oppose the democratic state in spite of a process of decentralisation that granted extensive home-rule powers to both the Basque Country and Navarre. The fourth section examines the counter-terrorist policy from the 1990s onward and argues that a process of social learning led to the refinement of security policy that eventually brought the demise of ETA. The fifth section gives a comparative view of the end of the violent campaign and discusses the effectiveness of terrorism. Finally, conclusion summarises the explanatory variables that account for the upsurge and decline of ETA between 1975 and 2011.

ETA and radical Basque nationalism

The history of ETA during the democratic period requires an understanding of radical Basque nationalism, the ideology that legitimised the use of terrorism and the movement that provided social and political support for its actions (Mata 1993; Sáez de la Fuente 2002; Casquete 2006; Muro 2008; Bullain 2011; Fernández and López 2012). It is also known as the nationalist left or *izquierda abertzale* and without it ETA would not have been a resilient insurgent group but an underground movement incapable of fighting a 'long war' or a tactical combination of violence and political activism. The existence of a stable radical milieu (up to 15 per cent of the Basque electorate) allowed ETA to fight a war of attrition against the Spanish state with the goal of forcing the authorities to sit round the negotiating table (Ibarra 1989; De la Calle and Sánchez-Cuenca 2009, 39). The issues to be discussed during peace negotiations would have been the political independence of the Basque homeland, the unification of Navarre with the Spanish and French Basque Countries, the decommissioning of weapons and the release of prisoners. Nonetheless, the two principal antagonists – the Spanish government and ETA – viewed territory as both valuable and indivisible, and were unable to resolve their differences in the numerous talks held between them. This is fully consistent with the literature that predicts the emergence of political violence when both the state and a dissatisfied minority come to view control over the same territory as an issue that affects their own survival (Toft 2003).

Radical Basque nationalism could be defined as the political ideology and social movement, led by ETA, which argued that the Basque homeland (under Spanish and French sovereignty) deserved an independent socialist state and that the use of political violence or terrorism to achieve that strategic goal was justified. More specifically, the Basque Movement of National Liberation (*Movimiento de Liberación Nacional Vasco* – MLNV) was a self-named network of organisations founded in 1974 and made up of a number of interconnected political groups, social agents and NGOs with interests in the fields of feminism, environmentalism, internationalism, Basque culture, youth, students and prisoners' rights. Some of the most important members of this web were the trade union LAB, the electoral coalition Herri Batasuna (and successors) and the terrorist group ETA. The key characteristic of all the satellite organisations was their ideological and strategic dependency on ETA, which they nourished with the necessary human, material, moral and logistical resources to continue acting as the front runner of the movement. ETA did select violent means for achieving the final goal and established a link between ethnicity and violence for members of the radical community. According to ETA, Basqueness was derived pre-eminently from active participation in the liturgy of national struggle (Muro 2008, 10).

The tactical history of ETA after the Franco dictatorship may be divided into two periods: 1975 to 1995 and 1995 to 2011 (Sánchez-Cuenca 2001, 65; De la Calle and Sánchez-Cuenca 2004, 59). The first was a period of democratisation when ETA launched a war of attrition to force the Spanish government to negotiate the principles of the so-called 'KAS Alternative'. It is important to point out that there were two ETAs competing between 1974 and 1986: *ETA militar* (ETA-M) and *ETA politico militar* (ETA-PM). ETA-PM was linked to the political party Euskadiko Ezkerra (EE) and partially disbanded in 1982 to pursue political tactics, whereas ETA-M continued its violent campaign, hence inheriting the name ETA (Fernández 2013). The war of attrition during this first period obtained some tactical results in the form of policy concessions and peace negotiations as well as provoking some excessive use of force on the part of Spanish security forces (as the theory of action–repression–action predicted). The second period of decline between 1995 and 2011 was characterised by the intimidating use of the 'socialisation of suffering' (De la Calle and Sánchez-Cuenca 2004; Calleja and Sánchez-Cuenca 2006), the gradual loss of support for the armed group and the increasing effectiveness of police efforts in both domestic and international arenas. This latter period was also characterised by a 'failed' peace process which eventually succeeded in bringing peace, as will be demonstrated later.

From the point of view of radical nationalists, the first period (1975–1995) was characterised by ETA's insistence that Spain was an autocratic state with only a democratic façade and that political violence was not only a legitimate but a necessary and effective form of coercion (Sánchez-Cuenca 2001, 15). In spite of the approval of the 1978 Constitution, the call for competitive elections and the process of political decentralisation, both ETA-M and ETA-PM continued to argue that nothing substantial had changed (Mees 2001). This opinion remained unaltered, even when the transition in the Basque Country was concluded with the approval of the Statute of Autonomy (1979) – which granted self-rule powers covering the collection of taxes, police (*Ertzaintza*), education, health care, language, culture as well as public media – and the return of the Basque president in exile, the *lehendakari* Jesús María Leizaola. Not even when regional elections were held from 1980 onward and Basque nationalism (with 45 to 65 per cent of the votes) became the indisputable hegemonic force over the next decades did the radical nationalist community ever accept that the regime was legitimate. In sharp contrast with the rest of Spain, the transition to democracy in the Basque Country was characterised by low support for the constitutional settlement and high levels of political violence and social mobilisation (Muro 2010).

Between 1975 and 1995 ETA was supported both morally and logistically by a segment of the Basque population and was a resourceful organisation capable of inflicting sustained damage on Spanish interests. As may be seen in Figure 2.1, the majority of deaths were concentrated during the transition years, especially between 1976 and 1981 when ETA killed 302 individuals. These years came to be known as 'years of lead' because ETA's violent actions made it to the headlines on a weekly basis. Many of those targeted by ETA were either policemen or military, and they responded with a 'rattle of sabres' and two attempted *coups d'état* during that period. The level of violence declined from the 1980s onward, as Figure 2.1 indicates.

ETA killed 845 individuals during its 52-year history, 802 during the democratic period (95 per cent) and 43 under the dictatorship (5 per cent). The data for

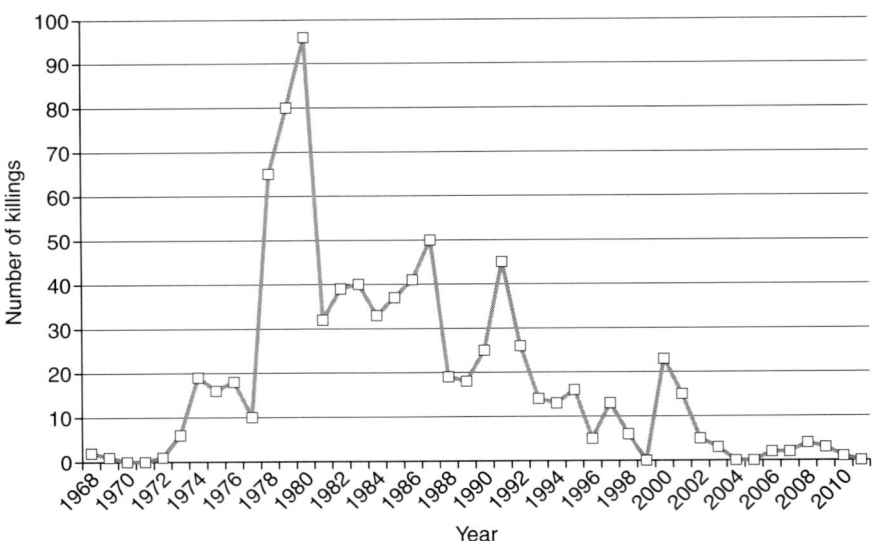

Figure 2.1 The number of ETA killings per year (1968–2011) (source: author's own elaboration).

these years combined all the killings of ETA and its multiple factions and splinter groups (ETA-M, ETA-PM, Comandos Autónomos Anticapitalistas (CAA), Iraultza, Mendeku, etc.). Of the different clandestine organisations and terrorist groups that killed in the Basque Country, however, ETA-M was responsible for 92 per cent of the attacks (López 2015). The high number of fatalities was the result of using car bombs and a failure to discriminate between combatants and non-combatants. Some of the attacks with the highest death-toll included the 1986 attack at the Republica Dominicana Square in Madrid (12 deaths and 32 injured) or the 1987 car bomb in the supermarket Hipercor in Barcelona in 1987 (21 deaths and 45 injured). The military compounds of the Civil Guards (*casa cuartel*), where both policemen and their families lived, were also attacked: in 1987 in Zaragoza (11 deaths and 40 injured) and in 1991 in Vic (ten casualties and 44 injured).

The second period between 1995 and 2011 was characterised by ETA's realisation that a military defeat was impossible (due to the effectiveness of counter-terrorism) and by a growing popular rejection of its violent methods. In 1978, 48 per cent of adult Basques perceived ETA members as either patriots or idealists, and only 7 per cent of those interviewed in opinion surveys from the Euskobarómetro called them plain criminals. In 2007, however, only 23 per cent of Basque citizens referred to them in favourable terms and those who portrayed members of ETA as simply criminals had risen to 18 per cent. The key elements of this period were: (1) the socialisation of suffering; (2) the Pact of Estella; (3) the failed attempts to bring about a peaceful resolution of the conflict (which will be dealt with in the section on counter-terrorism); and (4) the impact of 9/11.

To start with, the so-called 'socialisation of suffering' was a tactic by which ETA expanded its range of legitimate targets. From 1995 onward, politicians from non-nationalist parties (e.g. Gregorio Ordoñez) were increasingly targeted in an attempt to push them to the margins and polarise Basque society and its party system. Violent incidents of street fighting (*kale borroka*) also targeted the offices of non-nationalist political parties, especially the PSE and the PP, which were often the target of arson attacks together with ATMs, bank offices, public transport, trash containers, etc. As part of this new tactic of intimidation, approved in the *Oldartzen* document, ETA kidnapped Miguel Ángel Blanco, a 29-year-old town councillor, in the Basque town of Ermua on 10 July 1997. ETA then released a statement that contained a 48-hour ultimatum: either the government transferred all ETA inmates to jails close to the Basque Country or it would kill the hostage. In spite of massive demonstrations across Spain demanding Blanco's release, his body was found shortly after the ultimatum expired. This cold-blooded assassination contributed to a growing dissociation of important sectors of Basque society from the terrorist group, as evidenced in an increasing mobilisation of citizens demanding the end of violence (Muro 2008). The popular objection to the murder of a minor local politician also fostered a temporary unity of political parties against ETA following the spirit of the Ajuria Enea Pact. But union and public anger against ETA's intimidation and harassment was something of a mirage, as the pact between Basque nationalist organisations demonstrated.

The Pact of Estella (Lizarra in Euskera) of September 1998 sharply divided the nationalist parties (PNV, EA and HB) from the so-called constitutionalists (PSOE and PP) and the Basque party system came to be described as 'polarised pluralism'. The PNV and EA had approached HB with the intention of favouring the disarmament of ETA in exchange for replacing the Statute of Autonomy of 1979 with calls for the right to self-determination. Inspired by the Good Friday Agreement signed months earlier, the PNV failed to import the Irish model when it decided to negotiate single-handedly a ceasefire with ETA behind the back of the constitutionalist political parties. Indeed, the main consequence of the Estella–Lizarra pact was additional polarisation between nationalists and non-nationalists and a deep sense of betrayal by pro-Spanish forces. ETA responded by declaring a ceasefire of 14 months that greatly benefited its political wing of the time (Euskal Herritarrok – EH), that had replaced the banned Herri Batasuna, and which had doubled its number of seats in the regional Parliament from 7 to 14 per cent. ETA returned to violence because its leadership was unhappy about the slow progress and immediate lack of results.

Finally, the international dimension also contributed to the decline of ETA. Israelis and Palestinians had negotiated at Camp David and Oslo, and the IRA had managed to find a landing strip with the Good Friday Agreement, but nothing of that sort appeared on the Basque horizon. By the turn of the century, Basque public opinion was much less supportive of terrorism, and the international context became even more unfavourable to clandestine and insurgent groups. The coordinated Al Qaeda attacks of 9/11 on the USA ended the romantic view that terrorism was the 'weapon of the weak' (Crenshaw 1981). As a consequence, ETA found it more difficult to justify its use of political violence in an increasingly hostile environment characterised by a fourth wave of religious terrorism and the internationalisation of the fight against jihadism (Hoffman 2006).

To recapitulate, the factors that account for the decline of ETA during the 1990s and early 2000s were the 'socialisation of suffering' tactic, the backlash of public opinion, the counter-terrorist policy (which will be examined later in this chapter), and the changing international environment which favoured the exchange of information and international collaboration, especially among EU member states. Ultimately, all these events triggered an internal debate about the usefulness of violence and its role in obtaining policy concessions and resolving territorial disputes. The idea that terrorism could be counterproductive for Basque independence was gradually internalised by ETA sympathisers and helped trigger the process of internal deliberation in the 2000s.

Why did ETA last so long?

The survival of ETA into the transition years warrants an explanation. Born under the dictatorship, it could have disbanded as Spain consolidated its democracy. After all, this was the option taken by ETA-PM, a splinter organisation that was dissolved in 1982. The argument of the *polimilis* was that the new political scenario justified a change of course and disbanded both the terrorist group and the political wing, Euskadiko Ezkerra, a party that in 1993 joined the Basque social democrats (Partido Socialista de Euskadi – PSE) (Fernández 2013). But why was ETA-PM disbanded in 1982 while ETA-M continued to use violence? What were the tactical and organisational variables that explain the longevity of ETA?

The ETA of the 1980s and early 1990s had few reasons to give up weapons. The use of the 'war of attrition' (*guerra de desgaste*) had brought considerable returns as successive Spanish governments were willing to sit down to negotiate with ETA. Calls for political negotiations were not uncommon and many believe that a stagnant conflict could not be resolved by the use of force but only by a negotiated settlement where both sides would have to make concessions. Actually, it could be argued that the process of democratisation created a set of devolved institutions (or political opportunity structures) that facilitated the elite's decision to promote nationalism and ethnic conflict, including terrorist campaigns (Snyder 2000, 37). Besides, ETA's discourse about Spanish authoritarian practices resonated with the Basque population which learned about the odd case of ill-treatment and torture under police custody.

The longevity of ETA may also be explained by the organisational needs of the group. It is commonly assumed that terrorist organisations tend to follow the logic of self-maintenance and to value their own survival (Della Porta 1995, 196). Terrorism can cease to be a tactical means to achieve a strategic goal and become an end in itself as both a way of life for terrorists and a tool to assure organisational continuity. This is why organisations devote considerable attention to financing their activities through voluntary donations or extortion. A study from the University of Deusto estimated that between 1973 and 2011, ETA collected €161 million in kidnappings, robberies and the so-called 'revolutionary tax', extorted from small to medium-sized businesses. Furthermore, as a consolidated non-state actor, ETA competed with other nationalist terrorist groups (Iraultza, ETA-PM, CAA, etc.) in the violent marketplace, while its political wing, Herri Batasuna, tried to erode the hegemony of the PNV in the nationalist camp. While ETA was engaged in a strategy of 'outbidding' other terrorist groups, Herri Batasuna followed a similar approach in the political arena. The strategy of both the 'political' and 'military' wing of radical Basque nationalism needed a significant degree of action and 'resource mobilisation' to be effective.

Besides the tactical and organisational reasons, an ideological component helps explain why ETA continued to kill. As argued above, its justification for the use of violence during democracy was that no significant change had taken place since the death of the dictator. Furthermore, the agent responsible for Basque oppression was not a system of institutions (democratic or autocratic) but Spain, an entity that had historically mistreated Basques. According to this nationalist interpretation, the opponent responsible for the occupation and oppression of the Basque nation was Spain, regardless of the 'political roof' it took. ETA's violence was a reaction to decades – perhaps even centuries – of Spanish aggression and injustice. In the words of one of the ideologues of Herri Batasuna, Telesforo Monzón, the logic of violence would be simple: 'It is not ETA that has bred violence. It is violence that has bred ETA' (Monzón 1995).

But why did this nationalist interpretation of Basque history resonate? Did Basques believe that Spain was not a full democracy? How did ETA manage to convince its supporters that political violence could be an effective tactic? This nationalist interpretation was facilitated by the fact that, in spite of the growing opportunities to influence the decision-making process democratically, key sections of the PSOE government and the security forces continued to display undemocratic attitudes and behaviour. According to ETA supporters, there were three indicators or areas that undermined the democratic system, namely (1) torture; (2) the GAL; and (3) the policy of dispersing prisoners. In the eyes of some Basques, these excesses confirmed the widely held idea that the territorial conflict was a war between two extremes.

First, cases of ill-treatment while in police custody were not uncommon. When basic human rights were abused, those responsible were not always brought to justice, and a sense of camaraderie and corporatism led policemen to protect each other. With the incorporation of *habeas corpus* (or the right to object before a judge regarding the legality of one's imprisonment) and the introduction of 24-hour CCTV for ETA detainees, torture was gradually abandoned and by the late 1980s Amnesty International confirmed that systematic torture had completely disappeared (although the odd case of abuse could still be detected). Radical nationalists instrumentalised and politicised the issue of torture and argued that cases of ill-treatment were not occasional but systematic practices Ultimately, the authoritarian behaviour of sectors of the security forces strengthened their image as a hostile force and made it easier for ETA supporters to persuade new generations that the Basque Country was an occupied territory (Aguilar 1998; Muro 2009).

Second, the dirty war of the Grupos Antiterroristas de Liberación (GAL) was also highlighted to emphasise the autocratic tendencies of state institutions. In their effort to prevent civilian loss in another attack, the security forces' response to terrorism diminished democracy more than the acts of terrorism themselves (Crenshaw 2010, 2). The GAL was a state-funded paramilitary group responsible for shootings, bombings and kidnappings in the French Basque Country between 1983 and 1987. The 'dirty war' against ETA claimed 27 deaths, including nine individuals whose connections to radical nationalism were unclear (Woodworth 2001). The 'dirty war' had the support of the upper echelons of the Ministry of Interior and was aimed at ending the 'French sanctuary' for ETA members, facilitating the extradition of suspected *etarras* to Spain and forcing the French government to cooperate in anti-terrorism operations, assistance that was provided from 1984 onward (Bew *et al.* 2009, 202). In this respect, the state-sponsored death squads accomplished their undeclared objective of ending the cross-border sanctuary but also backfired, as they discredited the Spanish government and security forces while renewing ETA's support and membership. Having said that, it is important to point out that the number of victims in the dirty war of the GAL and similar groups – the Anti-communist Armed Groups (AAA), Anti-terrorism ETA (ATE), the Spanish Armed Groups, the Warriors of Christ the Kings, and the Basque Spanish Battalion (BVE) – account for 7 per cent of all the victims killed between 1968 and 2011, whereas ETA was responsible for 92 per cent of all the remaining victims (López 2015).

Third, the dispersion policy for ETA detainees confirmed the 'political nature' of the conflict in the eyes of radical nationalists. The dispersion policy was initiated in 1989 following the failed peace negotiations of Algiers. The goal of the policy was to break the internal cohesion of these detainees (who defined themselves as 'political prisoners') by scattering the prison population and transferring the hardliners to jails as distant from the Basque Country as possible. This penitentiary policy became controversial, as it punished not only ETA detainees but also their families, which had to travel hundreds of kilometres to visit their relatives. Demonstrations against the policy became ritualised, and banners, posters and graffiti in favour of 'Prisoners to Euskal Herria' became part of the Basque urban landscape. At the same time, the policy neither facilitated a substantial number of cases of disengagement nor did it facilitate the establishment of clear pathways out of terrorism as the Italian repentance laws of the 1970s had done. In fact, the perception of an unjust penitentiary policy further increased the coherence of organisations and campaigns favouring ETA prisoners and prevented de-radicalised individuals from abandoning a group under siege, because they became martyrs and reference points for the whole movement (Casquete 2006).

To reiterate: ETA had few incentives to disband during the 1980s because the radical cause continued to attract a substantial minority of supporters and sympathisers, as indicated by Herri Batasuna's electoral support (12–18 per cent of the Basque electorate). In addition, the participation of ETA in environmentalist causes led to some tactical successes against large infrastructures in the Basque Country. On the one hand, it targeted the construction of a nuclear power station at Lemoniz (which was later cancelled) and was responsible for 246 acts of sabotage and the killing of five people, among them the chief engineer of the plant, José Maria Ryan, and 18 months later his successor, Angel Pascual. On the other hand, it also targeted the construction of the Leizaran highway by organising 158 acts of sabotage so that the road layout was ultimately modified (Domínguez 1998). The two campaigns ended in deaths and huge economic losses, despite having very little to do with the ultimate goal of secession from Spain. However, ETA could argue that political violence was effective in transforming social reality in a positive manner. Their sympathisers disseminated the idea that Spain was not fully democratic and that the Basque homeland was still occupied by a foreign force, and used the cases of torture, the collusion between the state and the GAL death squads and the ad hoc dispersion policy as empirical evidence justifying their political and ethical concerns. At the same time, a questioned counter-terrorist effort did not have the support, effectiveness and legitimacy it would acquire in the 1990s, when Basque public opinion finally turned its back on ETA (Llera and Retortillo 2004).

What constitutes a successful counter-terrorist policy?

According to Robert P. Clark, most violent campaigns over territory tend to end in one of two ways. One is for the government's police and armed forces to lose their taste for combat or their confidence in the political system, and for the executive itself to lose its popular legitimacy. This insurgent victory either sweeps away the existing regime or leads to territorial separation from the core state. The other way is for the government in power to combine a vigorous policy of repression with a judicious programme of reforms to isolate the insurgents from their base of popular support and to ultimately defeat them militarily, ideologically and politically. The end result of this defeat may be a negotiated truce and ceasefire which leads to a formal settlement with provision for a general amnesty and facilities for the members of the insurgent group to integrate into civil politics (Clark 1990, 1–5). The latter model fits well the strategy followed by the Spanish government to deal with the internal threat of ETA.

The turning point for the counter-terrorist policy against ETA was 1992, when the French police arrested the leadership of ETA (*Pakito, Txelis, Fitti,* etc.). The coordinated action across the border signalled the recalibration of the counter-terrorism strategy and the abandonment of old practices. At the core of the new strategy there was an understanding of the appeal of ETA's campaign and a new focus on counter-mobilisation and counter-recruitment. The range of actions was expanded from a security policy focused on weakening ETA to a wider counter-narrative strategy that also aimed at winning hearts and minds. The counter-terrorist policy would ultimately interlock a programme of investment in security, legal reforms and political initiatives at the domestic and international level to counter violence in the medium and long term.

From 1992 onward, the policy became more efficient by incorporating new elements and continuing some other long-term ones. The fight against ETA continued to be based on multiparty initiatives like the anti-ETA pacts, collaboration with France and the dispersion policy. Attempts to sit down with ETA and negotiate an agreement continued to be tried by governments of all colours but they all ended in failure. Finally, a novel approach, namely the banning of political parties close to ETA, proved to be a controversial yet effective measure. In what follows, I will highlight some of the security, legal and political elements of this successful and dynamic counter-terrorist effort: (1) Franco-Spanish cooperation; (2) anti-ETA pacts; (3) banning of parties; and (4) peace negotiations.

The collaboration between France and Spain was possibly the most significant external factor contributing to the decline of ETA (Reinares and Alonso 2007, 130; Alonso 2012). The Franco-Spanish cooperation was a necessary but not sufficient factor in causing the decline. When there was no collaboration between the two countries, ETA members could target objectives in Spain and cross the border to their safe haven in Southern France. The idea of France as a 'land of asylum' was gradually eroded with the signature of the *Acuerdos de la Castellana* in 1984, the Sokoa operation in 1986 and especially with the Bidart arrests of 1992, both in Southern France (Morán 1997, 196). Indeed, as the year 1992 was approaching, the collaboration between the two countries increased. Fearing that ETA would use either the Barcelona Olympic Games or the Universal Exhibition of Seville to make an attack and gain publicity, the authorities of the two countries devoted more resources to weakening ETA and curtailing its ability to launch an attack. The high point of this collaboration was the arrest of the ETA leadership in the French Basque town of Bidart in 1992. The Franco-Spanish operation at Bidart forced the organisation to contemplate the possibility of military defeat for the first time in its history. Its operational capabilities and ability to extort a regular income from business leaders were seriously undermined. But more importantly, the arrests at Bidart marked a turning point in the collaboration between the two EU member states. From the 1990s onward, the fate of ETA was linked to the collaboration of the French authorities, and it is telling that the last victim of ETA was Jean-Serge Nérin, a French policeman shot down in the outskirts of Paris on 16 March 2010.

The second key element of the counter-terrorist policy were the multiparty anti-ETA pacts signed at both state and regional levels against the elected representatives who supported ETA's violence. Even though these political pacts did not affect security, they were very important in galvanising the opposition to ETA and marginalising its political representatives (Jaime-Jiménez 1998). The Spanish Parliament signed an agreement in 1987 (*Pacto de Madrid*), while similar pacts were approved the following year in Euskadi (*Pacto de Ajuria Enea*) and Navarre (*Pacto de Pamplona*). These arrangements also helped forge a new culture by which political parties agreed to exclude counter-terrorism from the political game. The two main state-wide parties – the social democrats of the PSOE and the conservatives of the PP – later signed the Anti-Terrorist Pact in 2000 which involved 'excluding the policies to end terrorism from the scope of legitimate political and electoral confrontation'. The signing made way for parliamentary approval, by 304 out of 350 votes, of a controversial law that made possible the banning of political parties who defended or justified the use of political violence.

The third key element of the counter-terrorist policy was the Law of Political Parties in 2002, a piece of legislation that allowed the government, if requested by Parliament, to demand judicial procedures to outlaw political organisations with links to underground terrorist groups. The law was an initiative of the PP government and was tailor-made to ban ETA's political wing – Batasuna – in March 2003. The idea was to stop the electoral gains of political parties that were either permissive or supported the means and goals defended by anti-systemic groups like ETA. Under Spanish legislation, the parties that gained representation (from townships to the Parliament) were provided with generous financial resources to carry out their political programmes. The Law of Political Parties was very much criticised by Basque nationalist politicians who claimed that it would trigger more violence and deepen the de-legitimisation of the state. However, the initiative was very effective in reducing deadly terrorism by eroding social support and cutting off radical nationalists from public funding. Furthermore, debates on the legality or appropriateness of the legislation ended when the European Court of Human Rights in Strasbourg ruled in favour of the Spanish executive in 2009 (Alonso 2010, 223–224). As a result, ETA sympathisers were unable to mount an effective legal response, and once they stopped having access to public seats (and the mass media), their ability to reach their supporters and wider public opinion was drastically reduced. It is not difficult to argue that fear of becoming irrelevant pushed the political wing to pressure ETA to enter political negotiations with the state.

Finally, the fourth key element of the counter-terrorist policy was the attempt to use secret dialogues to achieve ceasefires or a definitive cessation of hostilities. These 'contacts' were sometimes called peace negotiations but the truth is that none of them produced the desired effect (see Table 2.1). Analysts of peace studies tend to assume that holding negotiations is a clear indication that the two parties in conflict have reached a 'Mutually Hurting Stalemate', a situation in which neither side can win, but neither side wants to back down or accept loss either (Zartman 2000). However, the fact that there were so many 'failed' peace processes meant that the parties were not in equilibrium and used the negotiations to take the temperature of the opponent, gain time, reorganise and/or send a message to an audience.

Failure was the common element in the negotiations, and yet it is possible to argue that the last rounds in Geneva, Oslo and Loyola deserve special attention because these 'failed' negotiations 'worked'. The so-called 'conversations' failed in bringing a rapid resolution, but missing the last opportunity for a negotiated settlement favoured a wide-ranging transformation from a political-military movement into a political one. Despite the evidence that intra-state conflicts over territory rarely end in peace agreements (Bapat 2005; Toft 2003, 142; Cronin 2009, 201) there is also evidence that terrorist groups facing imminent defeat 'may lead to a group's transformation into a political party contestant for power in a democratic setting' (Weinberg 2011, 13). The main consequence of ETA's decision to end the negotiations was to lose the support of the constituency and widen the gap with its political wing Batasuna, a party which wanted to remain legal and which maintained that this was the last opportunity to lay down weapons and negotiate some concessions for disengaged prisoners and activists.

The 2005 to 2007 negotiations of Loyola (Gipuzkoa) were seen by several key actors as the last opportunity for a negotiated settlement. The Spanish government led by Rodríguez Zapatero obtained a parliamentary mandate to open negotiations with ETA on condition that no political concessions were made. Considerable political capital was invested in the initiative while openly pursuing a 'double strategy' of talks and repression (Whitfield 2014, 150). The peace

Table 2.1 Peace negotiations between the Spanish government and ETA, 1975–2011

Years	Party in government	Place of negotiations	Result
1976–1977	UCD	Geneva	Failed
1980–1982	UCD		Successful (ETA-PM)
1987–1989	PSOE	Algiers	Failed
1998–1999	PP	Zurich	Failed
2005–2007	PSOE	Loyola	Failed

process was heavily criticised by the conservative opposition of the PP and the associations of victims, who accused the government of 'betraying the memories of the deceased'. The nationalist left recognised the uniqueness of the situation and took into account Basque public opinion which had stopped listing ETA's terrorism as one of its top worries in the surveys carried out by the government-funded Centre for Sociological Research (CIS). It exerted considerable pressure on ETA to make concessions. The post 9/11 world provided the ideal context for the realisation of an agreement and, following the truce of 2006, many came to believe that ETA would grab the chance to bring a 40-year-old campaign to an end (Aizpeolea and Eguiguren 2011).

The abrupt end of the peace negotiations of 2005 to 2007 is well known. ETA blew up a van loaded with explosives in the car park of Madrid's International Airport of Barajas, killing two people. The Spanish government's response was that there would be no more negotiations and that counter-terrorism would now be the only possible reaction to ETA's demands. The contacts were perhaps broken because the concessions that the government was ready to make did not have the full support of the conservative opposition, and ETA feared that the agreement would not be implemented (Alonso 2010).

By leaving the political negotiations, ETA missed the last opportunity to lay down its weapons while negotiating some exit options for its prisoners and activists. The terrorist group marginalised itself from its constituency and the contact with ordinary Basques was severed. In the years that followed, Batasuna committed itself to an 'exclusively' peaceful and democratic process in a series of documents and statements (Argitzen, Alsasua Declaration, Zutik Euskal Herria, Brussels Declaration, Guernica Declaration, etc.). In addition to the backlash from the constituency, the Spanish executive gained new legitimacy in using repressive measures (against Batasuna and its successor parties), and both Spanish and French authorities continued to arrest ETA members between 2011 and 2016. That internal debate and the external counter-terrorist effort weakened the organisation to the point that it ended its terrorist campaign on 20 October 2011.

How do terrorist campaigns end?

The comparative literature on the decline and demise of terrorist campaigns has identified a variety of modes of how organisations die out. In what follows, the results of various studies that describe how terrorist groups end their violent campaigns will be examined (Jones and Libicki 2008; Cronin 2009; Weinberg 2011). The main goal of this section is to see how the Basque case fits into these comparative studies. Is the ETA campaign representative of the existing universe of cases or is it an unusual or deviant case? If so, how should comparativists refer to the end of ETA's terror campaign?

The work of Seth Jones and Martin Libicki first offers an empirical analysis of the rise and decline of 648 terrorist groups between 1968 and 2006. In this report from the RAND Corporation they concentrate on 268 groups for which they have reliable data and identify four major ways in which terrorist groups have ended their violent careers: military force, success, policing or politicisation. They maintain that governments which used military force against their terrorist opponents rarely defeated their opponents (7 per cent, whereas few terrorist groups disbanded after successfully achieving their strategic goals (10 per cent)). The most common way for groups to disband was to be on the receiving end of a calibrated campaign of policing (40 per cent) or to be part of a process of politicisation, which included creating political parties or holding negotiations (43 per cent). In other words, the evidence suggests that the indiscriminate use of force rarely produces clear instances of victory and defeat, and that the selective use of force and discriminating types of actions has been historically more effective in bringing about the desired results.

In her book *How Terrorism Ends* (2009), Audrey Kurth Cronin examines 457 terrorist campaigns from the past two centuries and identifies six pathways by which they met their demise: decapitation, negotiation, success, failure, repression and reorientation. According to Cronin, these pathways are not necessarily separate and distinct. For example, groups such as the Irish Republican Army (IRA), the Kurdistan Workers' Party (PKK) or ETA are cited recurrently to make the point that patterns overlap and that the pathways are not mutually exclusive. In her view, terrorist campaigns are complex and there is no single cause of failure. Her findings are consistent with Leonard Weinberg's *The End of Terrorism?* (2011) in which he distinguishes between three types of endings – defeat, success and transformation – and argues that uni-causal explanations are unconvincing.

The findings of these scholarly works about the end of terrorism encompass the experiences of ETA campaigns. ETA is a clear case of what Cronin calls 'failure' and Weinberg calls 'defeat'. Jones and Libicki published their report in 2008 before the unilateral truce of 2011 and treated ETA as an active group. However, it is very likely they would have put the end of ETA's campaign in their 'policing' category. The idea that it was a defeat is shared by Spanish scholars and journalists, who have argued that ETA's terrorism was not only inefficient but counterproductive in gaining policy concessions. A different view would be held by authors who argue that the story of the end of ETA was not the consequence of counter-terrorism and banning Batasuna but of self-defeat and negotiation (Whitfield 2014; Powell 2014).

The idea that violence carried out by underground organisations is inefficient in gaining policy concessions is also backed by existing evidence. Cronin has argued that 'the good news is that terrorism virtually always fails' (2009, 206) and Weinberg has concurred by stating that 'terrorist groups typically fail to achieve their goals' (2011, 72). The foremost expert on terrorist effectiveness, Max Abrahms, has also argued that very few terrorist groups have achieved their strategic objectives and that success only manifests itself in short-term tactical gains such as publicising grievances, attracting attention to themselves or increased coercive powers. Indeed, with the exception of a handful of cases of decolonisation (Algeria's FLN, Israel's Irgun or Cyprus' EOKA) it is safe to conclude that terrorists have rarely achieved their long-term objectives.

The end of ETA's campaign is not unusual and may be compared to the decline of other terrorist groups (Della Porta 2013, 273). To use Jones and Libicki's terms, both policing and politicisation account for its defeat. Needless to say, the move towards politicisation and the internal debate about the effectiveness of terrorism would not have taken place had it not been for the effectiveness of the counter-terrorist effort of Spain and the crucial support of France. It was the external pressure of counter-terrorism that ultimately triggered the internal debate.

Conclusion

ETA unilaterally ended its violent campaign for independence on 20 October 2011. The terrorist campaign lasted 43 years and claimed 845 lives, plus hundreds of displaced and injured people as well as an estimated economic cost of about 10 per cent of the region's GDP (Abadie and Gardeazabal 2003; López 2015). At the time of writing, the group had neither disbanded nor decommissioned its weapons. And yet there was widespread agreement that the extinction of the Basque organisation was irreversible. Terrorism had proven to be both ineffective and detrimental for the secessionist cause and, as the Catalan campaign for independence indicated, the time of using coercive methods to influence public policy had clearly passed.

Terrorist violence between 1975 and 2011 had considerable popular support, partly due to a legitimising narrative provided by radical Basque nationalism, the social and political movement that sustained ETA's campaign of political violence, extortion and threats. According to this nationalist discourse, there was political conflict between two opponents with incompatible goals – Spain and the Basque homeland (*Euskal Herria*) – that would explain why ETA emerged in 1959 (even though it had been founded a year earlier, in 1958, as Chapter 1 explains). Needless to say, the random targeting of violence, the marginalisation of victims and the brutalisation of society (which was prevented from freely expressing its political views) were conveniently forgotten by a nationalist interpretation that privileged an understanding of 'revolutionary violence' as the 'weapon of the weak' against an all-powerful state.

The idea of Basque victimhood and Spanish oppression was partly reinforced during the 1980s by a security policy that did not always abide by democratic principles. Instances of torture and the case of the GAL were some of the darkest moments of Spain's recent history. As the counter-terrorist effort was professionalised however, the idea of a Spanish overreaction ceased to resonate and more Basque citizens turned their backs on ETA's campaign of assassinations, kidnappings and extortion. In addition, the collaboration with France proved highly effective and the political initiatives designed to erode ETA's support network were also efficacious. The operational decline of ETA's radical building from 1992 was clear and was intensified after 2001, when the fight against terrorism took a global shape.

The end of ETA's campaign is a clear case of defeat caused by the 'external' pressure of political, legal and security measures and the 'internal' waning legitimacy of violence within the radical nationalist community. The Basque case is consistent with existing research on the effectiveness of terrorism which argues that political violence is generally an ineffective way for perpetrators to attain their demands. The proponents of the so-called Strategic Model of Terrorism assume that perpetrators of terrorism behave as rational political actors who attack civilian targets because of the unmatched effectiveness in pressuring government compliance (Dershowitz 2002; Pape 2003; Kydd and Walter 2006). However, the empirical evidence does not confirm the idea that violence works in resolving conflicts over territory (Toft 2003). In fact, terrorism is a suboptimal tactic for inducing government concessions and it is often the case that peaceful movements have traditionally been more efficacious (Abrahms 2006; Chenoweth and Stephan 2011).

The counter-terrorist effort was the main explanatory variable for the end of ETA. The coordinated actions of judges, prosecutors, police and intelligence services, not to mention the international campaign to isolate the group, reduced the membership of ETA to a handful of individuals who, in the words of a Minister of Interior, could 'fit in a mini-bus'. Besides the long-term weakening effect of the security policy between 1975 and 2011, other short-term variables were important in producing the unilateral ceasefire. First, the failed peace process of 2005 to 2007 helped dispel the widely held idea among some Basques that ETA's war of attrition and readiness to negotiate would only be met by the obstinacy of the Spanish state that was not willing to compromise. The explosion of a car bomb in Madrid's international airport in 2006 made a negotiated resolution impossible and deepened the cleavage between ETA and Batasuna. Second, the constituency of ETA experienced an important transformation as a result of the Madrid Airport bomb and the Nationalist Left proceeded to pressure ETA to disband. The combination of these long-term and short-term factors led radical Basque nationalism to transform itself into a political movement where bullets were definitely abandoned in favour of ballots.

Bibliography

Abadie, Alberto and Javier Gardeazabal (2003) 'The economic costs of conflict: A case study of the Basque Country'. *American Economic Review* 93: 113–132.

Abrahms, Max (2006) 'Why terrorism does not work'. *International Security* 31: 42–78.

Aguilar, Paloma (1998) 'The memory of the civil war in the transition to democracy: The peculiarity of the Basque case'. *West European Politics* 21: 5–25.

Aizpeolea, Luis R. (2013) *Los entresijos del final de ETA. Un intento de recuperar una historia manipulada.* Madrid: Los libros de la Catarata.

Aizpeolea, Luis R. and Jesús Eguiguren (2011) *ETA: Las claves de la paz. Confesiones del negociador.* Madrid: Aguilar.

Alonso, Rogelio (2010) 'Confronting terrorism in Northern Ireland and the Basque Country: Challenges for democracy and legitimacy'. In *The Consequences of Counterterrorism,* ed. Martha Crenshaw, 213–254. New York: Russell Sage Foundation.

Alonso, Rogelio (2012) 'El Estado contra ETA: Entre la victoria policial y la derrota política'. *Cuadernos de Pensamiento Político* 34: 139–170.

Azurmendi, José Félix (2014) *ETA, de principio a fin: Crónica documentada de un relato*. Donostia: Ttarttalo.

Bapat, Navin A. (2005) 'Insurgency and the opening of peace processes'. *Journal of Peace Research* 42: 699–717.

Batista, Antoni (2012) *Adiós a las armas: Una crónica del final de ETA*. Barcelona: Debate.

Bew, John, Martyn Frampton and Iñigo Gurruchaga (2009) *Talking to Terrorists. Making Peace in Northern Ireland and the Basque Country*. London: Hurst.

Bullain, Iñigo (2011) *Revolucionarismo Patriótico. El Movimiento de Liberación Nacional Vasco (MLNV). Orígen, ideología, estrategia y organización*. Madrid: Tecnos.

Calleja José María and Ignacio Sánchez-Cuenca (2006) *La derrota de ETA. De la primera a la última víctima*. Madrid: Adhara Publicaciones.

Casquete, Jesús (2006) 'Protest rituals and uncivil communities'. *Totalitarian Movements and Political Religions* 7: 283–301.

Chenoweth, Erica and Maria J. Stephan (2011) *Why Civil Resistance Works: The Strategic Logic of Nonviolent Conflict*. New York: Columbia Press.

Cid, Miguel (2013) *Ante el final de ETA. La fuerza del perdón (1998–2013)*. Madrid: La Catarata.

Clark, Robert P. (1990) *Negotiating with ETA: Obstacles to Peace in the Basque Country, 1975–1988*. Reno: University of Nevada.

Crenshaw, Martha (1981) 'The causes of terrorism'. *Comparative Politics* 13: 379–399.

Crenshaw, Martha (2010) 'Introduction'. In *The Consequences of Counterterrorism*, ed. Martha Crenshaw, 1–30. New York: Russell Sage Foundation.

Cronin, Audrey K. (2009) *How Terrorism Ends. Understanding the Decline and Demise of Terrorist Campaigns*. Princeton, NJ: Princeton University Press.

De la Calle, Luis and Ignacio Sánchez-Cuenca (2004) 'La selección de víctimas en ETA'. *Revista Española de Ciencia Política* 10: 53–79.

De la Calle, Luis and Ignacio Sánchez-Cuenca (2009) 'Domestic terrorism: The hidden side of political violence'. *Annual Review of Political Science* 12: 31–49.

Della Porta, Donatella (1995) *Social Movements, Political Violence, and the State. A Comparative Analysis of Italy and Germany*. Cambridge: Cambridge University Press.

Della Porta, Donatella (2013) *Clandestine Political Violence*. Cambridge: Cambridge University Press.

Dershowitz, Alan (2002) *Why Terrorism Works: Understanding the Threat, Responding to the Challenge*. New Haven, CT: Yale University Press.

Domínguez, Florencio (1998) *ETA: Estrategia Organizativa y Actuaciones 1978–1992*. Bilbao: Universidad País Vasco. Servicio Editorial.

Domínguez, Florencio (2012) *La agonía de ETA. Una investigación inédita sobre los últimos días de la banda*. Madrid: La esfera de los libros.

Elorza, Antonio (ed.) (2000) *La historia de ETA*. Madrid: Temas de Hoy.

Escrivá, Ángeles (2012) *Maldito el país que necesita héroes: Cómo los demócratas acabaron con ETA*. Madrid: Temas de Hoy.

Fernández, Gaizka (2013) *Héroes, heterodoxos y traidores. Historia de Euskadiko Ezkerra (1974–1994)*. Madrid: Tecnos.

Fernández, Gaizka and Raúl López (2012) *Sangre, votos, manifestaciones: ETA y el nacionalismo vasco radical, 1958–2011*. Madrid: Tecnos.

Garmendia, José María (1996) *Historia de ETA*. San Sebastián: Haranburu.

Hamilton, Carrie (2007) *Women and ETA. The Gender Politics of Radical Basque Nationalism*. Manchester: Manchester University Press.

Hoffman, Bruce (2006) *Inside Terrorism*. New York: Columbia University Press.

Ibarra, Pedro (1989) *La evolución estratégica de ETA: de la guerra revolucionaria (1963), a la negociación (1987)*. Donostia: Kriselu.

Jaime-Jiménez, Óscar (1998) *Policía, terrorismo y cambio político en España, 1976–1996*. Valencia: Tirant lo Blanch.

Jáuregui, Gurutz (1981) *Ideología y estrategia política de ETA. Análisis de su evolución entre 1959 y 1968*. Madrid: Siglo XXI.

Jones, Seth G. and Martin C. Libicki (2008) *How Terrorist Groups End: Lessons for Countering al Qa'ida*. Santa Monica, CA: RAND Corporation.

Kydd, Andrew and Barbara F. Walter (2006) 'The strategies of terrorism'. *International Security* 31: 49–80.

Llera, Francisco and Alfredo Retortillo. 2004. *Los españoles y las víctimas del terrorismo*. Madrid: CIS.

López, Raúl. 2015. *Informe Foronda. Los efectos del terrorismo en la sociedad vasca*. Madrid: La Catarata.

Mata, José Manuel (1993) *El Nacionalismo Vasco Radical. Discurso, organización y expresiones*. Bilbao: Universidad del País Vasco.

Mees, Ludger (2001) 'Between votes and bullets: Conflicting ethnic identities in the Basque Country'. *Ethnic and Racial Studies* 24: 798–827.

Mees, Ludger (2003) *Nationalism, Violence and Democracy. The Basque Clash of Identities*. Basingstoke: Palgrave Macmillan.

Morán, Sagrario (1997) *ETA entre España y Francia*. Madrid: Editorial Complutense.

Muro, Diego (2008) *Ethnicity and Violence: The Case of Radical Basque Nationalism*. London and Abingdon: Routledge.

Muro, Diego (2009) 'The politics of war memory in radical Basque nationalism'. *Ethnic and Racial Studies* 32: 659–678.

Muro, Diego (2010) 'The Basques after Franco: Terrorism and nationalism in a divided society'. In *Politics and Memory of Democratic Transition: The Spanish Model*, eds Gregorio Alonso and Diego Muro, 159–180. London and New York: Routledge.

Monzón, Telésforo (1995) *Últimos Artículos*. Egin: Biblioteca.

Pape, Robert A. (2003) 'The strategic logic of suicide terrorism'. *American Political Science Review* 97: 243–361.

Powell, Jonathan (2014) *Talking to Terrorists: How to End Armed Conflicts*. London: The Bodley Head.

Reinares, Fernando (2001) *Patriotas de la Muerte: Quiénes han Militado en ETA y por qué*. Madrid: Taurus.

Reinares, Fernando and Rogelio Alonso (2007) 'Confronting ethnonationalist terrorism in Spain: Political and coercive measures against ETA?' In *Democracy and Counterterrorism. Lessons from the Past*, eds Robert J Art and Louise Richardson, 105–132. Washington, DC: United States Institute of Peace Press.

Sáez de la Fuente, Izaskun (2002) *El Movimiento de Liberación Nacional Vasco, una religión de sustitución*. Bilbao: Editorial Desclée de Brouwer.

Sánchez-Cuenca, Ignacio (2001) *ETA contra el Estado. Las estrategias del terrorismo*. Barcelona: Tusquets Editores.

Snyder, Jack (2000) *From Voting to Violence: Democratization and Nationalist Conflict*. New York: Norton.

Toft, Monica D. (2003) *The Geography of Ethnic Violence: Identity, Interests and the Indivisibility of Territory*. Princeton, NJ: Princeton University Press.

Unzueta, Patxo (1988) *Los Nietos de la Ira. Nacionalismo y violencia en el País Vasco.* Madrid: El País-Aguilar.

Watson, Cameron (2008) *Basque Nationalism and Political Violence: The Ideological and Intellectual Origins of ETA.* Reno: University of Nevada.

Weinberg, Leonard (2011) *The End of Terrorism?* London and New York: Routledge.

Whitfield, Theresa (2014) *Endgame for ETA: Elusive Peace in the Basque Country.* Oxford: Oxford University Press.

Woodworth, Paddy (2001) *Dirty War, Clean Hands. ETA, the GAL and Spanish Democracy.* Cork: Cork University Press.

Zartman, William I. (2000) 'Ripeness: The Hurting Stalemate and beyond'. In *Conflict Resolution after the Cold War*, eds Daniel Druckman and Paul Stern, 225–250. Washington, DC: National Academy Press.

Zulaika, Joseba (1988) *Basque Violence: Metaphor and Sacrament.* Reno: University of Nevada Press.

3 Democratisation of the Spanish state

Between extreme right-wing violence and police brutality, 1978–1987

José Antonio Pérez

Introduction

The transition to democracy and its consolidation in the Basque Country was marked by a process of intense radicalisation of political violence (Wieviorka 1997; Mansvelt Beck and Markusse 2008). Undoubtedly the most important and large-scale violence was that exerted by ETA, whose terrorism totally determined the consolidation of the democratic system, but it was not the only one. Besides this terrorist organisation and others which would appear some years later on the extreme left-wing nationalist side (abertzale) such as the Autonomous Anticapitalist Commandos (CAA), there was a proliferation of extreme right-wing groups which began their terrorist activities from the second half of the 1970s, such as the Basque-Spanish Batallion (BVE), Antiterrorism ETA (ATE) or the Armed Spanish Groups (GAE) (López 2015). Moreover, all this happened in a climate of great tension, in which security forces resorted on many occasions to an abusive and out-of-proportion violent response, which left a terrible trail of dead and injured people.

Although there are already important academic studies on ETA terrorism, there are still some significant aspects left to be researched, such as those related to victims, the behaviour of the Basque society or the performance of terror mechanisms (Castells 2013). Nevertheless, the same cannot be said about the other two phenomena. Thus far, we barely have any rigorous research which has dealt with the importance of the extreme right-wing violence or with the use of excessive force by the police during those years in the Basque Country. This gap has been exploited by a combative literature in left-wing nationalist circles, which shows police violence and that perpetrated by the extreme right-wing groups to be part of the same 'genocidal strategy' against the Basque people (Agirre 2012; VVAA 2014). Thus, it is necessary to study both phenomena in greater depth from a rigorous academic perspective so that this helps us to accurately understand the importance of these signs of political violence during a particular time of our recent history.

This chapter intends to analyse how both phenomena occurred and to what extent they marked the democratisation process of the state during those years, the performance of the authorities in this field and the effects of their persistence in the legitimisation and consolidation process of democracy in the Basque Country.

Political violence at the end of Franco's regime

Most political parties and unions in the anti-Franco opposition discarded the use of the so-called 'armed struggle' from the 1950s. However, the irruption of ETA radically changed this situation. Since its inception, this organisation theorised on violence as a legitimate resource (Sullivan 1988, 54; Fernández 2013, 84) and had carried out certain symbolic violent activities. But it was not until 1968 that a tragic turning point would mark the history of the Basque Country. The murder of the Corporal of the Civil Guard José Antonio Pardines at the hands of Xabier Etxebarrieta, one of ETA's leaders, on 7 June changed everything. The strategy adopted by this organisation from that moment on started to promote a spiral of action–reaction–action with the aim of provoking the repression of Franco's authorities. As has been pointed out, ETA

> wanted to reveal their cruellest and most dictatorial side and to arouse some sympathy for the aims of the group as well as fomenting an insurrection as a reaction against the hard repression Franco's regime would use indiscriminately after ETA's terrorist attacks.
>
> (Fernández 2014, 290)

In any case, the fact that this organisation resorted to violence is in line with a particular international context where many other organisations put into practice the same kind of strategy from the 1970s (Baby 2012).

The Franco dictatorship in Spain was not prepared for that, though. The first crimes committed by ETA in 1968 stirred up great discontent among the highest authorities of the country. The Commission for the National Defence of the Spanish Parliament (Comisión de Defensa Nacional de las Cortes) agreed to urge the government to adopt 'as many measures either ordinary or extraordinary as it were necessary in order to relentlessly nip the separatist terrorist process in the bud' (Casanellas 2014, 61).

After the murder of Captain Melitón Manzanas, former collaborator of Gestapo and the most notorious figure of Francoist repression in Gipúzcoa, the police started to close in on ETA and managed to arrest a large number of members of the organisation between March and April 1969. Most of those arrested ended up being charged in the famous *Proceso de Burgos* (Burgos Trial). During the numerous demonstrations against this trial, murders were carried out by the Civil Guard, as had happened in Eibar in December 1970 when Roberto Pérez Jaúregui, an anti-Franco militant, was shot dead. But in this kind of operation against ETA there were also some victims who had no connection with the organisation, as had happened in Urabain when a local was killed by Armed Police.

The excessive force used by the police was not exerted exclusively against this group; it was also deployed against workers' protests and local demonstrations, as was the case in Erandio (Biscay) in October 1969 when the police were trying to break up a demonstration against the gas emissions from nearby factories. As a consequence of this intervention two people were shot dead.

However, the appearance of ETA was much more alarming than simple local protests, and it required a more professional and forceful response by authorities. In 1972, the Spanish Prime Minister, Admiral Luis Carrero Blanco, created the National Intelligence Service (at that time known as SECED). This new body would be responsible for investigating and curbing the different outbreaks of terrorism which arose during the final years of Franco's dictatorship and, especially, the most active and deadliest of all of them: that of ETA. To that end, they urged the creation of a mercenary network made up of Spanish citizens or foreigners with rightist ideology and military training. However, the effectiveness of that body was soon questioned when they were unable to prevent the assassination of its driving force.

The terrorist strike against the President of the government on 20 December 1973 proved that the organisation was not only capable of murdering members of the security forces but that it had enough infrastructure, capacity and decision-making power to kill the most influential figure of the regime after Franco himself. A year later, ETA would kill 13 people in an outrageous, indiscriminant attack in Cafetería Rolando in Madrid. That bombing increased tensions within the organisation and this would end up with ETA splitting into two factions: ETA-M ('military') and ETA-PM ('political military'); but, above all, it meant a qualitative leap in the strategy of terrorism.

This string of events which took place during the last years of the dictatorship made the police intensify their fight against ETA, resorting to some ruthless methods. After Etxebarrieta's case and up until Franco's death, 15 members of ETA died in different confrontations with the security forces and over 20 died between then and 1982.

Civil Guard checkpoints, above all those set up at night and badly signalled, became the most usual resource to spot and arrest terrorists following an attack or, at least, to block their escape. However, far from achieving their purpose they turned into scenarios of terrible events where innocent people were killed. Between 1970 and 1982 19 people were killed in these circumstances and over 30 were injured by shooting by the Civil Guard and the police at these checkpoints (Pérez and Carnicero 2008). Most of them had nothing to do with ETA nor offered any resistance. The mere presence of these checkpoints during those years helped spread fear in the Basque Country and Navarra, and somehow highlighted the idea of an occupied country which ETA and the left-wing nationalists were successfully disseminating.

The bloody end of Franco's dictatorship

Police excesses increased from 1975 onward. At the end of January that year, Víctor Pérez Elexpe, a young anti-Franco activist, was shot dead by a corporal of the Civil Guard in Portugalete (Biscay) while he was handing out leaflets in favour of a strike. But the worst was yet to come. In the first months of that year there were no deadly terrorist attacks by ETA and the situation, al least on that side, seemed to give the government and the police some breathing space. It was simply a mirage. The murders of two policemen in March and April by ETA-PM forced the authorities to react. Aware of the potential of the terrorist organisation and for fear of losing control of the situation, on 25 April the Spanish government imposed the state of exception in Gipuzkoa and Biscay. According to police reports at that time, the dictatorship intended to 'strengthen the activity of the security forces to its full extent' (Casanellas 2014, 248). Police operations started one day later and in a very short time they managed to dismantle and arrest a large number of ETA militants in both provinces.

Although the organisation was badly affected, the state of exception could not completely put an end to the terrorist attacks. ETA military groups, less affected by the police action, intensified their activities, and on 6 May 1975 they murdered a member of the Civil Guard in Gernika and a day later a policeman in Bilbao. During these men's funerals there were moments of great tension. The most active extreme right-wing sectors both within the security forces and some other external groups started to mobilise. The newspaper *La Vanguardia* published a detailed compilation of some sentences which reflected that feelings were running high during the event organised after the funeral of both policemen on 12 May in Bilbao. Members of far-right groups demanded 'the persecution of the murderers to France'. These demonstrations took place amid strong emotions also shared by some high-ranking officials who were present (La Vanguardia 1975a).

The journalist José María Portell, who wrote the article and who was murdered by ETA three years later, underlined the climate of considerable apprehension felt during those days with heavily armed policemen storming into a large number of cafés, restaurants and discotheques, and clandestine far-right groups carrying out attacks against people, bars and shops with complete impunity. These actions also occurred in the South of France, where there was already an important community of left-wing nationalists and political refugees (abertzales). Between April and June 1975 several bars and meeting points in the French municipalities of San Juan de Luz, Biarriz or Hasparren were attacked. On 12 July, one of the first Spanish far-right groups, Antiterrorism ETA (ATE), made themselves known by means of a communiqué where, significantly, they dissociated their performance from the Spanish police and introduced themselves as a 'private initiative'. A clear statement in which they tried to distance themselves from the state apparatus reads:

> We know the murderers. We know their shelters and the protection they are benefiting from. They are not committed to a political fight. They escape from norms and the applicable laws but they won't escape from our justice. We'll use the weapons they use to kill innocents, even across the border while they are there. Terrorists only know the language of terror and violence. We'll serve them what they deserve.
>
> (La Vanguardia 1975b)

The state of exception imposed in 1975 was the toughest of that period and was used to provide cover for the police concerning any kind of infringement of human rights which they may have committed: widespread arbitrary detentions, indiscriminate searches, ill-treatment and torture. Through those weeks, the police killed several people who were involved in no political activity whatsoever, as happened in May in San Sebastián, where a German woman was shot dead at a checkpoint by police.

Gernika was one of the villages most violently struck during those weeks. On 14 May, the village witnessed a bloody night. In an operation mounted against an ETA cell, there was a shooting. As a consequence, a lieutenant of the Civil Guard and a member of the terrorist group died. But there were also two more victims: a couple were killed in that same police shooting.

The declaration of the state of exception favoured free circulation and the unpunished performance of different far-right groups who, in some cases, even acted under the protection of the security forces, especially the Civil Guard. These groups included the participation of members of SECED, GOSSI (Operative Group of the Secret Intelligence Service of the Civil Guard) and BIS (former Political-Social Brigade), which spread terror in the area of Gernika after attacking and setting fire to several shop premises and houses, as was the case of the farmhouse belonging to the sculptor Agustín Ibarrola, a member of the Spanish Communist Party (PCE) (Etxaniz 2005).

In the course of those months, the fight against ETA was quite successful. The most important operation was that provided by a member of the organisation, Mikel Lejarza (*Lobo*), recruited by the Spanish Intelligence Services. As a consequence of his undercover work within ETA, over 100 activists of the PM faction were arrested in the summer of 1975. In order to complete the police offensive, on 26 August the government enacted a decree law whereby the police were granted extensive prerogative powers with regard to anti-terrorism. The whole process resulted in a summary court martial against several activists of the organisation which culminated in the famous executions by firing squad of two members of ETA-PM (Juan Paredes Manot and Ángel Otaegui) and three members of the FRAP (Patriotic Revolutionary Anti-Fascist Front) on 27 September. This was one of the most shocking events at that time and, to a large extent, it served the purpose of declaring the members of the leftist nationalist organisation 'martyrs'.

ETA's response was immediate. On 5 October 1975 ETA planted a powerful bomb, and three members of the Civil Guard were killed and two seriously injured in Aránzazu (Gipuzkoa). This had been the bloodiest attack ever known committed by ETA in the Basque Country (Alonso *et al.* 2010, 59–60), and it left the barracks of the Civil Guard in a state of profound shock.

At about 11 p.m. on the same day, three masked, armed men stormed into a restaurant in Alto de Campazar (Biscay), which had already been attacked several months before by several strangers. In this new attack, the terrorists killed one of the owners of the restaurant, Iñaki Etxabe, brother of an ETA member. Although the Basque-Spanish Batallion (BVE) claimed responsibility for the attack, eventually it was never known and, as in some other cases during the same year, the action was attributed to a group of 'uncontrolled individuals'. However, there was some suspicion that members of the Civil Guard had planned it all. This was the first crime committed by this kind of conspirator. The event had a second consequence which was equally disturbing. A few days later a taxi-driver from Mondragón (Guipuzkoa), who had been one of the few witnesses of that criminal action, was found dead from a gunshot wound to his head in the vicinity of the Civil Guard barracks in Villarreal (Araba). It was a very strange event whose responsibility was attributed to ETA but which, eventually, was regarded as an attack by the BVE. Such was the political and social atmosphere, plagued with tensions and deadly attacks, in which the Basque Country was immersed following the executions on 27 September 1975.

The 'years of lead' of the transition in the Basque Country

Transition would be neither a bed of roses nor an exemplary transfer of powers. That process, which would later be idealised as an example of coexistence and reconciliation (Baby 2012), was being built up over a big pool of blood. Five days after Franco's death, ETA murdered the mayor of Oyarzun, Antonio Echevarría, making it clear that they would not change their strategy even after the dictator had died. In addition to the violence of this group it is necessary to mention the brutal repression exerted by the police during those years and the actions of different far right-wing groups which had started during the last months of the dictatorship. The years before the 1978 Constitution was passed were the hardest regarding excesses by law enforcement officers in their zeal to preserve public order, since they were used to a military concept of such order and to the use of disproportionate and sometimes indiscriminate violence against civilians.

One of the most dramatic events during those first months following Franco's death was that which took place in Vitoria on 3 March 1976, when the police forcefully cleared a peaceful workers' meeting in a church, leaving five workers dead and almost 100 wounded (Carnicero 2009). Some days later a young boy was shot dead in Basauri (Biscay) by the Civil Guard while he was taking part in a demonstration against the events happened in Vitoria.

Meanwhile, conspiracies and plots committed by right-wing extremists, covered up by some members of the repressive state apparatus who allowed them free movement and even encouraged them in their actions, started to spread at the beginning of that complicated year (Sánchez 2000; Carcedo 2004). The most serious incidents took place on 9 May 1976 during the traditional pilgrimage climb of Montejurra (Navarra) held by the Carlist Party, a group which had evolved towards self-management federal socialism. During the ascent to the sanctuary, two men were killed and dozens of people were injured in a shooting which seemed to be part of a perfectly organised operative called 'Operación Reconquista'. According to former General Sáez de Santamaría, one of the most outstanding members of the anti-terrorist fight during those years, this operation included:

Army men upset with the democratic reform of the regime, extreme right-wing parties as New Force, violent activists as those who belonged to the Apostolic Anticommunist Alliance (Triple A), Spanish Basque Battalion, The Warriors of Christ the King ... mercenaries recruited from foreign organizations: the Portuguese PIEDE, the Argentinian Triple A and so on ... and some other isolated members of the security forces of the State which, because of their ideology, did not fit in the Reform of the Regime.

(Carcedo 2004, 152)

The plot was financed by José María Oriol y Urquijo, President of the Council of State, and was supported by such important people as the Director-General of the Civil Guard and its Deputy Director-General, and other high-ranking officials of Gipuzkoa and Navarra (Sánchez 2010, 25).

During those years hundreds of demonstrations were held in villages and towns of the Basque Country in favour of the amnesty of the last political prisoners. These places also witnessed terrible crimes committed by 'uncontrolled' people and far-right extremist groups like the one which took place in Santurce (Biscay), where a woman was murdered on 9 July 1976, or in Madrid, where a group of right extremists killed a student on 23 January 1977. This crime was carried out just one day before the massacre of Atocha, where some lawyers, specialists in labour law, were killed in their offices, one of the most atrocious crimes during those years of the transition.

Between 12 and 18 May 1977, five people were killed (four by shots from the security forces) and dozens were injured as a result of the violence the police used to break up the demonstrations which took place in favour of the amnesty. Most of the victims were not even taking part in the protests. The excesses were barely investigated and when judicial procedures were started the cases were dismissed, which helped spread the feeling that security forces enjoyed a high level of impunity.

If anyone happened to think the Amnesty Law passed in October 1977 would halt political violence, they were proved wrong. Quite the contrary: ETA terrorism charged with all its intensity at the 'newly born democracy'. It was precisely at that moment when the new regime decided to intensify police pressure on both factions of the terrorist organisation. However, that reaction was loaded with numerous displays of brutality by the police.

A new phase of police repression between the end of 1978 and 1980 together with paramilitary actions in contexts of complete impunity revealed the limitations, deficiencies and lack of coordination with which the different police groups were encumbered. Besides, it also highlighted the incapacity of the highest-ranking officials of the Ministry of the Interior led by Rodolfo Martín Villa to find a clearly defined anti-terrorist strategy and to engage France in the dismantling of ETA's 'safe haven' which the group was enjoying 'across the border' of the Basque Country.

All this made it possible for law enforcement agencies and security forces to generate completely autonomous dynamics of performance either by the initiative of their nostalgic leaders longing for a military intervention of yesteryear or by policemen who were implicated in illegal repressions of civilian protests, or who collaborated with violent groups of a clearly extremist right-wing sign. These performances increased the range of grievances suffered by a large part of Basque society, especially those linked to the radical nationalism, and fostered an interpretation of the political violence in the Basque Country as an issue of national identity, which became fairly widespread among that social sector which expressed the sense of living in 'an occupied country full of martyrs'.

Police excesses reached dramatic levels, especially during the summer of 1978. On 8 July during the San Fermín festivities of Pamplona, a group of the National Police entered the bullring and charged the crowd with the aim of crushing the riots caused by supporters of Basque radical nationalism. This resulted in the death of a young militant of the Revolutionary Communist League (LCR). A few days later another young boy was shot dead in San Sebastián during violent street protests. On 13 July, some shop premises in Rentería (Gipuzkoa), were vandalised by members of the National Police. This abuse and impunity increased in cases such as the murder of the young ecologist Gladys del Estal, who was shot dead in June 1979 in Tudela by a member of the Civil Guard during an anti-nuclear demonstration.

When Juan José Rosón became Minister of the Interior in the mid-1980s, he introduced a significant change in public order laws. The new Minister promoted the creation of a single chain of command for the anti-terrorist effort; he also improved the coordination and performance of the intelligence services and intensified the replacement policy of those officers suspected of extreme right-wing tendencies. In addition, and thanks to the negotiations with the leaders of the political party Euskadiko Ezkerra, the Minister managed to dissolve ETA-PM (Fernández 2014, 235–238)

These changes were the first results obtained after the long process of democratisation and compliance with the legal code which the UCD governments had been applying to the institutions of the state, especially to those more rigidly attached to the past dictatorship such as the army, the forces of public order and the judiciary system (Palacios 2010, 437–439). Until that moment those forces had had a majority of leaders supporting the same militarised, centralised and unified perspective of public order, a concept which prevented them from gaining an insight into the special characteristics of the terrorist phenomenon in the Basque Country. In addition, the different police forces had inadequate training and lacked practical expertise in anti-terrorism.

These police contingents arrived in the host localities thinking that they were being sent to a territory in a 'state of war', an impression they later confirmed when they experienced outright rejection and fear of the locals. There were many cases of children suffering segregation by classmates and teachers in their schools simply because their parents were members of the Civil Guard or the police. Consequently, these contingents moved in temporarily but did not settle and waited until they could apply for another posting. Sheltered in their barracks (separate fortified housing blocks) with barely any contact with the locals, these

people internalised their hostility and suspicion, convinced that they were prefer-
ential victims of terrorism, and thus displayed an attitude of rejection and deep
distrust of the people who hosted them (Martín 2009).

Under such extreme living conditions, both police forces started to show an attitude of constant provocation, which did not help them earn great public respect.
There was an overwhelming sense of militarisation of public spaces and the police
believed that 'they were implicitly playing the same role as "forces of occupation",
which paradoxically had been the same term the Basque radical milieu had applied
to the intelligence organizations' (Jaime-Jiménez 2002, 150–165).

One of the constant images attached to these security forces was that of 'torturers'. The motto the radical Basque nationalism and left-wing groups painted
in their graffiti and chanted in their demonstrations was 'Police tortures and
murders'. The anti-terrorist legislation covered these practices both because
those arrested were isolated (many of them were captured in indiscriminant
raids) and because there was a shortage of laws or appropriate disciplinary measures against these practices. The Basque General Council reported many accusations in addition to the ones made by organisations of radical nationalists,
left-wing parties, the PNV (Basque Nationalist Party) or the most progressive
Spanish press (Castro 1998, 195–196).

The torture inflicted upon those arrested with practices such as chocking by
total immersion, beating, foot whipping, etc. represented one of the most sinister
legacies of the dictatorship, and its gradual disappearance was a slow process
which depended on the introduction of changes in penal law, the reinforcement
of internal sanctioning processes and the interest of the judges and the political
class in allocating responsibilities. In February and May 1981 the two most
despicable crimes of those years came to light. The first was the case of José
Arregui, a member of ETA-M, who was tortured to death. This event deactivated
the protests against terrorism which had been organised following the kidnap
and murder of José María Ryan, a chief engineer of Lemóniz nuclear station, a
few days before.

In May, there was a second even more tragic event: the 'Almeria case'. Three
young boys were mistaken for the members of ETA who had just carried out a
terrorist attack against Lieutenant-General Joaquín Valenzuela in Madrid. After
being arrested, they were tortured, murdered, dismembered and burnt by a group
of civil guards and a high-ranking officer of the headquarters in Almeria. The
judicial attestation contained innumerable mistakes and the members of the Civil
Guard and the officers who had been charged received all kinds of prison benefits. They were even provided with money from the reserve funds from the Ministry of the Interior during their suspension from duty (El País 1999).

Meanwhile, extreme right-wing groups were acting freely, particularly in
some areas of Gipuzkoa and Biscay, as part of an upward violent right-wing
movement in Spain in general. On 3 April 1978 the Basque General Council
condemned all these groups which 'keep some kind of connection with the
security forces or, at least, they are known by the latter ... [being] on some occasions even aided and picked up by police vehicles' (*El Correo*, 4 April 1978).

Police passivity before these actions helped to prove that these condemnations were right and allowed these groups to connect their violence with other, more specialised clandestine cells who had the protection of the state, especially in the southwestern part of France. These groups operated with complete impunity in that area and the Basque Provinces. Some of these retaliation attacks against militants or supporters of the two ETAs were performed by members of the intelligence services of the state, taking advantage of the cover provided by the several acronyms of extreme right-wing groups such as Triple A, ATE, ANE, GAE or el BVE.

The goal of this paramilitary violence was to spread terror and confusion among the refugees and ETA militants settled in the 'French sanctuary'. Many of these attacks resulted in the killing and wounding of some who had nothing to do with terrorism, as happened in the machine-gun attack at the bar *Hendayais* on 23 November 1980, where two people were killed and nine wounded. In the aftermath, the criminals crossed the border and handed themselves over to the police at the control post, who let them escape when they produced a document which showed their contact with the highest authorities of the police, in particular, with Manuel Ballesteros, head of police intelligence and director of the newly established Unified Counter-terrorist Command (Woodworth 2002, 31–32; Pérez and Carnicero 2008, 121–122).

Other attacks did affect members of ETA-M directly. Between July 1978 and 1981 ten militants of this organisation were murdered in the Basque Country both in Spain and in the southern part of France. The most dramatic was the one against José Miguel Beñarán, *Argala*, the main ideologist of ETA-M, on 21 December 1978, allegedly committed by a death squad group made up of members of the three corps of the Spanish Army, in revenge for his participation in the terrorist attack against Carrero Blanco (Woodworth 2002, 41).

Seemingly, the people responsible for all this violence were independent individuals who did not have any clear anti-terrorist strategy, as happened in the criminal actions by Ladislao Zabala and Ignacio M. Iturbide between 1979 and 1981. These two inhabitants of Sebastián were members of the bloodiest right-wing group who committed seven murders (besides wounding a large number of people and serious ravages) in the 'triangle of death' made up of San Sebastián, Rentería and Andoain (Gipuzkoa). All the actions were devised as an impulsive response to ETA attacks and their victims were sometimes chosen at random by the mere fact that they were suspected of supporting left-wing nationalists and some others selectively, as happened to a councillor of the Herri Batasuna Party in San Sebastián, Tomás Alba, who was killed by this group in September 1979. They acted autonomously, taking advantage of the impunity of their activities, well known not only by the authorities but also by many locals. They started to claim responsibility with the name of Triple A but soon switched to the acronym BVE. Only pressure from neighbours and political parties eventually led to their arrest by the police in March 1981, the year in which these kinds of activities tailed off. The officer in charge who had permitted them to carry out their activities was not only allowed to continue in his duties but was also promoted to head of the intelligence service of the police. That same year, a reformed terrorist of one of those groups submitted a written confession to the police court in San Sebastián involving a captain of the Civil Guard, several policemen and the two extreme right-wing civilians mentioned above in innumerable attacks committed by these groups (Sánchez 2010, 139–147).

The most terrible year of this sectarian right-wing violence was 1980, precisely the most intense year of ETA-PM activity. On 20 January, four people died as a consequence of the explosion of a bomb planted in a bar owned by an activist of the PNV (Nationalist Party). That same year two young girls were raped and murdered in two appalling and dark episodes, whose responsibility and political purpose will forever remain in the dark. Twenty-one people were murdered that year by these extreme right-wing groups or paramilitary forces. In many cases the victims had no connection with the political sphere of radical Basque nationalism against which they were said to be acting, as happened in the case of Yolanda González. She was a militant of the Socialist Workers' Party (PST) from Bilbao who was kidnapped, tortured and murdered in Madrid on 1 February 1980 by a group of well-known extreme right-wing members of Fuerza Nueva, in an operation which had the collaboration of a member of the National Police (González 2012; Woodworth 2002, 41–43). These are just a few of the most notorious crimes committed by these kinds of groups during those years.

Anti-terrorist Liberation Group (GAL)

The victory of the PSOE (Spanish Socialist Workers' Party) in the parliamentary elections of 1982 did not bring about a change in the counter-terrorist policy of the French government, despite the fact that both cabinets were led by social democrats. At least until 1981 France held that 'Basque terrorism was an exclusively Spanish issue'. They also refused to accept the evidence that ETA had their 'safe haven installed in the Pyrénées-Atlantiques department and reluctantly believed Spain was a democracy' (Morán 1997, 395). This stance was reinforced following the failed *coup d'état* on 23 February 1981.

As has been argued above, the persistence of ETA terrorism and the lack of French collaboration were the main reasons why

> from some sectors of the government and other external groups, there were people who considered the need for developing some irregular complementary strategies with the double objective of frightening ETA in French territory and prompting a change of attitude in the authorities of that country.
>
> (Jaime-Jinémez 2002, 312–313)

There is every indication that some of the highest authorities of the Ministry of the Interior followed the same dynamics as those implemented by the previous governments resorting to illegal methods in the counter-terrorist campaign. Besides, on this occasion the court even proved that these groups had the aggravating factor that they were managed and financed directly by the highest authorities of the Ministry, such as the Minister himself, José Barrionuevo, and the Secretary of State for Security, Rafael Vera, in the 1990s (Carcedo 2004, 384). The similarities were so clear that certain members of the right-wing squads operating during the former government were involved in the activities of this 'second dirty war', such as Jean Pierre Cherid and Mohamend Talbi, among others, who had already participated in the events of Montejurra in 1976. The fact that some of the most outstanding members responsible for the anti-terrorist policy continued in power made things easier.

The first action of GAL was a consequence of the kidnap and murder of Alberto Martín Barrios, captain of the army, committed at the beginning of October 1983 by a faction of ETA-PM known as ETA-PM VIII Assembly. In reaction to this, members of the Civil Guard kidnapped two militants of ETA-M, José Antonio Lasa and José Ignacio Zabala, in the South of France. They were taken to Spain, where they were interrogated, tortured and murdered. Among those responsible for these crimes were two members of the Intxaurrondo barracks, headquarters of the Civil Guard in Gipuzkoa under the command of General Enrique Rodríguez Galindo (Miralles and Arqués 1989, 155–156; Woodworth 2002, 56–58; Carcedo 2004, 374–375). A few days later, on 18 October, several members of the Special Operations Groups (GEO) unsuccessfully tried to kidnap another Basque refugee in Hendaya, José María Larretxea, member of ETA-PM VIII, who they wanted to exchange for Captain Martín Barrios. This string of actions would spark off the tragic story of GAL, one of the gloomiest chapters of the young Spanish democracy.

In December that year several mercenaries were hired by the National Police Superintendent stationed in Bilbao, José Amedo Fouce. By mistake, they kidnapped a French citizen of Spanish descent, Segundo Marey, confusing him with an ETA leader. Amedo was later accused and convicted for this crime. This was the first operation with GAL's signature and the first 'mistake' in a long list which would become longer over the years (Miralles and Arqués 1989, 63–67; Woodworth 2002, 69–71; Carcedo 2004, 385–386).

One of the most shocking killings was that committed in Bilbao against Santiago Brouard, leader of Herri Batasuna (HB), on 20 November 1984. It was one of the few actions GAL carried out on Spanish soil and it drew widespread condemnation in the Basque Country, triggering numerous strong reactions in many places. The suspicion that it had been the responsibility of 'state terrorism' grew among Basque citizens, undermining the credibility and legitimacy of the Spanish government and arousing considerable public sympathy for ETA's armed campaign.

Five years after Brouard's assassination – and theoretically two after the dissolution of GAL – Josu Muguruza was killed, also on 20 November when, together with two other elected members of te Herri Batasuna coalition, he was about to collect the certificate of election in the Spanish Parliament in Madrid. This also represented a shocking event for the Basque citizens. Despite the fact that GAL claimed responsibility, the suspicions pointed to some mysterious 'Bases Autónomas' (Spanish neo-Nazi groups). Eventually, two people were arrested: Ángel Duce, a policeman, and Ricardo Sáez de Ynestrillas, the son of a Spanish army commandant murdered by ETA in 1986.

According to General Sáenz de Santa María, GAL worked autonomously from other extreme right-wing and paramilitary groups until 1981, ruling out the possibility that senior members of the government had direct control over illegal anti-terrorist groups. In this version, the level of responsibility in the illegal fight against ETA of both the UCD and PSOE governments was quite similar (Carcedo 2004, 410–415).

In February 1986, GAL murdered two people who had nothing to do with ETA, an elderly man and a young girl, in a little village in the South of France. The organisation admitted in a communiqué that it had been another mistake. This, and another deadly attack the following year against a Basque anti-militarist refugee who had no connection with ETA, was the last operation performed by GAL.

The diplomatic efforts which the Spanish government was progressively making were eventually fruitful, above all following the 'Pactos de la Castellana' in 1984. There was a change in the attitude of the French government at the same time as the negotiations to make it possible for Spain to become a member of CEE began. From 1986 France began to collaborate actively in the persecution of the Basque terrorists and counter-terrorism served only to mount tensions with the neighbouring country. The truth is that though at first GAL operations managed to spread fear among the most radical left-wing nationalists and ETA militants, in the medium term those attacks prompted the de-legitimation of the legal fight against terrorism and by extension the very democratic system itself.

Conclusion

The brutality and large number of excesses committed by the security forces during the years of the Spanish transition to democracy and the activity carried out by extreme right-wing groups were different phenomena with different goals. The impunity enjoyed by the latter led a great many citizens and, in particular, the most radical left-wing sector to believe that both were part of the same strategy whose aim was the persecution and punishment of 'the Basque People'. A significant number of the victims of police violence had not even liaised with radical nationalism, nor evinced any particular violent attitude. They were victims of a disproportionate, abusive response, the consequence of an age where the government, despite the strength it seemed to project through such violence, was actually very weak and unable to control a situation in which by the minute it appeared to be losing control. As the state apparatus became democratised in the mid-1980s police abuses started to dwindle, but their effects and memories lingered for many years, which had far-reaching political consequences and contributed to the weakening of the consolidation and the legitimacy of democracy.

The violence inflicted by extreme right-wing and paramilitary groups which emerged in the mid-1970s during the decline and dissolution of Franco's regime reached its deadliest height in 1980, the same year ETA was at its peak. Everything seems to indicate that these groups, under different acronyms, performed their activities with great impunity and undercover by the some members of the state apparatus until the early 1980s, when eventually, thanks to the consolidation of democracy. it was possible to make them disappear.

It is difficult, both strategically and ideologically, to put together all these different forms of violence. Their appearance and further development were favoured by the existence of certain stagnant, fossilised police structures which were used to practices imposed during the last decades but also by the slow, doubtful reforms carried out by the consecutive UCD governments:

> The State and particularly the Spanish law enforcement agencies (FSE), by which it was represented, moved in a game of polarity: on the one hand, trying to settle its legitimacy on new democratic grounding and on the other, keeping pro-Franco lingering legacy in existence.
>
> (López 2015, 49)

Within this framework, the operations carried out by the different extreme right-wing groups, which in many cases had close contact with the security forces, were rather an impotent response against the events than the consequence of the 'strategy of tension', as happened in other places (Casals 2009). In any case, these kinds of violence strengthened the de-legitimation of the security forces and gave rise to social sympathy for terrorist violence thanks to a discursive mechanism that was present in the debate which existed at that time, claiming that one kind of violence annulled the other.

The GAL phenomenon was, to a large extent, quite different, as may be seen in the direct implications of the state in its funding, participation and coverage, and which the courts managed to prove. Its persecution by the law also marks a crucial difference from the previous terrorist actions that enjoyed complete impunity. It would be convenient to remember that all these plots, including the one GAL set in motion, were responsible for 7 per cent of the political murders committed between 1968 and 2010, whereas during the same period ETA and other groups were directly responsible for the remaining 93 per cent (López 2015).

The persistence of all these phenomena gave the impression that the new democratic system lacked the tools and, above all, enough will to put a stop to the violence. However, despite the great difficulties it had to overcome until it was eventually consolidated in the Basque Country, democracy, through its own mechanisms, got rid of extreme right-wing and paramilitary terrorism and established the necessary tools to dramatically reduce the abusive and disproportionate behaviour of the security forces.

Bibliography

Agirre, Joxean (2012) *No les bastó Gernika. Euskal Herria, 1960–2010*. Andoain: Euskal Memoria Fundazioa.

Alonso, Rogelio, Florencio Domínguez and Marcos García (2010) *Vidas rotas. Historia de los hombres, mujeres y niños víctimas de ETA*. Madrid: Espasa.

Baby, Sophie (2012) *Le mythe de la Transition pacifique. Violence et politique en Espagne (1975–1982)*. Madrid: Casa de Velázquez.

Carcedo, Diego (2004) *Sáenz de Santa María. El general que cambió de bando*. Madrid: Temas de Hoy.

Carnicero, Carlos (2009) *La ciudad donde nunca pasa nada. Vitoria, 3 de marzo de 1976*. Vitoria: Gobierno Vasco.

Casals, Xavier (2009) '¿Existió una estrategia de la tensión en España?' *Historia del Presente* 14: 25–38.

Casanellas, Pau (2014) *Morir matando. El franquismo ante la práctica armada, 1968–1977*. Madrid: Los libros de la Catarata.

Castells, Luis (2013) 'La historia del terrorismo en Euskadi: ¿entre la necesidad y el apremio?' In *Construyendo memorias. Relatos históricos para Euskadi después del terrorismo*, eds José María Ortiz de Orruño y José Antonio Pérez, 210–244. Madrid: La Catarata.

Castro, Raimundo (1998) *Bandrés, memorias para la paz*. Madrid: HMR.

El País (1999) 'Los guardias del caso Almería cobraron fondos reservados'. *El País*, 24 October.

Etxaniz, José Ángel (2005) 'El último estado de excepción en Gernika-Lumo'. *Aldaba* 13.

Fernández, Gaizka (2013) *Héroes, heterodoxos y traidores. Historia de Euskadiko Ezkerra (1974–1994)*. Madrid: Tecnos.

Fernández, Gaizka (2014) 'El simple arte de matar. Orígenes de la violencia terrorista en el País Vasco'. *Historia y Política* 32: 271–298.

González, Juan Manuel (2012) 'Balance de víctimas mortales del terrorismo y la violencia política de extrema derecha durante a transición, 1975–1982'. *Historia Actual Online* 27: 7–17.

Jaime-Jiménez, Oscar (2002) *Policía, terrorismo y cambio político en España (1976–1996)*. Valencia: Tirant lo Blanch.

La Vanguardia (1975a) 'Gran Acto de afirmación patriótica en Bilbao'. *La Vanguardia*, 13 May.

La Vanguardia (1975b) 'Los comandos "Antiterrorismo ETA" dan a conocer su programa en el suroeste de Francia'. *La Vanguardia*, 13 July.

López, Raúl (2015) *Informe Foronda. Los efectos del terrorismo en la sociedad vasca*. Madrid: Los libros de la Catarata.

Mansvelt Beck, Jan and Jan Markusse (2008) 'Basque violence: A Reappraisal of culturalist explanations'. *European Journal of Sociology* 49: 91–118.

Martín, Oscar (2009) 'Separatismo, subversión y violencia colectiva en el País Vasco (1968–1976): nuevas perspectivas del cambio político desde las fuentes del foreing office'. In *Culturas políticas del nacionalismo español: del Franquismo a la Transición*, ed. Manuel Ortiz de las Heras, 101–132. Madrid: La Catarata.

Miralles, Melchor and Ricardo Arqués (1989) *Amedo. El Estado contra ETA*. Barcelona: Plaza y Janés.

Palacios, Diego (2010) 'Repressive legacies and the democratization of the Iberian police systems'. *South European Society and Politics* 15: 429–448.

Pérez, José Antonio and Carlos Carnicero (2008) 'La radicalización de la violencia política durante la transición en el País Vasco. Los años de plomo'. *Historia del Presente* 12: 112–128.

Sullivan, John (1988) *ETA and Basque Nationalism*. London: Routledge.

Wieviorka, Michel (1997) 'ETA and Basque political violence'. In *The Legitimization of Violence*, ed. David Apter, 293–348. London: UNRISD/Macmillan.

VVAA (2014) *La guerra no declarada. Terrorismo de Estado en Euskal Herria*. Euskal memoria.

Woodworth, Paddy (2002) *Guerra Sucia, Manos limpias*. Barcelona: Crítica.

4 Democratic politics and the strength of the rule of law, 1992–2015

Óscar Jaime-Jiménez

Introduction

The aim of this chapter is to define the context and evolution of the confrontation that developed between the firmly established Spanish democratic regime and the terrorist organisation ETA between 1992 and 2015. The starting date of this phase is relevant insofar as it marks two events: the Barcelona Olympic Games and the Universal Exposition of Seville, whose success visibly marks the beginning of ETA's growing operational ineffectiveness. The chapter identifies the main factors that contributed to the decline of the terrorist organisation. The starting hypothesis is that complementarity and coherence between the political and police responses proved decisive in causing the structural deterioration of ETA and its practical dismantling. The explanatory variables would be the police response, political consensus/dissention and the international factor. The complexity of the scenario is defined by the dependent variable shaped by the dialectic established between the democratic state and ETA during this period that marked the definitive decline of the organisation. The information used and interpreted here is taken from secondary sources of very different types, including publications, specialised studies and articles, data proceeding from the Spanish Ministry of the Interior, as well as verified news reports.

Following decades of the terrorist phenomenon in Spain and the application of diverse responses, the accumulated experience makes it possible to draw certain conclusions from a comparative perspective with other contexts (Reinares 1998, 2003; Holmes 2001, 2008; Remiro and Espósito 2002; Woodworth 2002; Estévez *et al.* 2006). The empirical evidence confirms the challenges for terrorist organisations to emerge in stable totalitarian and authoritarian regimes. This is due to the control that these regimes exercise over society, limiting any dissidence to an extraordinary degree and preventing publicity for such violent actions, an inalienable element in any terrorist strategy. Nor can it make use of the values offered by asymmetry. Terrorism emerges in democracies and authoritarian regimes that are in crisis, with the Spanish case providing a very representative example. It is open societies or those that are in a precarious and fragile process of moving towards greater political openness that inevitably generate favourable structural conditions that enable diverse actors to explore violence as a course of political action. Unstable regimes that provide opportunities to terrorist groups tend to overreact and generate significant problems whose solution in the short term is difficult for later democratic regimes. It is in open, plural and democratic societies where terrorism tends to develop to a greater extent due to the structural opportunities they offer. Contexts characterised by the coexistence of varied legal political actors, even in antagonistic positions, and unsupervised civil societies where the state limits its space of activity, constitute a favourable setting for certain actors to explore alternative forms of action like political violence.

The end of terrorist organisations is closely linked to the state's ability to isolate them from their social milieu and to respond efficiently through force directed with precision, professionalism and the appropriate intelligence. Experience shows that a police response is only sufficient in cases where terrorist groups lack social roots. However, where terrorist organisations can count on the support of significant community backing, such as the cases of ETA or the IRA, defeat can only result from the concerted action of state and social responses with the aim of isolating the activists from their milieu and increasing their vulnerability (Funes 1998; Lennon 2003; De la Corte 2006). The lack of a clear definition of terrorist spaces in such scenarios makes it necessary to develop and implement very precise strategies and tactics that solely affect those responsible for terrorist activities and do not criminalise entire communities. An efficient response is a long, complex and coordinated process that covers different fronts (Domínguez 1998; Chalk 2000; Jaime-Jiménez 2001, 2002; Cronin and Ludes 2004; Cronin 2009). There is no doubt about the difficulty of predicting the consequences of violence (Hewitt 1993; Carr 2008). It may, however, be asserted that the principal threat of terrorism's challenge to democratic and plural societies is not that it might upset coexistence and destabilise the institutions. Instead, its threat is that it could destroy the political principles on which our model of society is based (Ganor 2005; Donohue 2008; Hocking and Lewis 2007; Wilkinson 2011) and that citizens could accept a curtailment of rights as necessary for successfully confronting terrorist violence. An uncritical acceptance of that scenario would be terrorism's greatest victory. Relevant errors committed in the past decade and a half in response to global terrorism (Anonymous 2004; Bergen 2011; Aid 2012) have resulted in its becoming relatively stronger.

The different sections in this chapter follow a chronological order that includes periods considered significant for analysing the reasoning set out above. The first section covers the period from 1992 to 1996 and includes the final phase of the governments of the *Partido Socialista Obrero Español* (PSOE – Spanish Socialist Workers' Party). These were marked by disillusionment with respect to the policy of contact with ETA and a deepening of political consensuses, which was translated into an increase in the efficiency of the anti-terrorist response. The second period starts in 1996 following the victory of the conservative *Partido Popular* (PP – People's Party) in the general election and concludes in 2004 with that party's defeat in the general election. This period of time was characterised by the full implementation of the PP's policies. It became clear that the state's response to terrorism was significantly subordinated to the variable political geometry of the period and to short-term strategic calculations, as shown in the changes in the attitude of the party in office. It promoted contacts with ETA and later committed itself to a policy of isolating the organisation and responding forcefully on all fronts. The third phase is characterised by the victory of the PSOE in the general election of 2004 – strongly conditioned by the jihadist terrorist attacks carried out a few days before – up until the party's defeat in the general election of 2011. During this period of time direct relations between ETA and the government were re-established but ended in total failure. The terrorist organisation resumed its armed activity but in conditions of highly pronounced organisational and operational precariousness. The organisation thus moved further into almost definitive structural decline, a process also conditioned by the growing emergence of a nationalist sector of the radical left (*Izquierda Abertzale*, IA – Patriotic Left), which had formerly been dependent on ETA and then committed to the political path. Finally, the victory of the PP in this election meant that the fight against terrorism was partially redirected through highly demarcated socio-political spaces in which the new government had limited room for manoeuvre.

During the period from the end of the dictatorial regime in 1976 until the political transition, the terrorist organisation ETA consolidated itself and grew stronger, at the same time as the foundations of the democratic regime and the new institutions were being established. This paradoxical evolution resulted from the peculiar Basque scenario in which there was a dynamic interaction among multiple actors with coinciding, converging, parallel, diverging and opposing interests. Their relative positions, established according to their formal attitude towards terrorism, did not prevent each actor from holding a discrete micro-strategy serving its immediate interests in terms of cornering influence and power. In this way the confrontation between the constitutional state and ETA was distorted. Holding a position in favour of peaceful political change following Francoism did not necessarily mean condemning the use of political violence (the *Partido Nacionalista Vasco* – PNV, Basque Nationalist Party). Nor did the fact of having been a victim of Francoist repression imply renouncing the use of terrorist practices to carry out illegal violence in favour of the state (senior figures in the Ministry of the Interior and their relationship with the *Grupos Antiterroristas de Liberación* (GAL, Anti-terrorist Liberation Groups)). All of this would become apparent over the following decade. The starting point inherited from the late 1970s was characterised by the existence of political elites in confrontation with each other; inadequate anti-terrorist legislation; terrorist activities encouraged from within the institutions; police forces developing practices characteristic of non-democratic regimes and inhibited societies, thereby generating a space favourable to the arguments of those who challenged the system and their terrorist practices (Jaime-Jiménez 2002).

Following the convulsive decade of the 1980s (Ballbé 1985; Del Águila and Cotarelo 1992; Cotarelo 1992; Unzueta 1997), in 1992 there was a widespread conviction that a new phase had begun, although this did not necessarily mean the immediate end of terrorism. The change of decade was strongly influenced by the perception of the need to establish a new framework in relation to ETA's violence in a fully established democracy. Besides, Spain had joined the European Economic Community in 1986. During the final years of the previous period the different parties with parliamentary representation in Madrid and the Basque Country had recognised the need to reach agreements against the violence practised by ETA. This had resulted in the pacts signed in 1987 and 1988 among the parties at the state level (the Madrid Pact) on one side, and among those with representation in the Basque Parliament (the Ajuria Enea Pact) on the other. All of this contributed to a fall in terrorist activities (Reinares and Jaime-Jiménez 2000; Jaime-Jiménez 2002, ch. 3).

Similarly, in the early 1990s police cooperation with France had appreciably improved following the signing of the Castellana agreements in 1984 (Morán 1997, 196). Spain's priority was to strengthen relations with France in all spheres, giving less importance to cooperation with other countries at a multilateral level. The appearance of the GAL in 1983, which carried out 28 murders on French territory, did not significantly affect relations between the two countries. Nor did it accelerate a change of attitude in France, as some have argued, given that this had started previously. The figures show France's commitment throughout that decade. Between 1986 and the start of 1988, 189 ETA members were expelled from French territory. This forced the organisation to move further underground (Guenaga 2015), which underscored a clear change of attitude with respect to the years of the transition and the early 1980s (Jaime-Jiménez 2002, ch. 5). Police strategy had improved noticeably over that decade and a new actor had been incorporated: the Basque Autonomous Police (*Ertzaintza*).

The slow and sustained decline, 1992 to 1996

A new stage began in 1992. This was marked by a prior increase in the level of understanding between the central government of the PSOE and the Basque government under the leadership of the PNV. There were no significant crises until the GAL scandal surfaced. Although the paramilitary organisation had acted against ETA during the 1980s, it was not until the 1990s that the institutional plot that had sustained it was uncovered and a legal process begun.

With the appointment of José Luis Corcuera as the new Minister of the Interior in 1988, there was no re-emergence of the conflict with the Basque government over issues of police organisation, as in the earlier phase when José Barrionuevo had been Minister of the Interior. A period began that was characterised by the search for agreements. The attitude of the socialist government had been to maintain certain permanent, discrete contacts with the terrorist organisation with the aim of 'taking its pulse' (Pozas 1992). This course of action did not bring any significant success, which is why the next Minister of the Interior, Antonio Asunción, decided to abandon it in 1994, on the consideration that its only contribution was to create expectations in ETA (Jaime-Jiménez 2002, ch. 3).

At the operational level, a highly relevant success occurred in 1992 with the arrest of the entire ETA leadership in Bidart, France (Domínguez 2002), although a significant blow had already been struck with the discovery of an important logistical infrastructure in Sokoa (France). Thanks to the Bidart operation, ETA's financial infrastructure was also broken up and its system for collecting funds dismantled. In this way the organisation began to lack regular income. This operation had a strong impact, although little further profit was derived from it. All of this was a consequence of the increase in collaboration with France due to the approach of the Barcelona Olympics and the Seville Expo in 1992. Both events were a cause of serious concern to the Spanish authorities and ETA itself perceived this scenario as an unrepeatable opportunity to give its actions greater resonance. For that reason, at the start of May that year, 30 members of the Spanish police forces were temporarily assigned to strengthen the response to events in France. The Bidart operation was a direct result of the convergence between the two countries. In the following months there was a dramatic fall in the number of terrorist actions in comparison to the same periods of time in previous years. Similarly, more members of the organisation were arrested over the following weeks, which deepened the crisis in the organisation even further. The police of the two countries worked in a concerted and efficient way with the aim of impeding the logistical reorganisation of the terrorist structure. Finally, in 1993, thanks to these efforts, it was possible to dismantle an important arms and explosives factory in Anglet (France), thus extending the success obtained the year before at Bidart (Jaime-Jiménez 2002, ch. 5). France continued the policy of collaboration and proceeded to arrest numerous members of the structure, in exchange for Spain's maintaining its vigilance of potential Islamic fundamentalist activists who might cross the border. This was an aspect upon which the French Minister of the Interior, Charles Pasquá, had insisted.

The GAL scandal broke out at the end of 1994. It had negative consequences for relations between the two countries, a deterioration that was reflected in a significant fall in the number of ETA arrests made by the French during the first months. At the same time, the General Attorney of the Department of the Atlantic Pyrenees ordered action to be taken against any Spanish agent detected carrying out investigations on French territory, of which there were some cases. There started to be talk of a 'French GAL' and of money being received by French police officers for collaborating with, and providing information to, the Spanish security forces. As a result, the French authorities limited themselves to strictly fulfilling the law during that phase. This had a negative repercussion on the counter-terrorist effort against ETA (Jaime-Jiménez 2002, ch. 5). Following the French presidential elections of 1995 and the victory of the right, the Spanish government entertained the hope that France would assign more resources to the fight against ETA, in which no more than 30 agents were involved at that time. At a meeting between the Ministers of the Interior held in June 1996 it was agreed that the human resources assigned would be increased and more facilities would be provided to the Spanish police to carry out intelligence gathering in France (Jaime-Jiménez 2002, 297).

The changes in the policies of the People's Party, 1996 to 2004

The victory of the conservative PP in the general election of 1996 marked a turning point in government anti-terrorist policy. The new party in office was to oppose any process of negotiation, which put an end to more than 20 years of contacts, although the need to obtain support from right-wing Catalan and Basque nationalists was to influence the policy developed during this period. The relationship with France continued to develop and in March 1997 the French recognised that numerous Spanish police agents were in their territory carrying out different activities, with the exception of making arrests. However, no advance was made in the plan for operational cooperation (Jaime-Jiménez 2002, ch. 5). The new variable that appeared during this phase was the danger of a split among the signatories of the Madrid Pact in relation to the reinsertion of ETA inmates convicted for violent crimes. As a result of this situation, the Ajuria Enea Pact was also weakened and the PP began to distance itself from the consensus that had been achieved up until then among the different political forces on these questions.

One of the strongest supporters of the central government during the first stage was the PNV, a party with a moderate conservative character. During the transition it had shown an ambiguous attitude towards the violence on numerous occasions. By supporting the central government the PNV avoided marginalisation and obtained certain commitments with respect to a later transfer of powers. This alliance generated a certain understanding over how terrorism should be tackled. The attitude of the PP, which occupied a radicalised position on this issue, was softened to the extent of starting talks with the terrorist organisation that gave rise to important expectations on both sides. There was thus a decline in political tension and the questions of the Ministry of the Interior were once again considered matters that should basically be subject to consensus.

ETA suffered a significant setback in 1997 when the security forces freed Jose Antonio Ortega Lara, a prison official who had been kidnapped for 532 days, the longest lasting action of such characteristics to date. Ten days later, in order to demonstrate its continued operational ability, the organisation kidnapped the PP town councillor Miguel Ángel Blanco. He was murdered following hours of anguish, when no answer was received to ETA's demands that its prisoners be moved to prisons in the Basque Country. The organisation always knew full well that the state was not going to cede to its demands. Blanco's death triggered a rapid and powerful process in which the political forces and a large part of Basque society forcefully positioned themselves against terrorism, a rejection expressed in overwhelming form in demonstrations and public statements. The main political consequence was that the PP felt it had enough social support to alter the course of its strategy and it took advantage of the favourable context to confront moderate Basque nationalism.

For its part the PNV, perceiving that it had lost the initiative, set in motion a renovated political process, bearing a nationalist and exclusive stamp, which consisted in isolating the state forces and tensing relations with the PP government. This resulted in the so-called Lizarra–Garazi agreements (Onaindía 2000, ch. 11; Gurruchaga and San Sebastián 2000, ch. 19) that implicitly established a commitment to finding a solution among the Basque political, trade union and social forces. At the same time, ETA undertook to observe a truce, with the particular characteristic that it did not depend on the state's answer but on the attitude of the PNV government and, concretely, on foundations being put forward that could lead to self-determination. In this context of détente, ETA declared a total and indefinite ceasefire in September 1998. For its part, the PP government, feeling itself strengthened by the good electoral results obtained in the Basque elections in May that year, announced in November that it was willing to negotiate with ETA. The government did not want to be excluded from the positive returns that it might derive from a successful outcome to the Lizarra–Garazi agreements (Aizpeolea 2013, ch. 7).

The reason for the failure of the process must be sought in the debate that took place among the Basque parties. This was broken off in November 1999 when strong recriminations were directed against the PNV by the terrorist organisation. The most intransigent sectors of ETA finally imposed their line, arguing that few advances had been achieved. ETA's decision to end the truce was determined by two reasons: the PNV's hesitant attitude towards Udalbiltza (an informal association of Basque municipalities whose aim was to promote nationalist principles and collaboration to that end in the municipal sphere); and the consideration that this party was continuing to develop an ambiguous and opportunist political position with the sole aim of perpetuating itself in power. ETA's decision to break the truce even came as a surprise to its political wing, altering the latter's timid strategy of openness to the legal political sphere. However, the resumption of terrorist actions did not reach the intensity of the late 1970s, which showed up the organisation's operational limitations. For ETA this was a scenario marked by growing operational paralysis and problems in selecting new militants, the majority of whom proceeded from the *Kale Borroka* (street struggle). This source of human resources enabled it to recruit a large number of radical youths, but they lacked the training, skill and determination of previous generations, which made them very vulnerable. The data referring to the number of cells broken up and members arrested from the 2000s (see Table 4.1) are a clear sample of the organisation's decline.

Table 4.1 Effectiveness of the police response to ETA terrorism

	1999	*2000*	*2001*	*2002*
Cells broken up	3	6	15	13
Arrests	50	99	171	191

Source: Ministry of the Interior (2003) Balance sheet 2002. Madrid: Oficina de Relaciones Informativos y Sociales.

Facing a situation of terrorist virulence, the PSOE proposed the signing of an anti-terrorist agreement. The PP was not particularly inclined to doing so because of its political strategy of confrontation with the PSOE, which was considerably weakened at the national level. However, considering the possibility of projecting a negative image before public opinion and fearing that the PSOE might disassociate itself from the state commitment on anti-terrorist questions, the PP signed the Agreement for Liberties and against Terrorism in December 2000. This new political regulation, united to the exclusion by law of those political formations that showed a permissive attitude towards violence or that identified with ETA's means and objectives, meant that a greater limitation was placed on the organisation's influence.

During this period, the terrorist actions carried out by Al Qaeda in the United States in 2001 laid the foundations for an initial reflection within ETA and its milieu on the role that violence should play in the political processes in the Basque context (Barbería and Unzueta 2003, ch. 6). This reflection was not so much the result of an internal intellectual process; instead it was imposed by the global offensive against terrorism on all fronts. ETA began to see itself as implicitly discredited and to understand that the terrorist tactic could pose significant problems in an increasingly hostile international setting. This attitude started to be perceptible in the response received by other organisations that had nothing to do with jihadism. In its turn, pressure in favour of greater international cooperation against terrorism was increasing in different forums like the United Nations, the North Atlantic Treaty Organisation and the European Union, among others. This pressure was explicitly supported by Spain, which linked itself to the North American proposals in this respect. Similarly, the jihadist actions generated a certain feeling of being overwhelmed in numerous sectors of radical Basque nationalism. The idea emerged forcefully that continuation of the armed struggle in such a context of generalised hostility towards terrorism would prove to be totally counterproductive.

In 2004 the replacement of Xabier Arzallus – identified with the more pro-independence sectors and favourable to a political negotiation with ETA – by Josu Jon Imaz at the head of the PNV marked a radical change in this party's strategy. The PNV's internal divisions became apparent and from the start there was a commitment to regenerating a climate of understanding with the central government. There were varied consequences, among which it is worth underscoring a sharpening of the problems for the radical sectors, whose sensation of isolation was increasing. In this scenario, new dynamics developed such as a deepening of the differences between ETA and the sectors of the IA more favourable to advancing exclusively along the political path. While a split did not take place, two forms of understanding future strategy became established, with ETA tending to cede public prominence to the political sectors. The latter aimed to gain access to the institutions with a different image, one disconnected from violence, which would enable them to advance towards the goal of attaining independence by other means.

Cooperation with France increased thanks to the boost it received from the judicial sphere. At two high-level meetings held in 2001 between the governments of the two countries, a series of far-reaching decisions was taken. Formal backing was given to the temporary handing over of terrorists awaiting trial or who had been sentenced in France so that they could be tried in Spain. In addition, open, complete and reciprocal access to intelligence on anti-terrorist questions was provided and joint investigative teams were set up, the first of which was created in September 2004 for the fight against ETA.

The PSOE and the search for agreements

The effects on ETA and radical Basque nationalism of the terrorist attacks of 11 March 2004 in Madrid were highly relevant, as they were forced to reconsider the role that violence could play in the future, although this reflection had already begun in 2001 following the attacks in the United States. Violence had lost a large part of its effective impact as an instrument for applying pressure, since ETA was incapable of achieving the levels needed to continue provoking the effects it sought. In addition, it was highly probable that should such attacks be carried out, they would be very negative for the strategy of the IA and the survival of the terrorist organisation.

In the political sphere the defeat of the PP and the victory of the PSOE in the general election of March 2004 resulted in a noticeable change in government strategy (Alonso 2013). The PP's defeat was a consequence of its mistakes in the strategic and tactical handling of the jihadist bomb attacks that had taken place in Madrid a few days before the election – causing 191 deaths. Prior to the elect-oral victory, Jesús Eguiguren, a prominent member of the *Partido Socialista de Euskadi* (PSE – Socialist Party of Euskadi), the Basque branch of the PSOE, had begun to hold talks with the IA aimed at opening up channels for institutional contacts to facilitate a resolution of the Basque problem in the medium or long term, emulating the Irish process. This resulted in the start of a process that was taken up by the socialist government in Madrid whose members had not been previously informed, as it had been based on individual initiatives. This process, which lasted from 2005 to 2007, was characterised by profound disorder in the negotiations on the government's side. There was no team of experts working in support. Instead there was simply the will of individuals who even altered com-munications on the limited chain of command leading to the president of the government (Europa Press 2015a).

There was some haste on the government's side to advance in a process that was being developed at a highly favourable moment and towards which almost all the actors were favourable. The exception was the PP, which decided to break the anti-terrorist consensus and turn the issue into a political weapon. ETA's declaration of an indefinite truce in March 2006 triggered an atmosphere of enthusiasm and hope. While the PP initially maintained a cautious attitude towards the positive atmosphere generated by the truce, it went on to the offen-sive when it became known that there was to be a meeting between Patxi López, General Secretary of the PSE, and Arnaldo Otegi, leader of *Batasuna* (Unity), the abertzale left's political formation. This fact, together with a foreseeable transfer of prisoners as a result of future agreements, encouraged the PP to align itself with the most conservative positions and with like-minded associations of victims.

Meanwhile, ETA did not appear to be in tune with the abertzale left's proposals and questions of only minor importance were dealt with in the direct contacts between the terrorist organisation and the government. ETA's real hope was to negotiate political aspects, which the government envoys were not prepared to do. Nor does there appear to have been an informal agreement on this in the prior contacts between the PSE and the IA. There were evident difficulties due the differences of perspective. For the Spanish government the first objective was peace and there could be talk about politics later, while ETA's approach was the exact opposite. As the situation deteriorated, meetings were held among the PSE, the PNV and the abertzale left with the aim of energising the process and establishing certain commitments. These meetings would be known as the *Loiola Talks*. The discussions included the possibility of advancing towards a union between the Basque Country and Navarre, which posed enormous difficulties for the PSOE itself, because its definitive approval would need the support of the PP. ETA made clear its rejection of the plan unless it included a calendar, which was opposed by the rest of the forces. The organisation put an end to this phase by planting a bomb at Barajas Airport in December 2006, which killed two people.

Once again, the experience of negotiation had proved disappointing. The process itself underscored tensions and different interests within the IA, and between the latter and ETA. The organisation, at a time of maximum weakness due to successful police coercion, was under growing pressure to reconsider its attitude from more pragmatic sectors of the IA.

Unlike earlier occasions, the end of the truce in 2007 did not throw the police off balance. This was because the security forces had kept up pressure throughout the period of the truce, collecting information and elaborating intelligence. In February 2007 the head of ETA's logistical apparatus was arrested and by the end of the year five cells had been broken up, three of them before they had gone into action (Aizpeolea 2013, 117). Only four cells remained active. They only managed to murder two civil guardsmen and this was in an unplanned action. According to the General Intelligence Commission, the organisation had 100 militants at its disposal as well as significant logistical means (Irujo 2007).

In June that same year a *historic* summit was held between the Minister of the Interior, Alfredo Pérez Rubalcaba, and the Basque Councillor of the Interior, Javier Balza. The aim of the meeting was to reinforce the response to ETA, placing it above political disagreements on other issues. The intention was to increase collaboration and the exchange of information, a commitment that was to be upheld in the following years. The haste and inexperience of the new militants made the organisation vulnerable, with the number of arrests rising significantly. There was also a substantial increase in police pressure in France. At the end of that year the number of Spanish agents involved in the struggle against ETA in France rose to 200 (Rodríguez 2007).

In this situation and facing the lack of political initiatives, the president of the Basque government, Juan José Ibarretxe, wanted to progress by means of a pro-sovereignty plan. To this end a Consultation Law was approved in June 2008, which meant reinforcing the Basque political scenario facing the Spanish context. His proposal threatened to divide Basque society and met with the opposition of almost all the political parties. There was even strong opposition from within his own political formation, given that it shifted the PNV away from the centre of the political spectrum and posed a possible threat to its political hegemony. The PNV's inability to form a government following the election of March 2009 underscored the fragility of a project that did not obtain clear support from the majority of citizens. In this new scenario the PSE, supported by a moderate PP, occupied the presidency of the Basque government, where it was support by the central government, also socialist. This political configuration was favourable for the initiative of facilitating the transfer of certain prisoners willing to reject violence to prisons closer to the Basque Country. In this way a series of contacts between victims and terrorists was also begun. These initiatives were known as the *Nanclares Path*. They helped to acquaint numerous prisoners, who had been in jail since the 1980s, with Basque social reality and enabled them to perceive a changed society where violence made no sense. ETA's murder of a former socialist town councillor in Mondragón in March 2008 was a warning that the process was not proceeding along the path that the organisation wanted and underscored the break with the IA. The latter criticised the action through its spokesperson Otegi, who opted exclusively for the political route.

In an agonising headlong rush and under considerable pressure, ETA attempted to transfer its logistical base to Portugal, a move that was foiled by a stroke of luck in February 2010. From then on, very strong tensions arose within the organisation itself, which were resolved with the arrest of some of its leaders by the police. All of those arrested were well known and there were no more surprises in store. The situation was very favourable for internal movements to take place. ETA, paralysed by the police and challenged by the IA, entered a new phase characterised by its extreme weakness.

The terrorist organisation carried out different actions of limited impact and murdered a French policeman in March 2010. All of this served to exacerbate the differences with the IA, with Otegi accusing ETA of blocking any dialogue. The arrest in May 2010 of ETA's last leader, Mikel Carrera, facilitated the seizure of the political and symbolic space by the IA, which was ready to embark on the political route. In this context of unresolvable internal divisions, the IA requested the services of Brian Currin, a South African lawyer and an expert in negotiations, in order to internationalise the image of the conflict at a moment when it was rapidly losing international impetus.

In September, the organisation announced a unilateral truce for the first time in its history, and a permanent truce in January 2011. This made it easier for the IA to organise a political formation named *Sortu* with statutes that explicitly rejected violence, although the Supreme Court prevented it from standing in the municipal election of May 2011. The IA went into coalition with other national-ist parties in May to form *Bildu*, which was legalised, although this was opposed by the PP. The *Bildu* coalition achieved the greatest success in the IA's history, winning 26.45 per cent of the votes and significant institutional power, including the mayorship of San Sebastián. ETA had ceded the leading role in this situation to the IA, not out of conviction but because it could not avoid doing so.

The imminence of an early general election in November 2011 and the fore-seeable defeat of the PSOE due to the severe economic crisis afflicting the country led the IA to accelerate certain measures with the aim of forcing a com-mitment on the future government. Thus, an international conference was held in the Aiete Palace in San Sebastián in October 2011 which was attended by numerous international personalities. At this meeting a definitive cessation of violence was requested from ETA, which the latter declared on 20 October.

The inevitable and definitive end, 2012 to 2015

Following the conservative victory in the general election of 2011, the new PP government tried to reorient the policy developed by the socialists, although the structure of the scenario prevented it from radically changing the institutional approach. The situation at the time was marked by a defeated terrorist organisa-tion (Domínguez 2012); a political wing that had taken the imitative, advancing rapidly towards integration in conventional political life and willing to enter the institutions – a good example of this is the results of the local elections in May 2011 and 2015; a Basque civil society anxious to overcome the past – at the price of forgetting it in the case of some sectors; a Spanish civil society that was increasingly indifferent to Basque radical terrorism and its consequences; divided groups of victims that were becoming increasingly irrelevant; a col-lective of prisoners awaiting events; and finally, an indifferent international context more concerned with issues linked to jihadist terrorism. In this frame-work, the roadmap left a very narrow margin for manoeuvre. This was why the Spanish government adopted a do-nothing attitude, principally in those spheres where it was able (not) to act, such as the prisons.

The problem of the prisoners was what gave rise to the greatest concern, as the radical sectors opposed to the official line were becoming increasingly important in this milieu. This was in a context where the sectors of radical Basque nationalism most favourable to integration in the political system and to definitively ending the violence accepted that the prisoners were a burden that could affect the IA's strategy. The outgoing government informed the new pres-ident, Mariano Rajoy, that the political leadership of ETA was located in Oslo and was favourable to talks 'on its disarmament and disbandment in exchange for obtaining guarantees for its prisoners' (Aizpeolea 2013, 153). The new gov-ernment waited for the right moment in January 2013 to procure the expulsion of the ETA leadership from Norwegian territory. From the point of view of the PSOE and the PNV the prisoners could constitute an issue with enough symbolic weight to contribute to definitively ending the terrorist problem in the Basque

Country. If the issue was managed with flexibility, all the actors would be able to profit from it politically. This was not how the PP understood the question, due to the pressure it was under from the more conservative sectors and from some associations of victims. It opted for strategic inaction on this issue. The prison front was to suffer significant internal tensions, with the official line becoming progressively weaker due to the lack of progress, and the more radical line becoming established, a line that opposed individual solutions.

One of the most relevant police actions during this stage took place in January 2014 with the arrest of a group of prisoners' lawyers who formed the channel and structure by which ETA contacted and controlled the collective of prisoners. Subsequently, another series of arrests in January 2015 put a definitive end to this structure composed of lawyers responsible for defending numerous members of the organisation. Both actions had a very relevant impact on the ETA milieu.

The first real movement in the prisons resulted from the retroactive repeal of the so-called Parot doctrine – which was very unfavourable to imprisoned ETA members as it meant that prison benefits in the form of sentence reduction were applied to each crime taken individually – and the announcement of the release of prisoners. These releases were never massive, but instead were individualised, reaching a total of 137. In the first half of 2015 the number of preventive prisoners linked to jihadist terrorism for the first time exceeded the number of members of the Basque radical organisation in preventive prison. This fact underscored their continued rise and relative decline, respectively (Vasco Press 1730). The local elections of 2015 produced a scenario that could favour a significant change in the government's *impasse*. The defeat of *Bildu* in the province of Gipuzkoa and its relative victory in Navarre introduced an element of normality into the Basque and Navarrese political game.

The terrorist organisation was in a 'terminal state' in September 2015, according to the Minister of the Interior, Jorge Fernández Díaz. It was definitively broken up following the arrest of the last leaders of its political apparatus that month, although it had already been operationally annulled. The 20 or so clandestine militants scattered throughout France no longer formed an active structure, and likewise lacked the resources to provide cover to possible new activists (Europa Press 2015b). According to the Prosecutor's Office of the Paris Criminal Court, the organisation had some 30 operational members available. In this context of ETA's de facto breakup, although the organisation had not disbanded, it did not seem that alternative, critical movements could emerge in opposition to the official line. There had, however, been some episodes of street violence, resulting in the destruction of buses, and an internal current named *IBIL* had emerged that defended a violent, radical line of very limited relevance. To certain internal, dissident currents with limited influence, such as *IBIL* and *Amnistia Ta Askatasuna* (ATA) (in the prison area), must be added the letter signed by 93 former prisoners who continued to be in favour of an amnesty, against the criteria of ETA and the IA.

The IA is conscious that it is necessary to secure the support of France to advance the process and block possible retrogressions instigated by the Spanish government with respect to disarmament and possible negotiations. Brian Currin, the negotiator, has made moves in this direction, as he has held meetings with the French Minister of Justice. Significant figures in French politics support these initiatives and all of this is a cause of concern to the Spanish authorities.

The problem of political violence in its terrorist format in the Basque Country has been concluded, but the embers produced by the offences, the consequence of decades of abuses and murders, continue to occupy a space in the identitarian, symbolic and emotional structures of Basque and Navarrese citizens. There are some interpretations about the end of the process that are not particularly hopeful (Alonso 2010, 2012). But it is necessary to accept that due to its complexity (Batista 2011) and the difficulty involved in its management, there will inevitably be unresolved aspects that perhaps only the passage of time will make it possible to resolve. It is the future politicians and society itself that must occupy the spaces that have been freed of violence in order to elaborate new frameworks of coexistence built on memory and collective effort with the aim of maintaining democratic peace.

Conclusion

The evolution of ETA's terrorism from 1992 to the present makes it possible to be optimistic about the effective suppression of terrorism, so long as certain conditions are created. The opportunities provided to terrorism resulted, at least during this stage, from a lack of definition among the main political actors and, in the previous stage, from mistakes in handling the use of force and the application of the rule of law. All of this inflated the expectations of a terrorist organisation that was clearly on the decline but that still had enough capacity to prove lethal and intensely condition the country's political life, as well as diverting considerable resources. The development of the different stages shows how coordination and coherence of state action maintained over time have positive results, thus confirming the initial hypothesis. Moments of disunion create unoccupied spaces that are immediately detected by actors wanting to disrupt the system. Final responsibility for these scenarios is in the hands of the managers of the institutional powers and depends on their having a suitable perception of their respective responsibilities. But a relevant role is also played by the competence and professionalism of police officials who understand that anti-terrorist effectiveness concerns society as a whole and that they are inserted into a complex system of which they are an essential part, but one that is limited in scope.

Bibliography

Aid, Matthew M. (2012) *Intel Wars. The Secret History of the Fight against Terror*. New York: Bloombury Press.

Aizpeolea, Luis R. (2013) *Los entresijos del final de ETA. Un intento de recuperar una historia manipulada*. Madrid: Los libros de la catarata.

Alonso, Rogelio (2010) 'Confronting terrorism in Northern Ireland and the Basque Country: Challenges for democracy and legitimacy'. In *The Consequences of Counterterrorism*, ed. Martha Crenshaw, 213–255. New York: Russell Sage Foundation.

Alonso, Rogelio (2012) 'El Estado contra ETA: entre la victoria policial y la derrota política'. *Cuadernos de Pensamiento Político* 34: 139–170.

Alonso, Rogelio (2013) 'The Madrid bombings and negotiations with ETA: A case study of the impact of terrorism on Spanish politics'. *Terrorism and Political Violence* 25: 113–136.

Anonymous (2004) *Imperial Hubris. Why the West is Losing the War on Terror.* Washington, DC: Brassey's.

Ballbé, Manuel (1985) 'Fuerzas y cuerpos de seguridad en España'. *Revista Internacional de Sociología* 43: 373–380.

Barbería, Jose Luis and Patxo Unzueta (2003) *Cómo hemos llegado a esto. La crisis vasca.* Madrid: Taurus.

Batista, Antonio (2011) *Adiós a las armas. Una crónica del final de ETA.* Barcelona: Debate.

Bergen, Peter L. (2011) *The Longest War. The Enduring Conflict between America and Al-Qaeda.* New York: Free Press.

Carr, Caleb (2008) *The Lessons of Terror: A History of Warfare Against Civilians.* New York: Random House.

Chalk, Peter (2000) *West European Terrorism and Counter-terrorism. The Evolving Dynamic.* London: Macmillan.

Cotarelo, Ramón (ed.) (1992) *Transición política y consolidación democrática.* Madrid: CIS.

Cronin, Audrey K. (2009) *How Terrorism Ends. Understanding the Decline and Demise of Terrorist Campaigns.* Princeton, NJ: Princeton University Press.

Cronin, Audrey K. and James M. Ludes (eds) (2004) *Attacking Terrorism. Elements of a Grand Strategy.* Washington, DC: Georgetown University Press.

De la Corte, Luis (2006) *La lógica del terrorismo.* Madrid: Alianza.

Del Águila, Rafael and Ramón Cotarelo (eds) (1992) *Transición política y consolidación democrática, España (1975–1986).* Madrid: CIS.

Domínguez, Florencio (1998) *De la negocación a la tregua ¿El final de ETA?.* Madrid: Taurus.

Domínguez, Florencio (2002) *Dentro de ETA. La vida diaria de los terroristas.* Madrid: Aguilar.

Domínguez, Florencio (2012) *La agonía de ETA. Una investigación inédita sobre los últimos días de la banda.* Madrid: La esfera de los libros.

Donohue, Laura K. (2008) *The Cost of Counterterrorism. Power, Politics and Liberty.* Cambridge: Cambridge University Press.

Estévez, Lucana *et al.* (2006) *European Response to Terrorism. The Cases of Spain and Slovakia.* Bratislava: Ministerio de Defensa de España/Ministry of Defence of the Slovak Republik.

Europa Press (2015a) 'Eguiguren presume de que desobedeció al Gobierno al continuar negociando con ETA tras un atentado de la banda'. *Europa Press*, 7 April.

Europa Press (2015b) 'Ocho etarras se mantienen entre los más buscados, entre ellos "Josu Ternera" y De Juana Chaos'. *Europa Press*, 23 September.

Funes, María Jesús (1998) *La salida del silencio.Movilizaciones por la paz en Euskadi 1986–1998.* Madrid: Akal.

Ganor, Boaz (2005) *The Counter Terrorism Puzzle. A Guide for Decision Makers.* New Brunswick, NJ: Transaction Publishers.

Guenaga, Aitor (2015) 'La reacción al chantaje terrorista de ETA fue muy tardía (Interview with Florencio Domínguez)'. *El Diario Norte*, 18 July.

Gurruchaga, Carmen and Isabel San Sebastián (2000) *El arbol y las nueces. La relación secreta entre ETA y PNV*. Madrid: Temas de hoy.

Hewitt, Christopher (1993*) Consequences of Political Violence*. Aldershot: Dartmouth.

Hocking, Jenny and Colleen Lewis (2007) *Counter-terrorism and the Post-democratic State*. Cheltenham: Edward Elgar.

Holmes, Jennifer (2001) *Terrorism and Democratic Stability*. Manchester: Manchester University Press.

Holmes, Jennifer (2008) *Terrorism and Democratic Stability Revisited*. Manchester: Manchester University Press.

Irujo, Jose María (2007) 'La policía cree que ETA tiene un centenar de terroristas y una capacidad operativa inmejorable'. *El País*, 6 June.

Jaime-Jiménez, Óscar (2001) *Policía, terrorismo y cambio político en España (1976–1996)*. Valencia: Tirant lo blanch.

Jaime-Jiménez, Óscar (2002) 'Adaptación evolutiva y eficacia del contraterrorismo en el actual contexto español'. In *Políticas del miedo. Un balance del terrorismo en Europa*, ed. Eduardo González, 345–370. Madrid: Biblioteca Nueva.

Lennon, Alexander T.J. (ed.) (2003) *The Battle for Hearts and Minds. Using Soft Power to Undermine Terrorist Networks*. Cambridge: MIT Press.

Morán, Sagrario (1997) *ETA entre España y Francia*. Madrid: Editorial Complutense.

Onaindía, Mario (2000) *Guia para orientarse en el laberinto vasco*. Madrid: Temas de hoy.

Pozas, Alberto (1992) *Las conversaciones secretas Gobierno-ETA*. Barcelona: Ediciones B.

Reinares, Fernando (1998) *Terrorismo y contraterrorismo*. Madrid: Paidos.

Reinares, Fernando (2003) 'Democratization and state responses to protracted terrorsm in Spain'. In *Confronting Terrorism. European Experiences, Threat Perceptions and Policies*, ed. Marianne Van Leeuwen, 57–70. The Hague: Kluwer Law International.

Reinares, Fernando and Oscar Jaime-Jiménez (2000) 'Countering terrorism in a new democracy: The case of Spain'. In *European Democracies Against Terrorism*, ed. Fernando Reinares, 119–145. Dartmouth: Ashgate.

Remiro, Antonio and Carlos Espósito (2002) 'Spain'. In *Combating Terrorism. Strategies of Ten Countries*, ed. Yonah Alexander, 163–186. Michigan, OH: University of Michigan Press.

Rodríguez, Jorge A. (2007) '200 agentes españoles en la guarida de ETA'. *El País*, 3 December.

Unzueta, Patxo (1997) *El terrorismo. ETA y el problema vasco*. Barcelona: Ediciones Destino.

Vasco Press (1730) *Crónicas*.

Wilkinson, Paul (2011) *Terrorism versus Democracy. The Liberal State Response*. London: Routledge.

Woodworth, P. (2002) *Dirty War, Clean Hands, ETA, the GAL and Spanish Democracy*. Cork: Cork University Press.

Part II
The politics of fear

5 Epic, memory and the making of an uncivil community

Jesús Casquete[1]

Forging a collective identity

By the autumn of 2011, ETA (*Euskadi ta Askatasuna*, Basque Country and Freedom) had become the only remaining group in Western Europe seeking to force a majority of a population to submit to a political project imposed by means of terrorist violence. ETA's survival over more than half a century (it was founded in 1959 but caused no fatalities until 1968) would not have been possible without human, material, moral and logistical resources and the support of a dense network of political and social groups.

In this chapter I will analyse the terrorist phenomenon and its social concomitants in the Basque Country, from the transition to democracy in Spain at the end of the 1970s up until armed violence ceased in October 2011. The main question motivating and giving shape to this investigation may be stated as follows: How is a 'radical milieu' forged and perpetuated, fostering habits of exclusiveness, extremism, uncivility and parochialism among its members to the point of justifying the use of violence to achieve *political* goals that affect the entire social sphere? Following Malthaner and Waldmann (2012), by 'radical milieu' I mean the segment of a population that sympathises with terrorists and supports them morally and logistically. No terrorist group can survive in the long term without the resources provided by a dense and committed social support network. What distinguishes the milieu from simple sympathisers is that the former implies a social structure responsible for the observed in-group cohesion. Such a Basque milieu configures a radical milieu; inasmuch as it supports a terrorist group that threatens the rights, liberties and life of others, it may also be labelled an 'uncivil community' (Casquete 2006a). This kind of community in the Basque Country despised the three pillars of what Charles Taylor has called a 'philosophy of civility', namely: (1) respect for human rights; (2) equality and non-discrimination; and (3) democracy itself (2010, 32). Hate of the 'other' seen as an 'enemy' lies at the base of an uncivility that violates other people's basic rights, an attitude and praxis that may be seen as immoral (Kateb 2008, 382, 387).

Before launching into my case study on the radical nationalist movement in the Basque Country, some theoretical considerations are necessary regarding the manner in which a social group with a vocation to bring about social and political change constructs a collective identity. After identifying certain characteristic features of the radical nationalist movement, I will focus my attention on a specific mnemonic mechanism aiming at preserving its collective memory: the commemorative calendar around the dead heroes elevated to the altar of the homeland; that is to say, contemplated as a prefiguration of the 'new man' to be forged in the national community of the future.

It is widely accepted that collective action requires the fostering of commitment among members of a social collective in order to develop and attain any degree of substantive or mobilising success. Commitment and a sense of loyalty to the group are based on group solidarity, or the feeling of belonging to a comforting plurality, and mutual recognition among a group of actors that they compose a single entity. The development of tight fraternal bonds among participants is thus a defining feature of successful collective action, providing the actors with the 'nerve' that is vital to sustaining their activity and meeting their challenges. Given this, then, examining how this sense of group membership is created and re-created over time is foundational to understanding the dynamics of collective action in historical and contemporary movements.

Several paths are available to a social collective seeking its own recognisable identity, with characteristics and borders that distinguish it from the surrounding social context. One of these is the establishment of boundaries between 'us' and 'them' (Elias 1965; Barth 1969). Its most rudimentary dictum in the words of a classical author of social theory, which is valid for the study of terrorism and its social cohorts, states that 'It is *convenient* to hate the adversary against whom, for whatever reason, you are fighting, as it is convenient to love whoever you are allied with and have to coexist with' (Simmel 1992, 303; emphasis in the original). Within the friend–enemy logic, love for the endogroup and hatred towards an exogroup, which has previously undergone a potentially lethal process of socio-stigmatisation, are two sides of the terrorist coin and its social support network. A second path involves creating a network of sociability through associative enclaves such as consciousness-raising groups, clubs, discussion and reading groups, athenaeums, bars or workshops (Evans and Boyte 1986). In these contexts, members of a social group enjoy the opportunity to exchange experiences, information, leisure activities, etc. on the basis of what Blumer called 'informal fellowship' (1946, 207). The third path uses ceremonies and rituals (mass events, parades, marches, demonstrations, commemorations, etc.) as mechanisms to form and reaffirm the *esprit de corps* of close-knit social groups. Feelings of shared identity and sympathy among participants intensify thanks to the symbolic paraphernalia that invariably accompany these rituals, such as slogans, songs, salutes, greetings, flags, hymns, uniforms, identifying attire, etc.

The radical nationalist milieu in the Basque Country articulated itself around the so-called *Movimiento de Liberación Nacional Vasco* (MLNV), or the Basque National Liberation Movement. I will outline in turn the main features of this radical milieu.

A politics of the holy

The radical Basque nationalist movement that developed around the MLNV since the transition to democracy in Spain in the late 1970s until ETA's cessation of violent activities in 2011 once defined itself as follows:

> [T]he form or forms of expression, and the social and political stream composed of large portions of the Basque Working People who seek as their ultimate objective *full national sovereignty* for all Basque lands. This Liberation Movement and the social segments composing it find their historical expression specifically in the organizations that, with their own unique approaches (depending on specific fields of intervention) contribute to advancing this process.
>
> (Herri Batasuna n.d.)

On the MLNV, see, in addition, Mata 1993; Sáez de la Fuente 2002; Muro 2008; Casquete 2009a; Bullain 2011; Merino 2011; Fernández and López 2012). In other words, the MLNV was the organisational umbrella for the entire radical nationalist spectrum in Euskadi (the Autonomous Community of Spain that includes the provinces of Araba, Gipuzkoa and Biscay), Navarre and the French Basque Country, all of which radical nationalists refer to in geo-political terms as *Euskal Herria*.

Throughout the period between 1978 and 2011 the MLNV had branches in such areas as feminism, ecology, international solidarity, Basque culture and especially language, youth and students, solidarity with Basque prisoners held for terrorist crimes and the workers' movement (Mata 2006). All such sectorial organisations comprised the social milieu of the ethno-nationalist terrorist organisation ETA, which appears at the pinnacle of this particular structure, based on an elitist ranking principle: those who risk the most should have higher decision-making capacity regarding the direction of the movement than those with a lower level of commitment. In other words: whoever kills rules the entire movement.

The MLNV has had recourse to a variety of political forms of representation in order to present candidates for election (Leonisio 2015). The political presence of the party *Herri Batasuna* (HB), which from its foundation was understood to be the political arm of ETA, lasted from 1978 to 1998. It was re-founded as *Euskal Herritarrok* in 1998 and became *Batasuna* in 2001. Based on the so-called Law of Parties of 2002 which prohibited all political expression of the movement, in 2003 the Spanish Supreme Court ruled that this latter organisation was part of the ETA network and therefore illegal. *Batasuna* then made use of smokescreen party lists such as the PCTV-EHAK (Communist Party of the Basque Homelands) or ANV (Basque Nationalist Action), which in turn were also legally proscribed. From the restoration of democracy in Spain after Franco's death in 1975 until the Law of Parties was passed and shortly thereafter implemented, electoral support remained stable at around 16 per cent for the successive political parties considered to be close to ETA. This figure may serve as a reference point for quantifying the potential scope of the radical nationalist milieu in the Basque Country. In a court sentence of 30 June 2009 and in subsequent sentences, the European Court of Human Rights in Strasbourg legally backed proscribing *Batasuna* as a measure 'necessary in a democratic society' for 'maintaining security, defending order and protecting the rights and freedoms of others'. With these prohibitions, the judicial sentence implicitly accepted the 'militant democracy' perspective proposed by Karl Löwenstein at a time when fascism was on the rise throughout Europe and there was 'underground war on the inner front' (Löwenstein 1937, 432; see also Preuß 2002, 104–119). The German jurist and political scientist justified adopting exceptional measures such as outlawing parties and placing limits on the freedom of expression and assembly as a safeguard against opponents of democracy seeking to weaken it from within.

Inside the MLNV, ETA functioned as the armed vanguard in a unique division of labour towards the single objective of a Basque state. The vote-seeking political arm and the various social organisations (feminists, ecologists, labour unions, etc.) made use of popular mobilisation and socialisation strategies while ETA used bullets and bombs. If, following Michael Walzer, 'terrorism is the deliberate killing of innocent people, at random, in order to spread fear through a whole population and force the hand of its political leaders' (2002, 5), then ETA fits into the category of a terrorist organisation. Since its first killing in 1968 until it declared a 'permanent ceasefire' in October 2011, ETA and different breakaway organisations were responsible for the murder of 845 people, most of them (96 per cent) after Franco's death in 1975 and the beginning of democracy shortly thereafter (López 2015). To the extent that it sought to structure the entire Basque social panorama by twisting the sovereignty of the popular will as expressed in its representative institutions, this terrorist *modus operandi* was unequivocally political in essence and positioned itself in confrontation with the Spanish and French democratic institutional regimes (though Basque nationalism has a weak political presence in France).

In consonance with a 'politics of atrocity' (Rapoport 1977, 46–61; Waldmann 1998), the means employed by terrorist organisations are intrinsically brutal and inhumane. Thus, classifying an actor as a terrorist is fundamentally a matter of examining the means it employs to achieve its objectives. Power-seeking violence used in a confrontation with an established power, carried out by an actor in defiance of authority, is then the key interpretive datum for classifying an actor as a terrorist. Based on this, I will use the label *radical* nationalism for the entire social and political web of the MLNV. This refers less to its goals (the right to self-determination and independence of the Basque Country, or in their terms 'the territorial unity of *Euskal Herria*') than to the violent means and disregard for the minimum moral requirements applicable to every social and political actor in any democratic system. In an open and plural public sphere, it is permissible to propose secessionist objectives by peaceful means. Basque supporters of independence who simultaneously condemn the use of violence to achieve this goal have done precisely this. *Aralar* and *Eusko Alkartasuna*, two nationalist parties explicitly favouring the independence of the Basque Country, encountered up until 2011 (thereafter they merged into a broader coalition of nationalist parties led by radical nationalists) no major obstacles as legal parties with institutional representation and even participation in regional government and in town councils. In Catalonia, much the same may be said for *Convergència Democràtica* and *Esquerra Republicana*. What no democratic regime can even begin to contemplate without questioning its own legitimacy is the pursuit of secessionist objectives by destroying the right to life and restricting the freedom of its citizens.

There are two intertwined discursive features that condition the worldview of this movement and how it understands and practises politics. First is its religious conception of politics, involving the sacralisation of the homeland, an imagined political entity with an absolute value that supersedes the will of the citizens. This is in line with what Charles Taylor has defined as a *hypergood*: 'goods which not only are incomparably more important than others but provide the standpoint from which these must be weighed, judged, decided about' (1989, 63). In our case, an *Euskal Herria* composed of Euskadi, Navarre and the French Basque Country has been enshrined as the object of faith and devotion for all members and sympathisers of this community of believers. The ultimate test of the strength of one's faith was expressed by Horace's *pro patria mori*: the willingness to face martyrdom for the cause of the homeland whenever circumstances require it. However, the fundamental distinction between this case and other sacrificial formulas, such as the republican tradition of defending the homeland from an invader or dictator, is that here terrorists acting in the name of *Euskal Herria* enhance *mori* with *necare*, adding killing to dying. The *gudaris* (or 'Basque soldiers', meaning members of ETA who died in violent actions or as 'victims of repression'), these 'martyrs' fallen in an act of 'combat', become the most noble and complete guardians of that which is sacred to this nationalist community. Thus, on Mount Aritxulegi in the province of Gipuzkoa, radical nationalists have planted an oak tree for every deceased *gudari*. By early 2009, there were 225 oaks in this *lieu de mémoire* (*Gara*, 30 March 2009). Not all the deceased *gudaris* honoured there died as a result of violence, such as clashes with Spain's security forces, due to handling explosive artefacts, victims of 'para-police' vigilante groups or terrorists, due to torture, etc. The category of *gudari* was widened to include members of ETA who died of natural causes (heart attack, cancer, etc.), accidents (traffic, falls, etc.) or other causes (e.g. suicide). Any sort of commitment to those who think differently (the 'enemy') is then conflated with treason and anathematised in the vocabulary and practice of those who embrace the religion of the fatherland. Any willingness to compromise by those considered 'heterodox' or 'heretical' is considered equivalent to doubting the core or the purity of what is sacred. In the words of the philosopher Avishai Margalit, '[t]he politics of the holy is the art of the impossible. It makes long-run compromise untenable' (2010, 72). As with any nationalism, the territorial dimension of the Basque conflict is included in the identity question, linking it to another important aspect in the religious reading of politics: *irredentism*. It involves the effort to recover territories supposedly occupied by the Basques in the Middle Ages but lost to Castile through military defeat. This armed conquest marked the beginning of Basque subjugation without consent, due to the unresolved grievance of political, economic and cultural domination by Spanish and French monarchs and states. From the nationalist perspective, this historical injustice must be put right by recovering these dominated lands and restoring a hypothetical ancient cultural and territorial unity under a single political authority in order to avoid the irreversible dilution of the Basque identity into the Spanish and French identities. Of the two states deemed to 'oppress' the Basque Country, the Spanish one is by and large the main 'enemy' of radical Basque nationalism. Throughout the history of Basque nationalism since its inception as a political movement by Sabino Arana in 1895, the founder of the PNV (Basque Nationalist Party), hatred of Spain has been the common thread of every family of radical nationalism (De la Granja 2015).

A second discursive feature of radical Basque nationalism is its recourse to the synecdoche as a political trope: those who proclaim ethno-nationalist irredentism serve the palingenesic project by establishing themselves as the exclusive carriers and interpreters of the fatherland's interests and values. They consider their movement to be the part representing the whole of the Basque people, putting into practice the rhetorical figure mentioned above. Thus a minority presents itself as the ontological majority, the true representatives of the *herria*, the people. The arguments used to develop the synecdoche are immanent to totalitarian logic. With the armed vanguard of ETA as its charismatic collective leader, a status earned by sacrifice in radical nationalist structures, the spokespersons of the movement are convinced that they know and precisely express citizen sentiment without needing to actually hear it or develop institutional mechanisms for legitimately translating public opinion into political will. They side-step the citizenry and bias the democratic process by establishing themselves as the only qualified exegetes. The *quantity* or number of exegetes is of little significance when compared with their *quality*, especially if applying the specific *hierarchy of courage* that reserves a privileged place in the MLNV structure for those who risk well-being, freedom or life – the *gudaris*. I will shortly turn to this issue.

Examples of this fagocitatious strategy are the many radical nationalist marches with slogans such as '*X, herria zurekin*' ('X, the people are with you', where X is a deceased or imprisoned member of ETA or more often ETA itself), '*Herriak ez du barkatuko*' ('the people will not forgive'), or '*Euskal gazteria aurrera*' ('Basque youth, arise!'). Members and sympathisers in the radical nationalist core and milieu have no doubts that they themselves are the depository of the true will of the people. Reiterative recourse to this rhetorical figure was evident in the slogan that *Segi*, the youth organisation of the MLNV banned in Spain in 2002, called its activists and sympathisers to the town of Itsasondo in Gipuzkoa during Easter of 2004 with the following: '*Gu gera herria, egin dezagun bidea*' ('We are the people, we determine the way forward'). On 21 December 2003, during public acts honouring José Miguel Beñaran, *Argala*, a prominent ETA member assassinated in 1978 by para-police forces in the French Basque country, the leader of *Batasuna*, Arnaldo Otegi, proclaimed that 'the nationalist left is *Euskal Herria* and is the future of this people' (*El Correo*, 22 December 2003). There are variants to the invasive nature of a synecdoche: one is seen in the prior examples and relates to *being*; others imply *knowing*. In the *Ikasle Eguna* (Student's Day) that was held on 6 November 2010 in Amurrio (Araba), a flyer for the event upheld the latter use by stating that 'this is the time to build the National Education System that *Euskal Herria* needs'. However, the former use was also operative when the speaker at this act concluded with the statement 'we are the future'.[2] Another sample of a rhetoric expanding 'us' to invade the entire Basque social sphere occurred on 25 February 2006 when several hundred people called out by *Batasuna* marched in the French Basque town of Cibouru to demand 'the right to decide, and respect for the voice of *Euskal Herria*'. In the local canton elections of 2004 held in the French Basque Country, radical nationalism had received 2.67 per cent of the vote.

A piacular calendar

Nations and politically oriented groups, including the social milieux of terrorist organisations, make use of diverse mnemonic mechanisms to preserve and foster their collective identity. Functional 'artefacts' are used extensively by current and constituent powers seeking to shape or shore up their collective identities. These include monuments, flags, coins, stamps, cemeteries, museums, iconography, street and city names, and other 'sites of memory'.

The commemorative calendar is an ideal terrain for the social study of memory. The calendar links a group and preserves its systemic borders with the implicit goal of resisting the passage of time by providing more or less formally institutionalised occasions that foster a pedagogy of remembrance. It gives rise to cycles of celebrations deliberately intended to commemorate relevant events of the mnemonic community's shared past and keep them current. In the words of Aleida Assmann (2005), it offers a series of 'monuments in time'. As with other mnemonic mechanisms, the calendar is very useful for strengthening social bonds, which according to Georg Simmel 'hold the individual parts together by maintaining reciprocity between them, from which comes cohesion of parts, and hence a unity of the whole' (1897, 664).

Like all other mnemonic artefacts, calendar holidays identify *what* we remember; but unlike the more solid mechanisms for preserving the past (museums, monuments, currency, street names, etc.), they also identify *when* we remember. On the same day a community of memory synchronises its attention and projects it onto a single historical moment. This is by nature a shared act with other participating members of a community of remembrance; it surpasses the scope of the isolated individual. Each celebration in the annual commemorative cycle thus offers an invaluable occasion for the members of mnemonic communities to symbolically and affectively bond with each other and with a shared past, thus reinforcing their sense of collective identity.

Simultaneous physical concentration of members of a community of memory such as the MLNV around a single object of attention, with the calendar as the precipitating factor, offers an optimal opportunity structure for perpetuating enclaves of uncivility. Those congregated along with many others indirectly linked through sociability networks (clubs, bars, social movement organisation sites, etc.) and the supportive media are exposed to the influence of true *emocrats* (Casquete 2009b). These are manipulators of emotion with violent impulses who perceive the individuals participating in public events as 'a grain of sand among many others that are blown by the wind at its whim' (Le Bon 1983, 33).

Emocrats adhere to the laws of propaganda by engaging in affective and emotional appeals, as opposed to the enlightenment tradition of addressing the intellect. In this sense, they follow in the steps of the Roman rhetors and their Renaissance descendants, for whom the *ars rhetorica* consisted especially of exciting the emotions; in contrast with the Aristotelian tradition that perceived rhetoric more as a method of reasoning and persuasion (Skinner 1996, 121–122). The surest way to sway an audience to one's own perspective would be to address it in a way that both convinces and moves it. Studies of political religions such as National Socialism and Italian Fascism (Maier 1995; Gentile 2006) have shown that the intent is primarily an emotional rather than a rational connection; to create 'the feeling that one is with larger entities such as the People, the Nation, the Party, or the Führer, especially in acts of hysterical and drunken dissolution into the masses' (Küng 2009, 166). Emocrats always seek to transform a situation of impotence, fear, despair or collective shame into one of widespread effervescence, hope, adhesion and commitment. In our case study, according to the political religion of Basque nationalism as embodied by the MLNV (see Sáez de la Fuente 2002; Casquete 2009a), the identity of *Euskal Herria* is threatened by two powerful and oppressive neighbours; appeal must be made to various themes (some of which I will shortly examine) in order to renew commitment to the cause. Their struggle has endured for more than half a century through dictatorship and democracy, and has acquired truly dramatic dimensions in claiming the lives of 845 people. Thus, the implicit objective of their commemogram seen as a sacred time was to maintain the borders of the radical milieu while infusing it with renewed energy in order to achieve the stated objectives and finally overcome its critical state.

Regardless of the nature of the date that precipitates remembrance, the MLNV adopted modern forms of collective action such as demonstrations and public gatherings (Casquete 2006b). As Fernando Molina has rightly pointed out, 'nationalism is not just discourse, but also mobilization' (2009, 46). Like all rituals, demonstrations are also forms of communication; the MLNV used them to occupy the public sphere with *ad extra* and *ad intra* messages of their worthiness, unity, numbers and commitment (Tilly 2006), for which they deserve to be taken seriously. *Ad extra* refers to the transmission of their message to the public while seeking to gain respect and cooperation; *ad intra* refers to the physical congregating of members that revived commitment to the cause of 'freedom for

Euskal Herria'. The essence of the message in both cases is: we do not forget to remember *ourselves*. Thus memory was used to serve an uncivil cause.

There is an additional peculiarity to commemorations that is especially interesting for understanding the mechanisms that produce radical milieux in general and the Basque nationalist one in particular. This unique feature has to do with group dynamics and the law of *group polarisation*: 'when people find themselves in groups of like-minded types, they are especially likely to move to extremes' (Sunstein 2009, 2). In other words, after participating in a more or less structured deliberative process (a cell meeting, protest march, trade union meeting, etc.), individuals with common opinions who only dialogue with each other tend to adopt more visceral opinions and foster more aggressive responses than before the interaction took place. Sunstein adds that 'deliberating enclaves of like-minded people are often a breeding ground for extreme movements. Terrorists are made, not born, and terrorist networks often operate in just this way' (Sunstein 2009, 4). Open, plural and free debates in a liberal sphere are social order virtues that remain unquestioned by the law of group polarisation, so long as the individuals carrying strongly different opinions and notions respect the moral equality of others. A very different matter is that of individuals holding identical opinions with a political dimension that addresses the organisation of common life. In this scenario the virtues are at risk of becoming a pathology: the sense of injury is increased and aggressive responses towards the 'enemy' become more probable. Group endogamy can thus have unfortunate consequences for social order.

In light of this, delving into the dates highlighted in the commemorative calendar of a radical community such as the MLNV will prove extremely interesting as a way for gaining access to its mechanisms of reproduction. Those individuals present at such celebrations were subjected to the influence of the emocrats through a passive vertical communication process while informally fraternising with other individuals via horizontal face-to-face communication, thus sharing a single-category universe, at least with regard to what had brought them together.

Over the past four decades the MLNV's calendar up until 2011 was filled with a range of occasions or 'festivities' that offered a 'moratorium on everyday life' (Marquard 1988). Of interest here are the dates around the death of ETA members fallen for the holy cause of the fatherland, the *gudaris*. After Durkheim (2001), these dates conform a 'piacular calendar'.

Radical Basque nationalism placed the cult to the *gudaris* fallen in the name of *Euskal Herria* at the centre of its cosmovision and practice. They were held up as examples of the MLNV's best members. That is why I refer to its '*gudarismo*'. This is the practice of a socio-political actor that, for the sake of building a dreamed-of *Euskal Herria*, pays tribute to fallen martyrs because of their inestimable unifying and mimetic value. Such public veneration gives substance to an historical chain of struggle for the 'freedom' of *Euskal Herria* that has been unbroken since (imagined) ancestral times. Their generosity in faithfully continuing the dictum of *patriae totus et ubique* makes them deserving of their followers' recognition and, furthermore, an example to be imitated. Not because they sacrificed their lives for the sake of the community, something that also finds meaning in the republican tradition, but because they were able to take the lives of others. Their sacrificial willingness makes them into the beacon of the dreamed-of national community. One can therefore understand why the *gudaris* should figure at the epicentre of the commemorative calendar of radical Basque nationalism, and why this is much more than an anecdotal element in the latter's practice. It is a test tube category in which their ideology and imaginary are condensed. The anniversaries of the deaths of *gudaris* who hold a special value for the community were also opportunities for asserting their example: such are the cases of the *Gudari Eguna* every 27 September, the date of the executions of Otaegi, and especially of Txiki; 20 November, the anniversary of the murders of Santi Brouard in 1984 and Josu Muguruza five years later; or 21 December, the anniversary of the murder of *Argala* in 1978. The speeches in their honour, given year after year at these commemorations by prominent radical nationalist leaders, were intended to give meaning to individual sacrifice and frame it in an epic chain of ancestral struggle to throw off the Spanish yoke. The blood spilt for *Euskal Herria* thus figured at the heart of the sacred time of radical nationalist jingoism.

The *gudari* is the 'new man' of which the MLNV dreams. He is a being who has adapted to his condition as a cog in the higher machinery and has given up any project of leading an autonomous life; a condition, it must be said, that derives from his own conception of happiness. That is why those who believe in the cause promoted an *imitatio heroica* in order to fill the country with subjects satisfied with their service to the noble cause of the fatherland. Considered retrospectively, the cult to the fallen *gudaris* proved to be a fundamental factor in the reproduction of the violent sub-community around ETA, with the latter understood as a type of charismatic leader of radical nationalism. Their exaltation fed the spiral of violence. This was clearly seen by the German writer and social critic Kurt Tucholsky. In 1932, during the period of epic inflation fuelled by the Nazis, he wrote that 'Every glorification of a person killed in war means three dead in the next war' (1960, vol. 10, 98). Bertolt Brecht had something similar in mind when, in one of his plays, he makes Galileo say: 'Pity the country that needs heroes' (1997, vol. 2, 94).

Thus, a basic mechanism for reproducing the uncivil community that justified violence in the Basque Country and Spain for decades was the yearly calendar glorifying the heroes who died for the 'freedom' of *Euskal Herria*. The *gudaris* thus appeared as a prefiguration of the 'new man' to be forged in the dreamed-of fatherland. It is thus worth considering the dates marked in red on the radical nationalist commemorative calendar that were dedicated to exalting the *gudaris* who died 'on active service'.

The days linked to community martyrology were used exclusively by radical nationalists and not shared with any other political actor. These occasions glorified ETA heroes and martyrs who died in more or less epic circumstances. They conveyed the message that the ultimate sacrifice had not been in vain and that those absent were still present as a uniting force for the group. Individual deaths became a source of life for the group and the blood that nourished the fatherland, in a way reminiscent of Tertullian's observation that 'the blood of the martyrs is the seed of Christians'. A key message in the socialisation of participants was the idea that 'we all must give a bit so that a few won't have to give it all'. The exhortation *pugna pro patria* appealed to the believing community in every sense but was centred especially on youth, who enjoyed the spotlight in all commemorative celebrations of this type. They should always have before them 'the revolutionary generosity and honesty of the *gudaris*, an example understood as one more stimulus to encourage us to continue struggling for the full liberation of our people' (*Egin*, 27 September 1989). Making use of the expeditious logic that 'a revolutionary is not to be mourned, rather replaced' (Egaña *et al.* 1993, vol. 8, 281), youth were invited to become '*biharko gudariak*', the *gudaris* of tomorrow, carrying the torch of the dead *gudaris* forward in time.

As I have already mentioned, three commemorations are particularly relevant in this group.[3] First, the *Gudari Eguna* was celebrated in a decentralised manner in the form of demonstrations throughout the Basque lands every 27 September on the anniversary of the 1975 deaths of Txiki and Otaegi, two ETA members who were tried without procedural guarantees and executed before firing squads in the last days of the Franco regime. A wave of protest that spread across the Basque Country, Spain and Europe tried in vain to prevent the death penalties that had been handed down from being carried out. Chronologically, this date marked the start of radical nationalism's ritual exaltation of all the activists of the terrorist organisation who, whether in jail, exile or clandestinity, continued to sacrifice the best years of their youth for the patriotic ideal. Following the schedule of the calendar, radical nationalism exploited the date to glorify the *gudaris* of yesterday and today, to render public homage 'to the dedication and capacity of self-sacrifice of the militants who, accepting levels of total commitment – from clandestinity, prison ... even death – continue at the forefront of the confrontation between Euskadi and the State' (*Gudari Eguna*, 27 September 1989, leaflet, KAS). The *Gudari Eguna* celebrated by the MLNV was a date that spoke of the commitment to the cause of the national liberation of *Euskal Herria* of those who put their personal interests aside, sacrificing them in favour of the fatherland (*non sibi sed patriae*). Eternal memory was the coinage that corresponded to such sublime demonstrations of generosity and commitment. As a diary for 1990 published by *Jarrai*, the nationalist youth organisation, states: 'These *gudaris* will always have a place reserved for them in our *Euskal Herria*'. Today's *gudaris* became the referents when it came to *imitatio heroica*. They had shown the correct path that would one day lead to the liberation of the fatherland; in particular, they provided 'an example of commitment for the youth' (*Gara*, 28 September 2000). Public recognition was conceived as a humble payment to those who immolated their lives for the fatherland or, in any case, were willing to do so.

Second, 20 November commemorated *Herri Batasuna* leaders Santiago Brouard and Josu Muguruza, who were murdered on that date by para-police and extreme right-wing forces. At the time of his death in a terrorist action in 1984, Santiago Brouard had behind him a long trajectory of commitment to the most extreme vector of Basque nationalism. The former deputy mayor of Bilbao, a Basque parliamentarian, a member of the Representative Assembly (*Juntas Generales*) of Biscay, the president of HASI (People's Socialist Revolutionary Party, a member of the *Herri Batasuna* electoral coalition) and a member of HB's National Committee, he was shot dead at his paediatric practice in Bilbao by two mercenaries of the GAL (Anti-terrorist Liberation Groups) in 1984. The GAL were an expression of the 'dirty war', of state terrorism, as was demonstrated years later by the Spanish lawcourts when they handed down a ten-year sentence to José Barrionuevo, who was the Interior Minister between 1982 and 1988. Exactly five years later, on 20 November 1989, Josu Muguruza was murdered at midnight in Madrid. Muguruza was an MP for HB in the Spanish Parliament and a senior editor at the *Egin* newspaper, which was aligned with radical nationalism. He had travelled to the Spanish capital with three other leaders of HB to present his credentials as an elected MP and to attend the constitutive session of Parliament. Among those accused of his murder was the son of the army officer Ricardo Sáez de Inestrillas, the victim of an ETA terrorist action; he was finally acquitted due to lack of evidence. Another leader of HB, Iñaki Esnaola, was seriously wounded in the same terrorist action.

Finally, 21 December was a day of homage to José Miguel Beñaran, *Argala*, who was killed on that day in 1978 by an extreme right-wing group in his hideout in the French Basque country. Immediately after his death *Argala* was made into an icon of radical nationalism. This was because he combined, like no other leader before or since, intellectual ability with the credibility and charisma within the terrorist organisation provided by his experience and readiness for armed action – and martyrdom. At the time of his murder he was considered to have been the chief ideologist of ETA-M since its emergence in 1974. There are those, however, who consider that to call him an ideologist is in reality an overstatement and his profile was more that of an organiser (Juaristi 1999, 143). Radical nationalism remembered him punctually every year in its particular martyrs' calendar. His death at an early age, as befits heroes, meant that he had a brief apotheosis, but his memory was kept alive without interruption for four decades in ritualised events. In the case of *Argala*, who was 'as outstanding in the tasks of war, strictly speaking, as on the theoretical plane', there was a religious fulfilment of the promise made by his comrades one year after his death: 'No! We will not forget you, as we do not forget a single *gudari* who has given his life fighting' (*Monográfico KAS 2*, 1979, 25 and 30, respectively). Every 21 December, or on the nearest weekend, his unconditional followers organised tributes in his birthplace, the town of Arrigorriaga (Biscay), although during the six years immediately following his murder, until 1984, memorial events were also organised in other places in the Basque Country.

There were many lesser commemorative dates exalting or remembering the more than 200 people known as *gudaris*. These were generally local dates celebrated in the home towns and neighbourhoods of individual *gudaris*. For example, in late September, 2009, the former Municipal Councillor in San Sebastián, Tomás Alba, was still remembered and celebrated in the radical nationalist milieu, three decades after he was murdered (*Gara*, 29 October 2009). In such cases the opinion of the natural family regarding the holding of such events was of secondary importance, if not irrelevant. The case of Bakartxo Arzelus, one of the few women recognised as *gudaris* in the radical nationalist pantheon of martyrs (Hamilton 2007), illustrates this process of 'confiscation by the community'. She was the first female member of ETA to die in combat, shot dead by the Civil Guard in San Sebastián in 1986. Her father, at the time a member of the Basque Nationalist Party, 'insisted' (according to *Egin*, 18 January 1986) 'in depriving the funeral and burial of his daughter of their political character'. At the funeral he was rebuked by several of those attending, who shouted, 'Bakartxo is not your daughter, she is our daughter', and threw coins at him (*El País*, 18 January 1986).

Death and nation-building

The radical milieu that supported and legitimised ETA's use of terrorist violence in the Basque Country exploited the blood shed by its activists, who had fallen in the fight to achieve independence, in a propagandistic way (that is, by appealing to the emotions). Heroism as a group adhesive – as an ingredient facilitating collective identity – is a well-known resource in modern and contemporary nationalist movements (Eriksonas 2004). It is not something specific to Basque nationalist radicalism, examined here in the light of the MLNV. The commemorative calendar of this nationalist family was nourished by festivities whose protagonists were *gudaris* killed by the 'Spanish enemy' in diverse circumstances. Their glorification was a fundamental factor for the reproduction of an uncivil community in the period of Spanish democracy from transition until 2011. Since then (that is, since the cessation of ETA's terrorist activities), it has been the community itself that has softened public tributes to dead ETA members. At stake was the credibility of its opting for legal and democratic channels for obtaining the independence of the Basque Country. Exaltation of the *gudaris*, and hence of violence, would have served the Spanish government as an argument for illegalising any political expression of radical nationalism.

During its period of uncivility up until 2011, public expression of sympathy with those fallen in combat or completing a prison sentence for terrorist activities was considered equivalent to confessing unconditional identification with them, transmitting to the audience the message that *they are us*. Concatenation of the living and the dead was not a benign strategy.

The cult of the fallen fulfilled several functions that together fed a culture of violence. First, it served as an integrating mechanism for a community that sought cohesion markers, becoming all the more decisive in a hostile sociopolitical and cultural environment where armed actions had completely discredited the cause in the eyes of the population. Attending a ritual that glorified a member of ETA renewed the attendant congregation's commitment to the cause, and, vicariously, the commitment of all radical nationalist members. Second, by placing a deceased *gudari* or prisoner in its pantheon, the national cult offered present and future generations an active example of the path to be followed. The hero was lifted up as a pedagogic and socialising figure, a reference point worthy of emulation, whose example served to catalyse the valour and resolution of fellow believers. Third, exalting the hero fallen for the fatherland as an example of the most sublime and disinterested abnegation provided an occasion to publicly 'legitimise' violent actions past and present. Taking these three factors into consideration, we should not overlook the importance for the radical nationalist community of the commemorative rituals for the *gudaris*. They were something that, luckily for coexistence in Basque and Spanish society, we can now view as a phase of recent history that has fortunately been overcome.

Notes

1 This chapter is part of a research project funded by the University of the Basque Country Research Group (GIU 14/30).
2 www.ikasleabertzaleak.org/2010/09/29/egitarau-oparoa-antolatu-du-iak-ikasle-eguna-2010erako/ (accessed 10 August 2015).
3 Insofar as I am referring throughout this text to the period between the 1970s and 2011, I employ the past tense. However, in some cases, such as the following, radical nationalism continues to stage demonstrations in the public sphere, albeit with a lower profile and visibility.

Bibliography

Assmann, Aleida (2005) 'Jahrestage – Denkmäler in der Zeit'. In *Jubiläum, Jubiläum ... Zur Geschichte öffentlicher und privater Erinnerung*, ed. Paul Münch, 305–314. Essen: Klartext.
Barth, Fredrik (1969) *Ethnic Groups and Boundaries*. Oslo: Universitetsforlaget.
Blumer, Herbert (1946) 'The field of collective behavior'. In *New Outlines of the Principles of Sociology*, ed. Alfred McClung Lee, 167–222. New York: Barnes and Noble.
Brecht, Bertolt (1997) *Ausgewählte Werke in sechs Bänden*. Frankfurt am Main: Suhrkamp.
Bullain, Iñigo (2011) *Revolucionarismo patriótico. El Movimiento de Liberación Nacional Vasco*. Madrid: Tecnos.
Casquete, Jesús (2006a) 'Protest rituals and uncivil communities'. *Totalitarian Movements and Political Religions* 7: 283–301.
Casquete, Jesús (2006b) 'The power of demonstrations'. *Social Movement Studies* 5: 45–60.
Casquete, Jesús (2009a) *En el nombre de Euskal Herria. La religión política del nacionalismo vasco radical*. Madrid: Tecnos.
Casquete, Jesús (2009b) 'Emocracia, propaganda y martirio en el nacionalsocialismo'. *Revista Anthropos* 224: 80–91.
De la Granja, José Luis (2015) *Ángel o demonio: Sabino Arana. El patriarca del nacionalismo vasco*. Madrid: Tecnos.
Durkheim, Émile (2001) *The Elementary Forms of Religious Life*. Oxford: Oxford University Press.
Egaña, Iñaki (ed.) (1993) *Euskadi eta Askatasuna. Euskal Herria y la libertad* (8 vols). Tafalla: Txalaparta.

Elias, Norbert (1994) 'A theoretical essay on established and outsider relations'. In *The Established and the Outsiders*, eds Norbert Elias and John L. Scotson, xv–lii. London: Sage. First published 1965.

Eriksonas, Linas (2004) *National Heroes and National Identities: Scotland, Norway and Lithuania*. Brussels: PIE Lang.

Evans, Sara and Harry Boyte (1986) *Free Spaces*. New York: Harper & Row.

Fernández, Gaizka and Raúl López (2012) *Sangre, votos, manifestaciones. ETA y el nacionalismo vasco radical (1958–2011)*. Madrid: Tecnos.

Gentile, Emilio (2006) *Politics as Religion*. Princeton, NJ: Princeton University Press.

Hamilton, Carrie (2007) *Women and ETA*. Manchester: Manchester University Press.

Herri Batasuna (n.d.) 'Atzo, gaur eta beti: Gora Euskadi Askatuta. 1978–1988. Hamar urte askatasunaren aldeko burrukan' ('Yesterday, today and forever: Long Live free Euskadi. 1978–1988. Ten years of fighting for freedom. 1978–1988'). n.p.

Juaristi, Jon (1999) *Sacra némesis. Nuevas historias de nacionalistas vascos*. Madrid: Espasa-Calpe.

Kateb, George (2008) 'Morality and self-sacrifice, martyrdom and self-denial'. *Social Research* 75: 353–394.

Küng, Hans (2009) *Was ich glaube*. Munich: Piper.

Le Bon, Gustave (1983) *Psicología de las masas*. Madrid: Morata. First published 1895.

Leonisio, Rafael (2015) 'Basque patriotic left: 50 years of political and terrorist acronyms'. *RIPS* 14: 83–104.

López, Raúl (2015) *Informe Foronda*. Madrid: La Catarata.

Löwenstein, Karl (1937) 'Militant democracy and fundamental rights I'. *American Political Science Review* 31: 417–432.

Maier, Hans (1995) *Politische Religionen*. Freiburg: Herder.

Malthaner, Stefan and Peter Waldmann (eds) (2012) *Radikale Milieus. Das soziale Umfeld terroristischer Gruppen*. Frankfurt and New York: Campus.

Margalit, Avishai (2010) *On Compromise and Rotten Compromises*. Princeton, NJ, and Oxford: Princeton University Press.

Marquard, Odo (1988) 'Kleine Philosophie des Festes'. In *Das Fest. Eine Kulturgeschichte von der Antike bis zur Gegenwart*, ed. Uwe Schultz, 413–420. Munich: Beck.

Mata, José Manuel (1993) *El nacionalismo vasco radical. Discurso, organización y expresiones*. Leioa: UPV.

Mata, José Manuel (2006) 'Terrorism and nationalist conflict. The weakness of democracy in the Basque Country'. In *The Politics of Contemporary Spain*, ed. Sebastian Balfour, 81–105. London: Routledge.

Merino, Javier (2011) *La izquierda radical ante ETA. ¿El último espejismo revolucionario en Occidente?* Bilbao: Bakeaz.

Molina, Fernando (2009) 'El nacionalismo español y la 'guerra del norte', 1975–1981'. *Historia del Presente* 13: 41–54.

Muro, Diego (2008) *Ethnicity and Violence. The Case of Basque Radical Nationalism*. London: Routledge.

Preuß, Ulrich K. (2002) 'Die empfindsame Demokratie'. In *Verbot del NPD oder Mit Rechtsradikalen leben*, eds Claus Leggewie and Horst Meier, 104–119. Frankfurt am Main: Suhrkamp.

Rapoport, David (1977) 'The politics of atrocity'. In *Terrorism – Interdisciplinary Perspectives*, eds Yonah Alexander and Seymour Maxwell Finger, 46–61. New York: John Jay.

Sáez de la Fuente, Izaskun (2002) *El Movimiento de Liberación Nacional Vasco, una religión de sustitución*. Bilbao: Desclée de Brouwer.

Simmel, Georg (1897) 'The persistence of social groups'. *American Journal of Sociology* 3: 662–698.

Simmel, Georg (1992) *Soziologie*. Frankfurt am Main: Suhrkamp.

Skinner, Quentin (1996) *Reason and Rhetoric in the Philosophy of Hobbes*. Cambridge: Cambridge University Press.

Sunstein, Cass R. (2009) *Going to Extremes. How Like Minds Unite and Divide*. New York: Oxford University Press.

Taylor, Charles (1989) *Sources of the Self: The Making of the Modern Identity*. Cambridge, MA: Harvard University Press.

Taylor, Charles (2010) 'The meaning of secularism'. *Heghedog Review* 12: 23–34.

Tilly, Charles (2006) 'WUNC'. In *Crowds*, eds Jeffrey T. Schnapp and Matthew Tiews, 289–306. Stanford, CA: Stanford University Press.

Tucholsky, Kurt (1960) *Gesammelte Werke in 10 Bänden*. Hamburg: Rowohlt.

Waldmann, Peter (1998) *Terrorismus. Provokation der Macht*. Munich: Gerling Akademie.

Walzer, Michael (2002) 'Five questions about terrorism'. *Dissent* 49: 5–10.

6 The practice of killing
Perpetrators and accomplices

Javier Gómez

Introduction

In 1978, José Miguel Beñarán 'Argala', a prominent leader of ETA, said:

> [N]one of us like violence. Armed struggle is unpleasant, it's tough, and because of it one goes to jail, goes into exile, or is tortured. Because of it one can die, one feels obliged to kill, it hardens people, it causes them harm but armed struggle is essential to move forward.
>
> (Casanova 1999, 160)

Months later, he was killed in an attack by extreme right-wing terrorists. Considered to be a 'modern guerrilla fighter' and a martyr today by the organisations that make up the radical Basque nationalist movement (Egaña 2005, 100), his words sum up the thinking of a member of a clandestine organisation which uses violence to achieve the political goals that form its ideological backbone. However, killing and the possibility of dying while taking up arms was a choice but not the only one (Crenshaw 2011). The 'armed struggle' was unnecessary (Arregui 2015, 93). Even after resorting to armed struggle as the fastest and most useful avenue, an ETA member could certainly choose another destiny to avoid the violence he had once thought inevitable.

This chapter examines the trajectories of ETA members from their fateful choice to kill, until the announcement of their final ceasefire in October 2011. It considers who they were, what they thought, the ideological references and common imagery behind their militancy, and the manner in which they legitimised the attacks they carried out. In addition, given that the purpose of these individuals at the time of joining ETA was to physically eliminate those whom they considered enemies, the text explores the process of creation and dehumanisation of the victims and the role these victims have played in the recent history of the Basque Country.

Killing and dying for ETA

On 7 June 1968, Civil Guard traffic officers Diego Martínez and José Pardines were carrying out a routine road check near the Gipuzkoan village of Villabona when a vehicle caught the eye of Officer Pardines, who ordered its occupants to stop. They were ETA members Javier Etxebarrieta 'Txabi' and Iñaki Sarasqueta. While Pardines was checking the registration documents for the vehicle 'Txabi' continued arguing with his companion inside the vehicle about how to proceed if the officer discovered that the car they were driving had been stolen. 'If he finds out, I'll kill him', declared 'Txabi'. Surprised, Sarasqueta tried to dissuade him; disarming the officer and fleeing would be enough. But 'Txabi' ignored him and shot Pardines, who died instantly (*El Mundo*, 7 June 1998). After leaving the priest's house where they had taken refuge, Etxebarrieta and Sarasqueta were stopped and searched by the Civil Guard, who discovered the identity of both and the weapon that Sarasqueta was carrying. At that moment, a shoot-out began in which Etxebarrieta lost his life, and Sarasqueta was eventually arrested after fleeing. Félix de Diego, the other witness to ETA's first crime, was killed by two gunmen of the terrorist group in January 1979, when he was already afflicted with a serious illness and had retired from the Civil Guard (Alonso *et al.* 2010, 189).

Radical Basque nationalism considers 'Txabi' to be ETA's first martyr (Hordago 1980), and his memory remains shrouded in a legendary story that sacrifices facts in favour of myth and memory, to the detriment of history. As an example, the journalist and former ETA member Ángel Rekalde claims, without citing any sources, that Etxebarrieta was beaten by Civil Guard officers and then, already dying, finished off with bullets. According to Rekalde, Etxebarrieta's death was a 'summary execution' carried out by the Spanish state, to which ETA responded ten years later by taking the life of Félix de Diego, the man who killed him (Rekalde 1997, 85). According to José María Lorenzo (1994), a historian linked to radical Basque nationalism, Etxebarrieta was a hero whose romantic struggle was tragically cut short. The name of ETA's first victim is not mentioned, nor the circumstances of his death. Thirty years after the murder of Pardines, Iñaki Sarasqueta remembered what happened in no heroic terms. He recognised that killing was an option but it was not the only one. The crime, he maintained, could have been avoided if his comrade-in-arms had not taken a large quantity of drugs and stimulants. Moreover, he rejected the categorisation of victims; killing, he maintained, 'was never good'.

At the time, however, killing was considered legitimate by those who had never taken up arms but saw no other way to change politics, whether because of nationalist anxieties or because of an ideology influenced by radical Marxism-Leninism (Duplá and Villanueva 2009, 93). From the moment it started to commit murder until the end of Francoism, ETA gained a reputation not only for its doctrine or ideology but for the acts it had carried out, especially following the 1973 assassination of Prime Minister Luis Carrero Blanco. Killing the person seen as Franco's eventual successor gave ETA and its militants an anti-Francoist aura that legitimised their violent actions among older sections of the population (Merino 2011). However, violence was not a response to the Francoist regime's own violent practice, nor was it a display of rejection of the dictatorship. Instead, the dictatorship presented an excuse for ETA to engage in political violence. As Idoia Estornés recently pointed out with reference to the evolution of the Basque nationalist trade union ELA from 1968, not all young Basque people who supported nationalism and socialism in Francoist Spain believed that violence was the only possible solution (Estornés 2013, 302).

The debate within ETA on the use of violence and its value as a tool began almost as soon as the radical nationalist organisation was founded. In fact, by 1961 ETA had already committed its first violent act when it attempted to derail a train full of Francoist volunteers who were on their way to San Sebastian to commemorate the 1936 military coup. It was a symbolic rather than effective gesture related to the story of Basque nationalism and the Spanish Civil War of 1936 to 1939. According to this narrative, the Spanish defeated the Basques in battle and imposed a particularly tyrannical regime equivalent to a genocide of the Basque people and of 'all things Basque', understood to mean anything representing nationalist sentiment (Aguilar 1998; Molina 2010). Twenty years after the end of the Spanish Civil War, a generation of Basque nationalists who had not lived through the war themselves felt the need to face their alleged invader with more force and radicalism than their elders (Fernández 2013). Nevertheless, the socio-economic and political context of the Basque Provinces at the time of ETA's founding was very different compared with two decades earlier. A new process of industrialisation had clouded the Basque reality, making its society more complex and diverse following the arrival of immigrant workers from the rest of Spain.

This internal context, coupled with international emancipation and anti-colonialist movements, facilitated the introduction of Marxism into ETA. A theoretical bridge connected the radical Basque nationalism of the first ETA members to the anti-colonialist movements: the work *Vasconia* by the writer Federico Krutwig, one of the first members of the organisation and an intellectual reference among his peers (Garmendia 1996). The Basque Country was presented as a colony conquered by force and suppressed by two states, France and Spain, intent on acculturating the local population (Krutwig 2006). There was a moral obligation, or at least a legitimate reason, to use whatever means necessary to fight back, particularly within the rigid framework of a dictatorship. In any case, the prominence of Basque nationalism as the underlying ideological backbone of ETA was present from the beginning (Fernández 2015). According to one former ETA member active during the late 1970s, he and his companions were convinced that the priority was 'an independent Basque country, reunited and Basque'. The term 'socialist' was rarely used (Reinares 2001, 52).

The importance of Basque nationalism in ETA above any other ideology was crucial not only to the first rift in the group – which appeared as early as 1967, led by members who were more left wing and less nationalist – but to the very evolution of the debate on the use of arms and the final decision to kill. In this sense, it is telling that ETA members Patxi Iturrioz and Eugenio del Río, leaders of the aforementioned labour movement split, nearly became the first victims of the radical nationalist organisation when they were accused of being 'liquidators' and sentenced to death by their companions (Uriarte 2005, 67). The theoretical debate on whether to take the crucial step of killing was finally resolved in a manner as accidental as the one described earlier. Txabi Etxebarrieta predicted it himself when he wrote in the 1968 Aberri Eguna manifesto: 'it is no secret that it will be difficult to get through this year without a single death'. Killing – and dying – offered a choice but not the only one possible.

The dehumanisation of the victims

ETA's deliberate use of violence as an instrument of political action over more than 40 years required not only ideological protection but also the active involvement of everyday citizens. Francoism as a political regime and its continual use of force and coercion to maintain power would not have lasted as long as it did without the voluntary and determined participation of a large number of Spaniards: citizens who were convinced that their social, economic and cultural demands could only be met through violence (Cazorla 2002). Peace was possible and the civil war could have been avoided if a group of soldiers had not decided to carry out a coup against the wishes of the polls and half the population. However, the matter ended in tragedy. The other half of the Spanish population found it convenient to actively or passively support the perpetrators of the coup and, later on, its prolongation in the form of a dictatorship. The killing of Civil Guardsman José Pardines and nearly 850 more victims resulted from a free choice made by individuals who believed that of all the available options which had at first been limited by a dictatorship and then unlimited by a democratic framework, violence was the most effective and worthwhile. More importantly, a section of the Basque population participated freely and willingly in helping ETA carry out its mission (Juliá 2010; López 2015).

In August 1936, the schoolteacher in Salvatierra (Araba), Ángel Pinedo, was arrested by several Catholic traditionalists and accused of having spread hatred of religion among children during the Second Republic. After one year in prison, a military trial against him began in which the first Francoist mayor of the town, the head of the Spanish Falangist movement, and the father of a boy who had studied at the teacher's school, participated. All of them corroborated the accusations made against the teacher, which came from a collective complaint that they themselves had filed. The teacher was released from prison two years later thanks to the intervention of the Civil Guard commander of Salvatierra during the Second Republic, or in other words an individual unaffiliated with the town. During the trial, the complainants asserted that they had nothing personal against the teacher; what is more, several days after the coup the mayor himself had intervened to prevent the execution of about 20 neighbours who were active in or sympathetic to the Basque Nationalist Party, a group opposed to the military coup. But, unlike those nationalists, Pinedo was not Catholic, not right-wing, nor a *person of order*. He was not part of the moral community whose norms and rules had called the Republic into question. An outsider who did not share the values that had held together the community of the neighbours *since forever* was the ideal person to take on the role of scapegoat, thus transferring responsibility for the war. According to this logic, the perpetrators of the coup had been pushed into making a decision that they rejected but which had been necessary – and just – as a means to purge the red, atheist and Republican enemies. Although the trial of Pinedo was officially by the military, his real trial was by the village neighbours who had first accused him and later testified against him. A Civil Guard member freed him from jail but his former neighbours prevented his return to Salvatierra after his release (Gómez 2014, 191).

Forty years later, a new process of ideological purging took place in the same town in the southern Basque Country. Whereas in 1936 the army and the Civil Guard had acted as arbitrators in the use of political violence, allowing neighbours to administer *justice* over other members of the community, in 1980, it was the *people* who were in charge of forcibly removing those responsible for the 'conflict' between the Basque Country and Spain. On 4 October 1936, the annual celebrations in Salvatierra were to begin with a cycling race, with Civil Guard officers José-Luis Vázquez, Avelino Palma and Ángel Prado in charge of controlling traffic. Days earlier, the parish priest Ismael Arrieta had met with two members of ETA to give them information about the route of the race, which enabled the gunmen of the terrorist organisation to get close to the three officers and shoot them. The gunfire mortally wounded Palma and Prado but Vázquez was only shot in the arm. As he lay hidden behind the car of one of the participating cycling teams, neighbours warned the ETA members that there was still one officer alive. Seconds later, the gunmen retraced their steps and murdered Vázquez before finally fleeing (*El Mundo*, 19 October 2014).

On the afternoon of the crime, town mayor María L. Murguiondo, who was also a member of a neighbourhood platform linked to radical Basque nationalism, called together a special assembly in which she refused to cancel the festivities (*El País*, 5 October 1980). The priest had provided the information for the execution of the crime, the neighbours had wanted the gunmen to make sure that no officer remained alive and the mayor wanted the celebrations to start as if nothing had happened (*ABC*, 23 May 2002). None of them had pulled the trigger but all had contributed to the triple murder. Shortly afterwards, the Civil Guard left its barracks in Salvatierra and the officers were transferred to other locations. Just as with Ángel Pinedo 50 years earlier, the community was expelling those who represented the authority of a government they considered responsible for the suffering of all Basques since time immemorial. As in Elgeta (Gipuzkoa) during the decline of Francoism, the moral community founded on Basque nationalism expelled from its ranks the immoral and anti-Basque world of immigrants and non-nationalist locals (Heiberg 1985, 297).

Justifying the crimes committed against individuals or groups considered external to the image of the Basque national community was not particularly complicated. Seeing themselves as lay victims of a foreign occupation, radical Basque nationalists believed that their own particular militia (ETA) needed to inflict as much harm as possible on the enemy that had started the war (Spain) (Castells and Rivera 2015). Greater difficulty was encountered when attacking those Basque civilians who were not nationalists. A young perpetrator who joined ETA shortly before Franco's death dreamed of a Basque Country in which there were 'people who would go to Mass, people who would not go to Mass, people in [dining] clubs, people who were not in such clubs, people who liked gastronomy, people who didn't like it', but in any case all Basque nationalists (Reinares 2001, 53).

This ethnocentric and exclusionary longing drove young people such as the one mentioned above to begin to kill Basques accused of collaborating with the alleged enemy, snitches – in ETA terminology; for example, Carlos Arguimberri, of the neighbouring small village of Itziar (Gipuzkoa). Unlike the majority of people in Itziar at that time – who identified with Basque nationalism – Carlos came from a family linked to local Catholic traditionalism (a variety of Spanish nationalism) with a strong presence in the province going back decades. In that agricultural society, the Arguimberri family worked in minor but essential services such as the postal service, carpentry or transportation. As the church was practically the only non-clandestine channel allowing Basque nationalists to maintain and strengthen their cultural identity during the dictatorship, the Basque nationalist community of Itziar was forming itself politically through parochial organisations in which the complicity of the parish priest was fundamental. Carlos was a member of one such organisation, *Baserri Gaztedi*, until an atmosphere of mutual distrust developed between him and his companions. Based on nothing other than suspicion, Carlos' closest circle of friends gradually distanced themselves from him. He was singled out by the community as the only one responsible for any abuse or form of persecution coming from the regime against the village, such as the detention of individuals involved in clandestine political activities, economic sanctions or physical punishments imposed upon those individuals, or the forced transfer of priests who sympathised with Basque nationalism. In the late 1960s, the first graffiti threatening Carlos appeared, followed by insults, and eventually the burning of the bus which he regularly used to transport the residents of Itziar to Deba. There was no further warning; on 7 July 1975, two ETA members boarded his bus, this time not to set fire to it but to make an attempt on Carlos' life, shouting 'you are a dog'. Thus Carlos became ETA's first victim to die due to the accusation of a police informant (Zulaika 1990, 101–120). By 1992 another 78 citizens would be murdered on the same pretext (López 2015).

The process of dehumanisation and stigmatisation of the victims before and after each crime accompanied the rhetoric of the ETA militants since their 'original' crime. One member of ETA, who had participated in the first kidnappings carried out by the group in the 1970s, claims that although 'nobody likes to kill', if he had had to kill one of the kidnapped citizens he would have done it, because ultimately they were 'a gang of immoral people and bastards' (Alcedo 1996, 192). The former head of the ETA commandos in Biscay, Carmen Guisasola, described the attack against a Civil Guard lieutenant colonel in which she had participated as a 'dream' come true (Domínguez 2002, 184–195). Nevertheless, ETA's hierarchical separation of the perpetrators, forced to commit acts against their wishes, from the victims, who had been oppressing and persecuting Basques, created a powerful narrative that lasted for decades after the consolidation of democracy.

A good example is the statement given by the girlfriend of José-Luis Luengos, killed by ETA in 1992. The crime, which puzzled the police at first, was justified by the terrorist group as the consequence of the victim's 'collaboration with the special services of the Civil Guard'. In light of this announcement, the victim's partner did not demand that ETA be held accountable for its crime but she insisted that the organisation rectify what she considered a defamation, being willing to 'move heaven and earth for them to withdraw that lie' (*EFE*, 16 December 1992). Four years later, the family of Eugenio Olaciregui, a bicycle salesman killed by ETA for his alleged role in the denunciation and arrest of prominent ETA member, Valentín Lasarte, made a similar statement after the crime. The file on Eugenio's murder was reopened years later when Lasarte confirmed in a declaration that he knew he had been betrayed by someone else. This judicial truth came as a relief to the family, which had been forced to endure the 'contempt of a significant sector of society' because of their ties to an alleged informer (*El Mundo*, 24 March 2012). The sister of José I. Iruretagoyena, a town councillor of the Popular Party in Zarauz (Gipuzkoa) assassinated by ETA in January 1998, wondered how it was possible that her brother had been killed despite being Basque and speaking Basque, as if the perpetrators had ignored two reasons for exemption in commissioning the crime (*El País*, 10 January 1998).

The 'transfer of responsibility' from the perpetrators and accomplices of crimes to their victims (Domínguez 1998, 225) not only came as a shock to those enduring the violence but also reinforced ETA's warmongering narrative, largely through the collectivisation of its language of terror in the media (Molina forthcoming). This success at a narrative level survives into the present and permeates not just Basque society or the victims of terrorism but even those who carry out or have carried out the management and coordination of the state security forces. A good example may be found in the 2008 declarations by Interior Minister Alfredo Pérez-Rubalcaba. Following ETA's assassination of Civil Guard officer Juan Manuel Piñuel in Villarreal (Araba), the Interior Minister reproached the terrorist group for having taken the life of an innocent man (*El Mundo*, 14 May 2008).

The inner and outer sanctuary

The Basque writer Jon Juaristi, who was active in ETA for a short time from 1968 onward, said with irony that the climate of disappointment following France's May 1968 had left the extreme left-wingers without a 'revolutionary subject' once the proletariat seemed to have accepted the consumer economy. Led by Jean Paul Sartre, French intellectuals of the extreme left identified with ETA and its members despite the fact that those beginning to join the ranks of the group were more active in Basque nationalism than in left-wing organisations (Juaristi 1997, 361). This was the intellectual context that gave rise to strong French networks of support for ETA and Basque nationalism. It consisted of a complex infrastructure that allowed the members of ETA to develop what they called 'armed struggle' in secrecy. Above and beyond the anti-colonialist and third-world discourses that fed ETA militants during the early years of the organisation, France represented a comfortable and safe haven due not only to its proximity but also to the sympathy aroused by a movement rebelling against dictatorship. Thus, and paradoxically, one of the largest colonial powers, which included within its territory provinces that which Basque nationalists claimed as their own, became a 'sanctuary' for a Basque nationalist group inspired by anti-colonialist theory (Domínguez 2002, 81–124).

In 1961, the first ETA meetings were held in France, to which many members fled in the face of police crackdowns in Spain following the bombing of a train carrying former Francoist fighters. The French government issued residence permits and letters of political refugee status to ETA members who crossed the border in increasing numbers. Although the French government issued deportation or restraining orders against some members from the end of 1962, it was clear that the operational base of the organisation was located in France when ETA claimed the life of its second victim, Melitón Manzanas, chief of the Gipuzkoa Political-Social Brigade. Following the attack in Irún (Gipuzkoa), Franco declared a state of emergency, first in Gipuzkoa and later throughout the whole of Spain; meanwhile, the police made numerous arrests as repression became tougher and more widespread. The extent of police persecution and Officer Manzanas' reputation as a cruel torturer among sectors of the anti-Franco opposition only increased support for ETA while boosting the organisation's international prestige. As Eduardo Uriarte, an ETA member in 1968, recalled some time later, public sympathy for the armed organisation grew while its own members began to consider the usefulness of their violent actions (Uriarte 2005). A year later, in 1969, the police detained dozens of ETA militants and prosecuted 16 of them, including Uriarte, in a military trial in Burgos. The bloody crimes they were charged with included the killing of Fermín Monasterio, the first civilian victim of ETA. Monasterio had refused to help in the escape of Miguel Etxebarria Iztueta, a member of the armed group whom the police had not been able to arrest (Alonso *et al.* 2010, 25–26).

Right from the beginning, on 3 December, 1970, the example which the Franco regime intended to set with the so-called 'Burgos Trial' ended up working against the dictatorship. On the one hand, the democratic opposition took up a common cause with the accused ETA members; important members of the Communist Party like Jordi Solé-Tura or socialists like Gregorio Peces-Barba came to the defence of the accused. On the other hand, international pressure reached new heights. In France, where the *Comité Basque de Défense de la Personne Humaine*, chaired by the centrist senator Errecart, had operated since 1962 (Lafitte 1962), protests multiplied and the French government's passive stance towards ETA continued. In fact, during the Burgos trial, ETA held German consul Eugene Beihl hostage in Saint-Jean-de-Luz and the group announced his release on French soil with no interference from the French Gendarmerie. On 28 December 1970, less than a month after the trial had begun, five of the defendants were sentenced to death and another ten were given prison terms of between 12 and 70 years; only one was acquitted. Nonetheless, mounting international pressure resulting from the harshness of the sentences, and the mediation of the Vatican (two of the defendants were priests) forced Franco to back down and commute the death sentences to terms of life imprisonment (Molinero and Ysás 2008, 142–159; Onaindía 2001, 427–493).

The disproportionate response of the dictatorship led to the perception in the collective imagination of an anti-Franco, righteous ETA that used violence only to physically eliminate the regime's torturers or in self-defence against the Civil Guard, an approach still maintained by radical Basque nationalism. The implicit justification of ETA's tactics by the anti-Franco opposition and the idealisation of ETA's goals during the agony of Francoism formed the context for the gradual establishment of the structures of the armed group and its members in France. There, they were able to operate with impunity and were tolerated by the French government. Iñaki Rekarte, who joined ETA in 1991, acknowledged that the members of the group enjoyed an 'atmosphere of absolute peace and security' on French soil but he also knew when that sense of security would end. When Rekarte went underground he was protected by the priest Pantxoa Garat in the parish house of Espelette (in southeastern France). He indicated that the French Gendarmerie officers stationed in front of his hideout were perfectly aware of who entered and left the home but that they lacked the slightest interest in taking action. 'The day that this permissiveness of the French police changed, ETA's network collapsed' (Rekarte 2015, 107–108).

The fact is that the collaboration of successive French governments with Spain on counter-terrorism was irregular, sporadic and restricted to specific times and interests. In August 1978, the European Convention on the Suppression of Terrorism approved a new regulation that limited the definitions of political crimes and refugees. This sparked a heated debate in France about the Basque refugees (Morán 1997). In spite of confrontations between the French conservative government and its socialist opposition, in 1979 France abolished the status of political refugee for all Spaniards. In practice, however, nothing changed. This was obvious upon the arrest in Paris of the ETA militant Tomás Linaza, who was accused of participating in an attack a year earlier that had cost the lives of six Civil Guardsmen in Ispaster (Biscay). Gaston Deferre, the French Interior Minister at the time, maintained that ETA's struggle was of a political nature and that he, as a former underground member of the French Resistance, 'strongly felt that conceding extradition is contrary to all French tradition', adding that he would only collaborate with Spain on the matter of fugitives accused of common offences (*El País*, 19 July 1981). Things did not change, at least at first, when the Socialist Party came to power in Spain. While Mitterrand's government extradited members of Baader-Meinhof and the International Brigades arrested on French soil to Germany and Italy, ETA members continued to operate with some freedom in the neighbouring country. The lack of French cooperation on anti-terrorism and the ineffectiveness of the Spanish State Security Forces in tackling ETA's aggression led anti-terrorist policy in Spain to protect and finance strategies outside the law. The creation of the Anti-terrorist

Liberation Groups (GAL), whose actions were developed almost exclusively in France, marked the practical culmination of this strategy.

As Rekarte pointed out, the network collapsed when the French police arrested the leaders of ETA in Bidart on 29 March 1992 in an operation that marked a turning point in terms of the collaboration between both countries on anti-terrorism. However, as equally important as the 'French sanctuary' was the haven found in the Basque Country. The needs of ETA for shelter and contacts were the same on both sides of the border but while for France government involvement was sufficient in the fight against terrorism, in Spain finding out what and who were behind the machinery of terror was much more complex. In May 1997, the Civil Guard arrested Jesús María Uribetxeberría, a resident of Mondragón (Gipuzkoa). The officers had found his name written in code in some documents carried by the ETA leader Juan L. Aguirre. These associated Uribetx-eberría with the kidnapping of prison officer José Antonio Ortega Lara, whose whereabouts were unknown.

Two months later, on 1 July, the Civil Guard found the *zulo* (hole, in Basque) in which Uribetxeberría and three other ETA members had held Ortega hostage. It was in Mondragón, not far from Uribetxeberría's home and underneath an industrial cooperative (Delgado and Mencía 1998). Just a week and a half later, ETA ordered one of its most active commandos to kidnap a Popular Party councillor, who would be killed within 48 hours if the Spanish government did not comply with ETA's demand for the transfer of terrorist inmates to Basque prisons. The operation, however, was not simple; it required depending on a go-between who could provide information and infrastructure while attracting no attention. The man chosen for the job was Ibon Muñoa, a councillor in Eibar (Gipuzkoa) of the radical Basque nationalist party *Herri Batasuna*. A Popular Party member in Eibar described Muñoa as a 'quiet man', little more than a 'poor man' (*Crónica de El Mundo*, 29 October 2000). Muñoa worked for a family-run auto parts business from which he could observe Miguel Ángel Blanco on a daily basis; the Ermua (Biscay) Popular Party councillor worked at a consultancy just a few metres from Muñoa's shop. Muñoa was the one to provide accommodation, information and his own vehicle to the ETA militants who kidnapped and killed Miguel Ángel. Following Muñoa's arrest, councillors of Eibar from other political groups could not believe the accusation; it meant that ETA consisted of not only its activists but also shy and quiet men and women with whom they worked on a daily basis.

Militants without militancy: the perpetrators after ETA's decline

Contrary to what happened with ETA political-military in 1982, the process of self-dissolution of the group has not taken place, nor has it been formalised; nor have members of ETA shown any intention of making it happen. The main difference lies in the absence of an ethical standpoint within ETA on the usefulness of the violence it had practised. This complicates the explanation of the crimes committed over more than four decades. Some of the ETA prisoners released when the Parot doctrine was annulled later became partially or directly responsible for multiple murders.[1] Such was the case of Jesús M. Zabarte, known as the 'Butcher of Mondragón'. Zabarte spent 30 years of his life in prison, entering for the first time before the arrival of democracy. Benefiting from the 1977 Amnesty law, he returned to ETA upon his release from jail and later became involved as an instigator, accomplice or perpetrator in 17 murders. Zabarte feels that the bloodshed was justified and denies that he is a murderer, opting for the term 'executioner' instead. He openly demands that the Spanish state acknowledge its responsibilities because 'it was what pushed me. I did not take this decision [to join ETA and kill]'. In terms of asking for forgiveness, Zabarte believes that it is he who has suffered the real pain for having been forced to kill – something that forms part of a larger historical process including Francoism and the obligation (imposed upon Zabarte and his peers) to sing the Francoist hymn 'Cara al Sol' at school (*El Mundo*, 21 October 2014).

The historicist justification and the self-acquittal of the crimes themselves reflect a widespread feeling among former members of ETA and the abertzale left. Hasier Arraiz, a former member of the youth organisation Jarrai and president of Sortu since 2013, felt that the past radical Basque nationalism was neither objectionable nor negotiable. On the contrary, 'with all our errors, we stand for what we were and what we are' (*El País*, 19 November 2013). Justification of the past and legitimisation of political violence as the consequence of a third party (the Spanish state) form the backbone of Sortu's story of the past but also make up part of the discourse of the majority of formerly imprisoned ETA members.

In January 2014, the collective of imprisoned members of the terrorist group (EPPK) expressed their intention to get involved in the 'democratic process', which they claimed to have propelled forward. The collective viewed the Spanish and French governments as enemies of this process and urged these governments to 'repeal every situation and measure of exception', which meant modifying the prison policy to adapt it to the new circumstances (*Gara*, 5 January 2014). The statement, devoid of references to the past, was read in Durango (Biscay) by José-Antonio López 'Kubati'. Nearly three decades earlier, 'Kubati' had held up his former comrade-in-arms Dolores González 'Yoyes' in Ordicia (Gipuzkoa) and, in front of her three-year-old son, murdered her after identifying himself as the man sent to carry out the death sentence issued by some of her former comrades. The executioner of 'Yoyes', as a dragooned operator acting for a large group of participants, confirmed that he had felt compelled to participate in the 'struggle for social and political freedom of our people', to which he remained committed. In his particular case, this 'struggle' had claimed the lives of 12 victims from the 'enemy' and one more, 'Yoyes' herself, from the group's so-called 'traitors'. According to his reinterpretation he was only an executioner, a mere servant who was obliged to perform such dark tasks because of the political oppression suffered by the Basque people. As a victim of circumstances and not a killer, José A. López still played the role of the long-suffering, selfless militant who was both disciplined and loyal nearly three decades after the crime.

The increasingly demoralised atmosphere surrounding the terrorist group as they were pursued by police and the judiciary influenced members of ETA's decision to lay down their arms. Aware of the situation, in his second term Spanish President José L. Rodríguez-Zapatero led the Spanish government to push forward 'Vía Nanclares', a project to change penitentiary policy with the aim of dismantling the discipline imposed by ETA upon its imprisoned members. The project gave inmates the chance to benefit from reintegration if they broke away from the group. Almost 30 imprisoned ETA members accepted these measures, which involved transferring all of them to prisons near the Basque Country and, once the government had certified their willingness to separate from ETA, they were moved to the prison of Nanclares de Oca (Araba). The gradual release of nearly all of the ETA members who accepted these measures brought them face to face with two hostile groups: their former companions in the terrorist group and the families of their victims. The reformed ETA members all reject any justification of their participation in the terrorist organisation, but their experiences in prison led to conflicting testimony about their decision to abandon political violence. Iñaki Rekarte, who had murdered three residents of Santander in 1992, says he had no political leanings and did not even feel like a Basque nationalist but had joined ETA under the influence of a friend with whom he shared a 'certain fascination' with weapons (Rekarte 2015, 51–54). Carmen Guisasola, also mentioned previously, acknowledges deliberately joining ETA with a willingness to kill, without any particular justification for her decision (*El País*, 2 November 2015). However, while Rekarte has completely cut himself off from the environment of the abertzale left to the point of receiving threats, other inmates protected by 'Vía Nanclares' have accused him of having changed from 'hating some to hating others' after he blamed Sortu and its leaders for the decades-long survival of terrorism. Andoni Alza and Ibon Etxezarreta, among others, expressed this view, thus avoiding a complete rejection of the ideological core that was intended to legitimise the organisation (*El Mundo*, 15 October 2014).

In any case, the looming shadow of the period following ETA's ceasefire stems not only from the future of its former members but from the new role which its victims had to play. As Gaizka Fernández pointed out, as early as 1982, the victims were the ones who suffered most following ETA's relinquishment of arms (Fernández 2013). They were not taken into account, the crimes were not solved and preference was given with an impunity that became less acceptable following the constant appearance in the media of the former members of ETA political-military, who seemed to show no regret. With few exceptions, even now former members of ETA have not attempted to address the suffering their attacks caused to their victims. Nonetheless, it is also revealing that in the rare meetings between victims and attackers, a story has been sneakily imposed upon the reality of the victims which excludes not only the groups that suffered to the greatest extent (the army, state security forces and members of non-nationalist parties) but also any reflection on the social responsibilities for the history of terrorism in the Basque Country. This story has, furthermore, been made official through the production of reports like '*Retratos municipales de vulneraciones del derecho a la vida en el caso vasco*' published by the Basque government in 2014. The report absolves ETA of the responsibility for its terrorist nature and the various violent clashes promoted by ETA, the state police and right-winged paramilitaries.

Conclusion

Nearly half a century has passed since two ETA members inside a stolen vehicle argued over whether or not the Civil Guard officer who had stopped them should die, or if, on the contrary, fleeing would suffice. The decision to kill and, as a result, risk one's own life had already been taken by ETA but the organisation had yet to choose its first victim. 'Txabi' chose to kill, only to end up himself dying shortly afterwards. The same thing happened ten years later to 'Argala', one of the ETA militants who most widely theorised about the use of violence and terrorist strategy. The history of ETA members, which is still awaiting a thorough analysis, is dotted with choices that the context – social, political or family – affects but in no case determines the outcome. They knew that, if they chose to kill, they could die killing, be arrested or, at the very least, remain in hiding while on the run. They also had – and continue to have – another option: to renounce violence, as the militants of ETA-PM did in 1982, and as did 'Yoyes'. The options were there but 'Yoyes' chose the costly one and paid for it with her life.

In 2011, following increased social isolation and constant police and judicial pressure, the remaining active members of ETA (numbering only about 50, according to the Interior Ministry, *El País*, 4 September 2011) decided, at last, to lay down their arms. The context in which this renunciation occurred was very different from that which surrounded the founding of ETA or the ceasefire called by its 'political-military' wing in 1982; the terrorist group's loss of social prestige and the absence of a regulated reintegration process had made it difficult to organise the return of prisoners who were finishing their jail sentences and who had mostly not reflected on their violent past. A good example of this is the case of former ETA activist Inés del Río. After becoming an icon of the organisation's prisoners and being welcomed home with honours, the former ETA member soon experienced the loneliness that came from her neighbours' reluctance to associate with someone who had once killed.

Note

1 This is a common term for the Spanish Supreme Court judgement on 28 February 2006, according to which the reduction of punishment for appropriate inmates would be applied to each individual's total term and not to the legal maximum prison term which was 30 years. It owes its name to an appeal made by prisoner Henri Parot, a member of ETA. The European Court of Human Rights ruled against making this ruling retrospective in 2013.

Bibliography

Aguilar, Paloma (1998) 'La peculiar evocación de la guerra civil por el nacionalismo vasco'. *Cuadernos de Alzate* 18: 21–40.

Alcedo, Miren (1996) *Militar en ETA. Historias de vida y muerte.* San Sebastián: RB.

Alonso, Rogelio, Florencio Domínguez and Marcos García (2010) *Vidas rotas. Historia de los hombres, mujeres y niños víctimas de ETA.* Madrid: Espasa.

Arregui, Joseba (2015) *El terror de ETA. La narrativa de las víctimas.* Madrid: Anaya.

Casanova, Iker (1999) *Argala.* Tafalla: Txalaparta.

Castells, Luis and Antonio Rivera (2015) 'Las víctimas: del victimismo construido a las víctimas reales'. In *El peso de la identidad. Mitos y ritos de la historia vasca*, eds Fernando Molina and José Antonio Pérez, 265–305. Madrid: Marcial Pons.

Cazorla, Antonio (2002) 'Sobre el primer franquismo y la extensión de su apoyo'. *Historia y Política* 8: 303–320.

Crenshaw, Martha (2011) *Explaining Terrorism: Causes, Processes and Consequences.* London: Routledge.

Delgado, Belén and Antonio Mencía (1998) *Diario de un secuestro. Ortega Lara, 532 días en un zulo.* Madrid: Alianza.

Domínguez, Florencio (1998) *ETA: estrategia organizativa y actuaciones, 1978–1992.* Bilbao: UPV-EHU.

Domínguez, Florencio (2002) *Dentro de ETA. LA vida diaria de los terroristas.* Madrid: Aguilar.

Duplá, Antonio and Javier Villanueva (2009) *Con las víctimas del terrorismo.* San Sebastián: Gakoa.

Egaña, Iñaki (2005) *Quién es quién en la historia del país de los vascos.* Tafalla: Txalaparta.

Estornés, Idoia (2013) *Cómo pudo pasarnos esto. Crónica de una chica de los 60.* San Sebastián: Erein.

Fernández, Gaizka (2013) *Héroes, heterodoxos y traidores. Historia de Euskadiko Ezkerra (1974–1994).* Madrid: Tecnos.

Fernández, Gaizka (2015) 'Mitos que matan. La narrativa del conflicto vasco'. *Ayer* 98: 213–240.

Garmendia, José María (1996) *Historia de ETA.* San Sebastián: Haranburu.

Gómez, Javier (2014) *Matar, purgar, sanar. La represión franquista en Álava (1936–1945).* Madrid: Tecnos.

Heiberg, Marianne (1985) 'Inside the moral community. Politics in a Basque village'. In *Basque Politics, a Case Study in Ethnic Nationalism*, eds William A. Douglas, 285–307. Reno: University of Nevada.

Hordago, Equipo (1979–1981) *Documentos Y.* San Sebastián: Hordago, 18 vols.

Juaristi, Jon (1997) *El bucle melancólico. Historias de nacionalistas vascos.* Madrid: Espasa.

Juliá, Santos (2010) '¿Culturas o estrategias? Notas sobre violencia política en la España reciente'. In *Violencia política. Historia, memoria y víctimas*, ed. Antonio Rivera and Carlos Carnicero, 167–190. Madrid: Maia.

Krutwig, Federico (2006) *Vasconia.* Pamplona: Herritar Berri (first published 1963).

Lafitte, Pierre (1962) 'Lau eskualdun gazte gobernuak kasaturik, bazterrak airean "Comité Basque de Défense de la Personne Humaine" muntatua da'. *Herria*, Bayonne, France: 1–3.

López, Raúl (2015) *Informe Foronda: los efectos del terrorismo en la sociedad vasca.* Madrid: Los Libros de la Catarata.

Lorenzo, José María (1994) *Txabi Etxebarrieta: armado de palabra y obra.* Tafalla: Txalaparta.

Merino, Francisco Javier (2011) *La izquierda radical ante ETA. ¿Él último espejismo revolucionario en Occidente?* Bilbao: Bakeaz.

Molina, Fernando (2010) 'El vasco o el eterno separatista: la invención de un enemigo secular de la democracia española (1867–1979)'. In *Los enemigos de España: imagen del otro, conflictos bélicos y disputas nacionales (siglos XVI-XX)*, eds Xoxe Manuel Núñez and Francisco Sevillano, 293–323. Madrid, CEPCO.

Molina, Fernando (forthcoming) 'Violencia en comunidad. El terrorismo nacionalista y la política del miedo, 1976–1982'. In *Euskadi: Transición y democracia*, eds José Antonio Pérez and Juan Pablo Fusi. Madrid: Biblioteca Nueva.

Molinero, Carme and Pere Ysás (2008) *La anatomía del Franquismo. De la supervivencia a la agonía.* Madrid: Crítica.

Morán, Sagrario (1997) *ETA entre España y Francia.* Madrid: Universidad Complutense.

Onaindía, Mario (2001) *El precio de la libertad. Memorias (1948–1977).* Madrid: Espasa.

Reinares, Fernando (2001) *Patriotas de la muerte. Quiénes han militado en ETA y por qué.* Madrid: Taurus.

Rekalde, Ángel (1997) *Mugalaris. La memoria del Bidasoa.* Tafalla: Txalaparta.

Rekarte, Iñaki (2015) *Lo difícil es perdonarse a uno mismo. Matar en nombre de ETA y arrepentirse por amor.* Barcelona: Península.

Uriarte, Eduardo (2005) *Mirando atrás. Del proceso de Burgos a la amenaza permanente.* Barcelona: Ediciones B.

Zulaika, Joseba (1990) *Violencia vasca. Metáfora y sacramento.* Madrid: Nerea.

Plate 1 Aircraft waiting for the corpses of three policemen ambushed in Bilbao (13 October 1978). During the transition to democracy ETA's victims (mostly policemen) were quickly transported to their birthplaces without public knowledge (source: Archivo Municipal de Bilbao. Fondo Periódico La Gaceta del Norte).

Plate 2 A handful of flowers on the ground. A reminder of the killing of three civil guards in the town of Getxo (Biscay) (22 October 1978) (source: Archivo Municipal de Bilbao. Fondo Periódico La Gaceta del Norte).

Plate 3 Popular homage to two victims of paramilitary terrorism in Hernani (Gipuzkoa) (8 September 1980) (source: Archivo Municipal de Bilbao. Fondo Periódico La Gaceta del Norte).

Plate 4 Street fighting (*kale borroka*) in Bilbao after paramilitary terrorist attack in Hernani (Gipuzkoa). September 1980. Public disturbances were routine after paramilitary or police actions (source: private archive).

Plate 5 Citizen walking between two demonstrations. On the left side, a pacifist one, claiming liberty for a businessman abducted by ETA (José M. Aldaya). On the opposite side, radical Basque nationalists gather to intimidate the pacifists (June 1995) (source: *El Correo*).

Plate 6 Radical Basque nationalists demonstrate against Rentería's town councillor Manuel Zamarreño during a plenary session on 21 May 1998. He belonged to the conservative Popular Party and was killed by ETA a month later (25 June 1998) (source: *El Correo*).

Plate 7 Jesús M. Pedrosa (in the centre) distributing political leaflets with Radical Basque nationalists in the background. He was a member of the Popular Party and town councillor in Durango. He was killed by ETA (4 June 2000) (source: Roberto Nistal/ *El Correo*).

Plate 8 Covered corpse of José Luis López de la Calle, writer and journalist, shot dead by ETA (7 May 2000) (source: Ignacio Pérez/*El Correo*).

Plate 9 Popular demonstration in the city of Bilbao in protest against the killing of the Popular Party's town councillor Miguel Ángel Blanco (13 July 1997), abducted by ETA three days earlier (source: *El Correo*).

Plate 10 Citizens of Ermua (Biscay) protest in the streets during the arrival of Miguel Ángel Blanco's body, killed by ETA the previous day (14 July 1997) (source: *El Correo*).

Plate 11 Tribute to Santiago Brouard, town councillor in Bilbao for Herri Batasuna (HB), who was shot dead by GAL paramilitaries (20 November 1984) (source: Archivo Municipal de Bilbao. Fondo Periódico La Gaceta del Norte).

Plate 12 ETA sympathisers in a demonstration during the *Aste Nagusia* (Big Week, the festival of Bilbao) (source: *El Correo*).

Plate 13 The aftermath of an ETA car bomb in Granada (Andalusia), which killed the hairdresser working on a military base (source: *Ideal de Granda*).

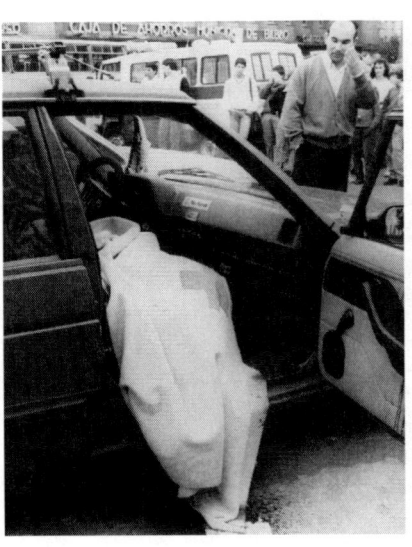

Plate 14 Covered corpse of Pedro Ballestero, a 24-year-old civil guard shot dead inside his car in Durango (Biscay) (19 March 1988) (source: *El Correo*).

Plate 15 Demonstration organised in San Sebastián by *Basta Ya*, a Spanish nationalist organisation that criticised Basque's 'compulsory nationalism' (source: *El Correo*).

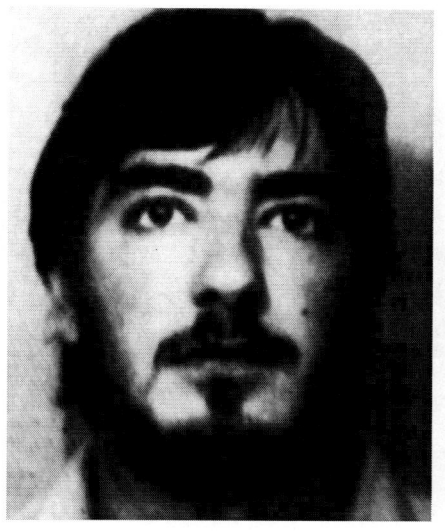

Plate 16 José Antonio Lasa and José Ignacio Zabala, two ETA members who were kidnapped, tortured and killed by the death squads of the GAL (source: *El Correo*/EFE).

Plate 17 A car bomb attack by ETA against the Hipercor supermarket in Barcelona (19 June 1987). Twenty-one people (four of them children) were killed and 45 wounded. They were all civilians (source: ABC).

Plate 18 People holding up signs protesting against ETA during a demonstration organised by *Basta Ya* in San Sebastian (Gipuzkoa) in September 2000 (source: *El Correo*).

Plate 19 ETA's attack in Madrid with a car bomb against a bus of the Civil Guard (14 July 1986). Twelve agents were killed and 32 severely wounded (source: ABC).

Plate 20 Three members of ETA declare a 'definitive cessation of its armed activity' on 20 October 2011 (source: *El Correo*).

7 The impact of ethno-nationalist violence

Comparing the experiences of victims of ETA and paramilitaries in Northern Ireland[1]

Javier Argomaniz

Introduction

The experiences of victims of terrorism remain an under-researched area within terrorism studies. Academic attention has predominantly been focused upon the perpetrators of violence (particularly when they are members of a sub-state group) and the state responses to such violence; the plight of those who have been directly affected by the violence remains secondary (Schmid 2012). While in many conflicts victims of political violence have and can experience relative neglect, the victims of ETA terrorism in Spain remain one of the few exceptions to the general disinterest that exists in the field. Spain is one of the few cases where the victims issue has received significant attention in the academic literature, generating a relatively sizeable body of work. A few representative examples are: Cuesta 2000; Pulgar 2004; Calleja 2006; Bilbao 2007; Etxeberria 2007; Sutil and Lázaro 2007; Mate 2008; Alonso 2009; Leonisio 2013; Rodríguez 2013; Alonso and Serranò 2015; Argomaniz 2015, and Muro 2015.

The reasons for this continued interest in victims' issues are twofold. First, and as described by other contributors to this volume, Spain has experienced varied forms of political violence over the past four decades. Naturally this has resulted in a large community of individuals having been personally affected by the violence, which constitutes a pressing issue in itself on a number of levels: for instance, whether their individual and social needs have been met by the government remains an important question (Lynch and Argomaniz 2015; Argomaniz 2015).

Second, and as will be explained later in this chapter, in Spain, victims of terrorism have come together to form a number of associations and, as a result, have become significant political actors in their own right. They have publicly campaigned to highlight their situation, in particular their rights as victims, but also in an effort to influence public opinion and political debate.

Addressing the issues surrounding the victims of terrorism is exceptionally relevant in this volume which focuses on ETA's terrorist campaign, both for the impact the violence had on individuals and their families but also the effect of the violence on Basque society more generally. Understanding the victimisation created by ETA is of course relevant to a key theme in this book – the direct consequences of the group's four decades of violence. Victimhood is obviously a direct outcome, and its social construction and political implications require specific attention.

As with terrorism more broadly,[2] the experience of being a victim of political violence is mediated by the context in which it occurs. With this in mind, a key issue is the extent to which it is possible to extrapolate from the Basque experience to other settings. In other words, we need to explain what the Basque case can teach us about terrorist victimisation as a process but also understand what is unique to this case as well as the characteristics that may be shared across regions that have experienced terrorism. Therefore, this contribution will not focus exclusively on victims of ETA terrorism but will also consider another example of ethno-nationalist violence, that which occurred in Northern Ireland. Northern Ireland is a key example of nationalist violence in Western Europe, overlapping in time with the Basque case. In addition, the IRA and ETA are the two most durable militant groups in the region, and have collaborated and developed strong links in the past while the political movements that gave birth to these two organisations have been sympathetic towards and actively supported each other. Unsurprisingly, these similarities mean that the situation in Northern Ireland and that in the Basque Country are often considered comparable and as a result, quite problematically, we often see the imposition of broad overarching categories upon the messy empirical realities of both contexts. As expected, given the goals of this edited volume, ETA victims will receive significant attention in this chapter but the Northern Irish case will serve as a comparable yet separate context where any similarities or differences in the victim experience may be analysed. Accordingly, this comparative approach is motivated by the joint objectives of illuminating the victims' experiences in both cases but also contributing to a better understanding of how the context to the violence impacts upon victimhood. The goal is to highlight distinctions and similarities in order to reveal potential structural trends about terrorist victimhood that may transcend the specificities of the Basque context.

This chapter is divided into three main sections. The first addresses ETA's victims, specifically their experiences, the work of statutory bodies and the provision of reparations, the emergence and evolution of victims' political activism, the formulation of a victim's discourse and prevailing claims of politicisation. The following section will examine the experiences of victims of political violence in Northern Ireland. It will then present the results of a comparative analysis focusing specifically upon the divergent political contexts underpinning the violence, the social construction of victimhood and the distinctive features of the separate support systems. In the process, important parallels across the two cases will be highlighted. Following this discussion, the chapter concludes with a set of claims about the context specificity of victimhood from terrorist activity and the important role that victims' associations can potentially play as actors in ethno-nationalist (post) conflict environments.

Victims of terrorism in Spain

Together with the UK, Spain is the European Union state that has experienced the highest level of sustained terrorist activity over the past 40 years. According to the *FundaciónVictimas del Terrorismo*,[3] more than 1,200 people have lost their lives as a result of the action of ethno-nationalist, jihadist, radical left and extreme right violent groups and individuals. Some 829 individuals died from attacks perpetrated by ETA and associated Basque armed separatists with 586 of these deaths occurring in Basque Country,[4] where most of ETA's actions have occurred.

Terrorist activity was particularly acute in the transition from the Franco dictatorship to a parliamentary democracy in the late 1970s and early 1980s. During this time violence was carried out not only by ETA but also by other ethno-nationalist organisations, such as the Catalan *Terra Lliure*, the radical leftist *Grupos de Resistencia Antifascista Primero de Octubre* (GRAPO), or by extreme right wingers including nostalgic supporters of the Francoist regime and disgruntled members of the security forces.

Therefore the period from 1978 to1980 was the bloodiest in the history of Spain's democratic existence, with more than 320 deaths.[5] During this time the fledgling democratic government was more concerned with limiting the damage from the wave of political violence engulfing the country than with protecting and compensating the victims. This was indeed a hugely difficult period for ETA victims. In addition to the neglect by government, the repression experienced by ETA during the Francoist era gave ETA an aura of legitimacy among some sectors in Basque society, leading to significant issues of non-recognition and re-victimisation for victims of ETA terrorism. While this legitimacy was short-lived, given the emergence of democratic institutions and Basque self-governance during the mid- to late 1980s, its impact was acutely felt; ETA's violence became normalised and an accepted feature of the political landscape. In conjunction with the tacit acceptance of ETA activity, victims were routinely dismissed as merely collateral damage of 'the conflict' (Cuesta 2000; San Sebastián 2003; Calleja 2006). In those early years, victims unquestionably suffered from institutional neglect and the absence of public recognition and social support (Leonisio 2013). Such 'recognition deficit', illustrated by the frequent instances of ostracism and isolation experienced by individual victims and the absence of an assistance system or a reference group, often resulted in processes of re-victimisation that hampered victims' families' recovery from the traumatic experience (Arteta 2007).

Given such 'recognition deficit', it is indicative that the first-ever victim association – the *Asociación de Víctimas del Terrorismo* (AVT) – was set up not in the Basque Country but in Madrid and by 'exiled' Basque citizens. Founded (together with two other ETA victims: Sonsoles Álvarez de Toledo and Isabel O'Shea by the widow of a Basque police officer, Ana María Vidal-Abarca),[6] the AVT became in time the largest and most influential victims' organisation in the country.

The gradual emergence of a large network of victims' organisations has ameliorated and eventually reversed the recognition deficit. Most of these groups were established in the 1990s and are considerably smaller than the AVT in membership size. Some of the best-known entities are *Colectivo de Víctimas del Terrorismo* (COVITE), *Fundación Miguel Ángel Blanco, Asociación 11-M Afectados Terrorismo, Asociación de Ayuda a las Víctimas del 11-M* or *Fundación Gregorio Ordóñez*. Although two of these most prominent groups (*Asociación 11-M Afectados Terrorismo* and *Asociación de Ayuda a las Víctimas del 11-M*) currently in existence emerged as a result of the 11 March 2004 Madrid train bombings and other victims' groups do have members victimised as a result of jihadist, left-wing and right-wing violence, most victims' associations were created in response to ETA's violence. Certainly the public activism of ETA victims and their families has overwhelmingly concentrated on the government's policies towards the terrorist organisation and its victims. Given the subject of this volume, this chapter will focus on these groups, even if it is essential to recognise the important role that the 11-M organisations have played in serving as advocates for victims of terrorism (Muro 2015).

The network of victims' groups is therefore very diverse. A select few groups (such as the AVT or COVITE) are relatively well resourced with, for example, the possibility to fund a full-time communication team as well as maintain a visible social media presence. This of course is important in terms of public presence but also in differentiating between the many victims' associations in existence. The majority of victims' groups are very small and manned by only a few (or sometimes one) staff members and/or volunteers, sometimes supported by interns. Both the larger more well-organised organisations and the small volunteer-based groups have been badly hit by the economic crisis of recent years and the reduction of public (state, regional and local) funding upon which they depend. In response, they have had to reduce staff levels and the scope of their activities, with some of the smallest groups being effectively in stand-by mode or even considering closure.

Despite their previous neglect it is precisely thanks to the tireless activism of the above-mentioned victims' groups that Spain currently has one of the most advanced and comprehensive victim support systems in Europe. Clearly, much has changed since the 1970s and the early 1980s when institutional support was almost non-existent and when available assistance was restricted to certain categories of state officials alone. It was during this period that initial steps were taken to address this statutory neglect. Initially, lobbying resulted in measures that were limited to specific categories of victims, but in the late 1980s and early 1990s financial assistance progressively expanded to other groups in the community as a result of the introduction of legislation on extraordinary pensions for victims (Argomaniz 2015). The passing of the 1999 Law of Solidarity constituted a landmark moment for victims of terrorism, as it was both a major sign of progress but also the catalyst for other measures that would ultimately lead to the creation of an advanced support system for victims and their families.

The framework then rapidly developed in subsequent years through the establishment of statutory bodies and the introduction of wide-ranging legislative initiatives at both the state and regional (i.e. Basque) levels to address the needs of victims of terrorism. For example, in 2002 the Victims of Terrorism Foundation was created; the same year the Basque Directorate for Care to Victims of Terrorism was established and, in 2006, the General Directorate for the Support of Victims of Terrorism emerged. The result of these developments was a complex, top-down and highly developed institutional framework where state agents not only deliver services but also mediate between the victims' community and the state and regional governments.

Importantly, over the past decade there was a progressive strengthening of the principle of 'integral support' as a result of the passing of the 2008 Basque Law on Recognition and Reparation for Victims of Terrorism and, in the Spanish Parliament, the 2011 Act on Recognition and Comprehensive Protection for Victims of Terrorism. The integral support principle recognises that victims' needs are complex and wide-ranging, and full reparation requires more than simply monetary compensation. In effect, both pieces of legislation acknowledge that victims' needs need to be both multi-dimensional and individually tailored. Victims require personal medical, psychological, monetary, legal, educational and employment support but, crucially, these laws also recognise victims as a political community deserving of recognition with the right to memory, dignity, truth and justice (Argomaniz 2015).

However, despite the existence of this legislation, it is questionable whether victims' public needs have been met satisfactorily by the state. As an illustration, representatives of victims' organisations have complained about the fact that more than 300 ETA murders have not been properly investigated by the Spanish justice system, which in their view represents an abuse of the victims' rights to truth and justice (Calderín 2014). As a result, victims' associations see themselves as not only being required to deliver individual support (i.e. psychological, legal, etc.) but also to act as centres for political action to ensure that the victims' public needs are met by government policy that is swiftly implemented.

Over the years, victims of ETA violence have sought to develop a clear and consistent narrative that serves to provide meaning to their suffering but also to reinforce their collective identity as a political community and to outline the parameters of their public activism. In this narrative, by virtue of their symbolism as public victims, they are presented as having a particular status due to the political nature of the crime they unjustly suffered. In effect, victims' organisations see their experience as one of sacrifice on behalf of the Spanish state, whereby their victimhood came about as a result of ETA's efforts to impose a totalitarian political project upon the Spanish citizens. This sacrifice came about as the victims were targeted by armed groups because they symbolised Spanish democracy and the rule of law (Alonso and Serranò 2015). In effect, victims' narratives thus construct their experience and identity as being linked to a public morality whereby victims become a countervailing moral force to the terrorists, deserving of public recognition due to the sacrifice they endured. Victims' narratives construct that society owes them a debt in the form of memorialisation and remembrance. As Sutil and Lázaro (2007) describe, for victims the failure to attain such recognition can aggravate the original traumatic experience and result in re-victimisation. Undoubtedly, the absence of strong moral support from society during the worst years of ETA's violence has consolidated this as a key claim by Basque victims.

Together with recognition, justice is arguably the other main public need for ETA's victims. This manifests as a call for retributive justice: the effective application of the Spanish legal system and a strict adherence to the rule of law, which would preclude the use of amnesties or political negotiation to deal with terrorist organisations (Martin-Peña *et al.* 2011; Serranò 2012). The importance placed on the right to justice helps us understand most victims' hostility to the government's release of ETA members following the European Court of Human Rights ruling on the Parot case.[7]

This opposition has resulted in a distinct cooling off of what was a previously close relationship between the AVT and the ruling centre-right party, *Partido Popular*. For example, both were involved in organising massive demonstrations during the administration of the former socialist president Rodriguez Zapatero to protest against the (eventually unsuccessful) negotiation attempt between the Spanish government and ETA. However, this relationship has been used to lay blame on *Partido Popular* for politicising the Spanish victims' movement, leading to accusations in the past that they had in fact co-opted political victim-hood in the services of the Spanish political right.[8] This politicisation and dominant position of the largest victims' groups has led to uneasiness among the heterogeneous victims' community. Smaller organisations and individual figures have resisted the attempt by the largest associations to claim for themselves the right to speak for the entirety of the victims' community.[9]

Victims of terrorism in Northern Ireland

In purely quantitative terms, political violence in Northern Ireland (NI) in the period know as the Troubles (1969–1998) was more lethal and widespread than in the Basque Country. According to Mesev *et al.* (2009), the Troubles resulted in more than 3,600 deaths, about 30,000 injured and tens of thousands displaced. Calculations from the McKeown dataset[10] attribute 55 per cent of fatalities to Republican groups, mainly the Provisional Irish Republican Army (PIRA) (2013); Loyalist paramilitaries (i.e. UVF, UDA and others) caused 1,018 deaths and the security forces were responsible for 378 deaths. The report suggests that 55 per cent of the victims killed were Catholics and 45 per cent Protestant (Mesev *et al.* 2009). While significant, these figures do not account for the all-encompassing nature of the violence in Northern Ireland: McAloney *et al.* (2009) reported that in some conflict areas as many as 80 per cent of the population knew someone who had been killed or wounded in the conflict.

The Troubles left a legacy of death and trauma that is still being felt in NI today. However, despite the vast number of victims affected by the violence, as well as their families, victims' issues were effectively neglected for almost 30 years. It was not until 1997, with Labour's victory in the British general election, and especially after the 1998 signing of the Good Friday Agreement (GFA), that support for victims became a policy priority. With time, the Northern Irish authorities developed what is now an advanced assistance framework that comprises a number of statutory bodies and associated legislation.

Currently, the Northern Ireland statutory support system comprises a tripartite system consisting of the Victims and Survivors Service,[11] the Commission for Victims and Survivors Northern Ireland (CVSNI)[12] and the Victims and Survivors Forum.[13] The work of the Commission for Victims and Survivors and the Victims and Survivors Service is overseen by the Victims and Survivors Unit,[14] a branch within the Northern Irish executive, the Office of the First Minister and Deputy First Minister (OFMDFMNI). Within this system the Victims and Survivors Service is responsible for the practical provision of assistance and allocates existing funding to support groups and individuals based on an assessment of needs. The Forum is a platform for consultation and discussion made up of victims that provides advice to the Commission. Finally, the CVSNI fulfils an important role practically and symbolically; the Commissioner (Judith Thompson at the time of writing) is tasked with promoting awareness of victims' issues, reviewing existing laws and services that impact upon victims and survivors, advising the government on related matters and engaging with the Forum in the commission of her statutory duties.

As the peace process progressed, due in large part to a considerable expansion in statutory provisions, there was rapid growth in the emergence of victims' organisations created in response to victims' and survivors' needs. In fact, three-quarters of the currently existing victims' groups were formed only after the ceasefires in 1994 (Lynch *et al.* 2013, 45). As with the statutory sector, community and voluntary groups benefited from the financial support of the British and Irish governments and the European Union. These organisations emerged in part to lobby the authorities on behalf of the victims, survivors and their families and, in addition to their advocacy work, sought to provide a variety of services: therapy, counselling, education and training, legal advice and more. When we look more closely at the composition of these organisations we find three distinct categories (each including dozens of groups): the organisations that serve the nationalist or unionist communities and cross-community groups. The latter serve members of both communities; the smaller groups in this category tend to have a greater public profile, prioritising the provision of individualised support to victims over advocacy work.[15]

In contrast, single identity groups, while also delivering services to individual victims, in general tend to be 'more politically divisive, have become engaged in political posturing, and have been manipulated by political actors' (Lynch and Argomaniz forthcoming, 2). Nationalist groups,[16] for instance, have been known to lobby against the illegal support of clandestine loyalist violent organisations

(Dawson 2003). On the other hand, some unionist victims' groups[17] have protested, together with anti-agreement unionist political figures, against the GFA and criticised the perceived injustices of the peace process (Nagle and Clancy 2012).

In addition, some nationalist and unionist victims' groups have sharply differing perspectives about who is a victim. While not an exclusive position, some nationalist organisations contend that former paramilitary prisoners be regarded as victims of the conflict; some unionist groups reject this position, which they regard as an exercise in moral equivalence (Lawther 2010). Their membership is generally more exclusive, including only those affected by Republican violence, especially relatives of murdered members of the security services.

Clearly in the Northern Irish context the divide running across the victims' community reflects the dynamics of the Troubles. Thus, generally unionist victims' representatives adopt a hierarchy of victims' position, a perspective where victims are divided into categories in a scale from most innocent – and therefore most deserving of support – to the least (Gilligan 2003). In this vision, innocent victims and guilty perpetrators are separated into mutually exclusive types: victims cannot be perpetrators and vice versa. Representatives from other groups are more likely to blur this differentiation and to broaden the scope of the victim label: 'that is, that everyone is potentially a victim and that the concept of "truth" is subjective and based on personal experience' (Lynch and Argomaniz 2015, 141). This approach is closer to the existing peace discourse, which is necessarily very broad to accommodate the largest possible number of perspectives, but that is also rejected by many survivors, to whom their own identity of 'victim' becomes essential to understand and provide meaning to their traumatic experience (Lynch *et al.* 2013, 874).

Thus the notion of a hierarchy of victimhood has its roots at the psychological level but also reflects the post-conflict politics of Northern Ireland and the still problematic relationships between the two communities. In fact victims' issues in Northern Ireland have become embroiled in the political culture of both sides in the conflict, which are themselves founded on narratives of victimisation: republicans point at the actions of the British government, security forces and loyalist paramilitaries to justify their use of violence, which they describe as purely reactive, whereas loyalists portray themselves as victimised by the IRA and other Republican militant organisations' actions (Morrissey and Smith 2002).

This situation is far from exclusive to Northern Ireland: it is in fact common in post-conflict contexts involving two or more political communities to observe a situation of 'competitive victimhood'. In this environment groups vie to portray themselves as the most victimised side, a claim that is used to legitimise their own recourse to violence and as a mechanism to prevent sympathy for victims from the other side (Noor *et al.* 2012).

In addition, polarisation among those who suffered in the Troubles is reflected in partisan memorialisation practices. Given the absence of a general cross-community consensus on the issue of remembrance, acts of commemoration and memorialisation are generally carried out separately and independently by the different groups. Commemorative practices have been varied, frequent and abundant involving murals, monuments, commemorative gardens, cere-monies, parades and more (Graham and Whelan 2007). These are however mainly intra-community activities and carried out at the local level, which means that they do not effectively serve as mechanisms for reconciliation through the representation of a shared loss (Brown and MacGinty 2003). This has an important effect on the question of social and political recognition for the victims. There is a broad understanding among survivors that, given the existing cleavages, it would be unrealistic to expect in the short term a national memorial or similar commemorative practices. They tend therefore to seek recognition for their loss or injury locally, from their close neighbours and com-munity. Thus memorialisation has the potential to work in terms of individual reparation but not to contribute towards bridging the gap between communities (Lynch and Argomaniz forthcoming, 14).

Comparative analysis

The overview of the two cases presented above demonstrates that there are important distinctions but also common patterns in victims' experiences in both NI and Spain. Among the key differences we highlight the varying political con-texts, the distinct roles that victims play within the local and national political culture and the dissimilar institutional frameworks of support. As we will see below, these crucial distinctions reproduce the different character of the violence experienced in each setting. At the same time, there are also important similar-ities found across the two cases. These are obviously crucial because they point towards the existence of commonalities in both post-conflict scenarios. We will now examine these questions below.

Diverging political contexts

As we have seen above, victims' communities in the Basque Country mostly comprise victims of ETA and other Basque separatist groups.[18] The largest victims' association in the Basque Country, COVITE, includes those afflicted by the violence of extreme right-wing groups and state terrorism, including the *Batallón Vasco Español* (BVE) or the GAL-*Grupos Antiterroristas de Lib-eración*, both covered in other parts of this volume. This important consideration aside, members of victims' associations belong to a large group of people who disagree and/or oppose the activities of the *Izquierda Abertzale*, the Basque Patriotic Left (BPL), the political movement that in the past supported ETA's violence and political goals.[19] This has traditionally facilitated the formulation of a common discourse, a shared sense of identity and ultimately collective action, irrespective of the diversity found among the large network of actors who represent the interests of victims.

On the other hand, the victims' community in Northern Ireland is largely divided along the community lines that characterised the conflict. Undoubtedly this is a product of the different forms of violence that occurred in each scenario:

one is a long-running campaign by a terrorist organisation supported by a political movement in opposition to the Spanish state; the other is a society divided along cultural lines represented (albeit involuntarily) by a number of violent groups with the involvement of the state.

The fact that in Northern Ireland there were multiple parties to the conflict means that the notion that there were wrongs on all sides has strong roots, whereas in Spain ETA is overwhelmingly blamed for the violence. This fundamental aspect completely shapes the question of victim identity in these two contexts.

Victims' identity, status and rights

In the Spanish case the dominant narrative is that ETA was the main party to the violence. In addition, the victims are constructed in opposition to the violence of ETA by reinforcing the fact that the victims did not retaliate violently against the group. This is important because it gives credence to the claim of innocence, a key element for the identity of the Spanish victims. Thus, in the case of Spain, there is a strong belief in the necessity of a hierarchy of victims, a clear separation between the innocent victim and the guilty perpetrator.

As such, the political action of Spanish victims' associations is shaped precisely by such distinctions as they see themselves in opposition to the goals of the political movement that traditionally embraced ETA. Being a self-defined victim in Spain often carries with it a principled defence of democracy and rule of law and the ethical opposition to any form of political violence. This victim identity is founded on the belief that there is an objective truth about ETA's indiscriminant violence and that society needs a historically accurate representation of ETA's activities. They have therefore pushed against the attempts by some actors within the Basque Patriotic Left to play down or justify ETAs past and have contested the narratives of the perpetrators themselves. In a way, 'victims are identified by who they are not' (Lynch and Argomaniz 2015, 146).

In the Basque context, attempts to blur the line between victims and perpetrators have been carried out by groups and individuals associated with the Basque Patriotic Left, who have also tried to broaden the definition of victims to include ETA members who died in action. The stretching of the victim's concept has been assimilated – to a certain extent – by some figures within the current nationalist Basque government, more specifically the Secretary for Peace and Coexistence.[20] Nonetheless – and very importantly – this particular perspective has so far roundly failed to gain popular support within Basque society, outside the minority BPL, to diminish the importance of the notion of victimhood or to erode the social status and political presence of ETA victims.

In Northern Ireland the label of victim has become irremediably politicised. Victimhood claims reflect community divisions, and determining who is a victim and who a combatant is a matter of debate that has fuelled political disagreement (Breen-Smyth 2009). There is no consensus on who is a victim and oftentimes the nature of the perpetrator is as relevant as the identity of the victim in determining identity status for victims. For one community, namely Republicans, there tends to be a more inclusive definition of victimhood; for the loyalist community, generally speaking, we can see similarities between the NI and the Spanish situation as they seek a clear differentiation between victims and perpetrators.

Disputes over the meaning of victimhood are not particularly rare: in many post-conflict situations assigning the label of victim is a highly contested process. Ambiguities emerge as victims from the different sides compete for recognition and reparation with accusations of responsibility being directed at the outgroup (Borer 2003). In the aftermath of internecine conflicts we often see competing hierarchies of worth (Flesher and Barberet 2012, 113).

In sum, Spanish associations but only some Northern Irish groups subscribe to an exclusive definition of victimhood. Victims' identity is more broadly contested in Northern Ireland, as different sectors of society aim to control the label; however, in Spain, claims to victimhood are, on the whole, less contentious due to the inherent exclusionary nature of the term as it is used by the vocal majority. In the Spanish context, the legitimacy of claims to victimhood is rarely challenged once the perpetrator is identified, and as such victims have a widely accepted status, and, by and large, the moral voice of victims' associations is not disputed by political actors (Lynch and Argomaniz 2015, 142).

The way victims' identities are articulated has important implications when it comes to demands for victims' rights. The right to truth, for example, is seen differently in both contexts: whereas in Spain victims' discourses highlight the importance of an objective truth, in Northern Ireland the fact that it is unlikely that communities will see the emergence of a shared account of the Troubles prevents victims from having a non-contentious victim identity. In the case of NI, the right to truth is seen rather as the duty of state authorities to provide victims' families with all the information they possess about the death of their loved ones; while this is also demanded by ETA victims, the right to truth is mostly understood as *el relato*, an accurate historical representation that does not whitewash ETA's crimes.

Victims' claims to justice are also impacted by social understandings of victimhood. For Spanish victims' groups the application of the rule of law is a key aspect of their political discourse. This results in an emphasis on retributive justice and establishing a blame for the past, within a criminal justice framework. As mentioned above, a key demand by victims' associations is for state authorities to investigate all ETA's murders and bring the perpetrators to justice.

Demands of retributive justice also exist in Northern Ireland but there is a wider acceptance that securing criminal convictions may be unattainable at this stage due to the scale of the Troubles, which would imply a very large number of potential prosecutions, the lack of information and evidence about many incidents and the potential destabilising impact upon the peace process. In response, restorative justice practices have been introduced at the local level to fill such gaps but also as a mechanism to ameliorate resentment and antagonism between communities (Dignan 2000). Restorative justice is often only vaguely defined but in practice it includes initiatives such as victim–perpetrator mediation, placing the victim at the centre of the process and aiming to foster reconciliation and understanding (Letschert *et al.* 2010).

In contrast, restorative justice in Spain has not enjoyed the wide use witnessed in Northern Ireland. The only major measure along these lines is the scheme carried out in the Basque prison of Nanclares centred around meetings between individual victims and former ETA members who repented and left the organisation (Pascual 2013). It is revealing that the initiative which took place between 2011 and 2012 was eventually blocked by the current centre-right government. Indeed, the programme has proven controversial with the political class and victims' associations; some have demanded that former ETA members collaborate with the police by providing intelligence before they can be considered for the programme,[21] but victims who participated in it have defended the personal and social benefits of the initiative.[22]

Different frameworks of support (macro vs. micro approaches)

Differing political realities contribute to explaining the emergence of alternative victim support systems in both NI and Spain (Lynch and Argomaniz 2015). In short, whereas the Spanish system may be described as a 'macro framework', the Northern Irish equivalent is better defined as a 'micro framework'. The latter is a bottom-up system where victims' needs are primarily addressed at the local level with funding support from national and international bodies. Due to the difficulties in constructing a top-down structure that serves and is supported by both communities, victims' needs are usually met by an array of community groups.

In contrast, the Spanish system is highly institutionalised and follows a top-down structure. Assistance is channelled by public bodies that also fund specific victims' associations' initiatives. These associations are managed by victims themselves, since only those who have been victimised are regarded as truly legitimate to defend their interests. Rather than multiple competing narratives and flexible victims' identities forcing a localised approach as in Northern Ireland, in the Spanish context we observe a coherent political narrative shared by victims' organisations and statutory bodies. Such a dominant narrative underpins the uncontested victim's identity and justifies claims for support and acceptance.

The obvious conclusion here is that the socio-political features of the post-conflict environment in these two settings fundamentally shape the available system of support, which in turn influences victims' personal experience and political action. These particularities mean that each framework is characteristic of the setting from which it emerges. We must note however that these categorisations are not mutually exclusive and should rather be viewed as ideal types: in fact, there are groups in Northern Ireland who seek national recognition and operate under strong political narratives, and victims' associations in Spain that limit their work to certain regions or cities or specific categories of victims (i.e. members of the security forces).

Similarities

As well as differences, important similarities and common themes coexist across these two cases. Apart from the obvious ones such as the fact that political violence had a widespread psychological impact in both scenarios, one of the most important shared features is public remembrance. If there is one public need that is widely recognised as essential by victims in these two settings it is that of memorialisation. In Spain, public recognition of the sacrifice of victims is extremely important, even more so because such acknowledgement was found lacking in the past when ETA was at its most active. Similarly, demands for memorialisation are common in Northern Ireland, even if this is carried out in a piecemeal fashion. In the absence of joint remembrance initiatives, acts of recognition of the loss suffered are carried out locally, often in the form of storytelling, the recording of personal accounts or small, community-level events (Lynch and Argomaniz 2015, 148).

Another common thread is that of politicisation, a frequent theme in the emerging literature on victimhood and political violence. Already, Hoffman and Kasupski (2007, xi) have categorised victims' associations into those focused on supporting the recovery process of survivors and families, and those which seek to shape public policy. The political dimension of victims' associations' work has been highlighted by other scholars who contend that these groups allow victims and their families to come together to break out of social isolation, make a stronger case to the state to recognise their needs, seek public solidarity and attempt to influence lawmakers and government officials (Schmid 2012, 11).

At the same time, victims of terrorism may be instrumentalised in political struggles, their voice and position used for other political purposes or encouraged to act as surrogates on behalf of political parties (Hamber 2009). Victims' groups themselves may enter the political arena in a way that is not necessarily conducive to the protection of victims needs; we have seen this occur in Northern Ireland and Spain. In both places victims' organisations have been co-opted by political parties to support certain positions or to put pressure on political opponents. As already discussed, some Northern Irish victims' organisations have behaved in a highly politicised manner. In Spain, the most salient example is the AVT. During the controversial chairmanship of Francisco José Alcaraz, the group mobilised together with the *Partido Popular* (right-wing mainstream political party) to oppose the Zapatero administration's negotiations with ETA. The massive demonstrations organised in tandem by both groups politicised the previously securitised area of the Spanish state's counter-terror policies, created disagreements within the victims' community and injected much tension into the country's political climate.[23]

Importantly, claims of politicisation can undermine the public image and even the perceived legitimacy of these groups. As Flesher and Barberet (2012, 113) contend, the more active and politicised victims' organisations are, the less they satisfy one of the criteria for the 'ideal victim': weakness. According to these authors, victims, as political actors fighting for their rights, are caught in a dilemma between conforming to an ideal type and rejecting the passivity expected of them.

Most significant is the fact that victims may be regarded as 'spoilers' by challenging attempts at reaching negotiations where they perceive that their needs are not being met and thus being blamed for destabilising peace processes. Brewer (2010) contends that mobilisation by some victims' groups in Northern Ireland has rekindled intercommunity hostility, keeping the flames of the conflict alive and weakening the peace process. The aggressive language used by some victim representatives in Spain has been described in the past as eroding political unity in the fight against ETA.[24]

A more subtle, insidious development is when victims are seen as inhibiting transformation by their mere presence in the public sphere. Victims in both places complain about feeling forgotten or left behind by their societies' efforts at post-conflict transformation. In Northern Ireland victims are publicly described as integral to the peace process but they have voiced concern that by making claims and demands they are seen as acting in opposition to the dominant peace discourse (Lynch *et al.* 2013, 81). In the Basque Country, organisations fighting for the rights of the victims have criticised the anomie present in most of Basque society, described as simply 'wanting to turn the page without reading the book'; that is, seeking to move on from the painful past without learning its lessons or removing the conditions that may lead in the future to the re-emergence of violence (Mateo and Pérez 2014; Fernández 2015).

The broader point is that, based on insights from both cases, it appears that attempts by the victims' community to behave as political actors in defending and lobbying for their rights almost inevitably lead to claims of politicisation.

Conclusion

In conclusion, the Basque case demonstrates that victims of terrorism can potentially impact upon the security environment insofar as they not only offer assistance to survivors and families but also become centres of political activism that seek to influence government's policies. They can also affect the post-conflict environment as they act to de-legitimise and challenge violent narratives and discourses of the perpetrators and their supporters.

However, the Northern Irish case serves as a counterpoint for the facile extrapolations of insights from the Basque context. Both scenarios may appear superficially similar, with subnational violence leading to a proliferation of victims' groups in the late 1990s dedicated to lobbying for their rights and the provision of services. However, when we examine the cases more closely, we see that the differences are substantial, since in NI the victims' community has evolved along community lines where historical identity and conflict divisions are relevant for conceptualisation of their experience. This has led to the politicisation of victims' issues in NI.

A comparative analysis can be especially effective in separating the features that are structural from those that are specific to the context in question. Clearly, overarching themes may be observed across both settings, such as politicisation and the importance of political rights, but the particularities of each case are essential.

Terrorism victims' status and position within a society are inextricably linked to the complexities of the violence experienced. The Troubles were a product of the role of the state and the antagonistic positions of two communities, whereas terrorism in the Basque Country erupted during the birth pangs of the emergent Spanish democracy and eventually became monopolised by a militant organisation pursuing a nationalist political project. The context to the victimisation not only affected the categories of need; it shaped the levels of contention surrounding the label, the final shape of the statutory support system and the parameters for political action available to victims as a community. Clearly, the emergent findings from these case studies point to the recurring lesson that in victimhood, as in many other aspects of political violence, context is key.

Notes

1 The analysis in this chapter draws upon the findings from a multinational research project on victims' needs funded by the European Commission and co-directed by Orla Lynch and the author himself. The results from the study were published in an edited collection and we will be revisiting frequently in the analysis the insights delivered there by the research team.

2 The Club of Madrid (2005) International Summit on Democracy, Terrorism and Security, 'Addressing the Causes of Terrorism', Volume 1, p. 7, available at: www.club-madrid.org/img/secciones/Club_de_Madrid_Volume_I_The_Causes_of_Terrorism.pdf.

3 See: www.fundacionvt.org/index.php?option=com_dbquery&Itemid=82.

4 See: www.fundacionvt.org/index.php?option=com_content&task=view&id=124&Itemid=98.

5 FVT website. See note 4.

6 See: http://ccaa.elpais.com/ccaa/2015/06/16/paisvasco/1434454067_622331.html.

7 See: http://politica.elpais.com/politica/2013/10/26/actualidad/1382811875_339148.html.

8 See: http://elpais.com/diario/2007/12/27/opinion/1198710011_850215.html.

9 See: www.publico.es/sociedad/rosa-rodero-pp-detras-avt.html.

10 The data and findings report are available on the CAIN website (http://cain.ulster.ac.uk/victims/mckeown/index.html#intro).The figures may be found on page 14 of the report; see: http://cain.ulster.ac.uk/victims/mckeown/mckeown01.pdf.

11 See: www.victimsservice.org/.

12 See: www.cvsni.org/.

13 See: www.cvsni.org/index.php/victims-and-survivors-forum.

14 See: www.ofmdfmni.gov.uk/index/equality-and-strategy/good-relations/victims-and-survivors.htm.

15 Examples include organisations such as WAVE and the Omagh Support and Self Help Group.

16 Such as Relatives for Justice, Justice for the Forgotten or the Bloody Sunday Trust.

17 Especially the West Tyrone Voice and FAIR.

18 ETA and related groups caused 92 per cent of the total number of deaths resulting from the Basque context (López 2014, 164).

19 For an exhaustive analysis of the composition and political evolution of the Basque Patriotic Left, see Leonisio (2015).

20 See: www.eldiario.es/norte/vientodelnorte/Aupa-Jonan-conflicto-olvidos-siempre_6_379422081.html.

21 See: www.elmundo.es/opinion/2015/03/16/55073a8aca4741ab648b456e.html?cid=MNOT23801&s_kw=el_gobierno_debe_endurecer_o_cerrar_la_via_nanclares_para_los_etarras.

140   J. Argomaniz

22 See: www.eldiario.es/politica/ETA-paralizando-encuentros-decision-politica_0_20577
9980.html.
23 See: http://elpais.com/diario/2008/01/24/opinion/1201129201_850215.html.
24 See e.g.: http://elpais.com/diario/2007/12/27/opinion/1198710011_850215.html.

Bibliography

Alonso, Martín (2009) *La razón desposeída de la víctima. La violencia en el País Vasco al hilo de Jean Améry*. Bilbao: Bakeaz.
Alonso, Rogelio and Ágata Serranò (2015) 'The needs of victims of terrorism in Spain'. In *Victims of Terrorism. A Comparative and Interdisciplinary Study*, eds Orla Lynch and Javier Argomaniz, 90–106. London: Routledge.
Argomaniz, Javier (2015) 'State responses to victims of terrorism needs in Spain'. In *International Perspectives on Terrorist Victimisation. An Interdisciplinary Approach*, eds Javier Argomaniz and Orla Lynch, 124–148. Basingstoke: Palgrave Macmillan.
Arteta, Aurelio (2007) '¿Qué víctimas? ¿Qué Justicia?' In *Las víctimas del terrorismo en el discurso político*, ed. Cristina Cuesta and Rogelio Alonso, 75–100. Madrid: Dilex.
Bilbao, Galo (2007) *Víctimas del terrorismo y reconciliación en el País Vasco*. Bilbao: Bakeaz.
Borer, Tristan A. (2003) 'A taxonomy of victims and perpetrators: Human rights and reconciliation in South Africa'. *Human Rights Quarterly* 25: 1088–1116.
Breen-Smyth, Marie (2009) 'Hierarchies of pain and responsibility: Victims and war by other means'. *Trípodos* 25: 27–40.
Brewer, John D. (2010) *Peace Processes: A Sociological Approach*. Cambridge: Polity Press.
Brown, Kris and Roger MacGinty (2003) 'Public attitudes toward partisan and neutral symbols in post-agreement Northern Ireland'. *Identities – Global Studies in Culture and Power* 10: 83–108.
Calderín, Juanfer F. (2014) *Agujeros del sistema. Más de 300 asesinatos de ETA sin resolver*. Vitoria-Gasteiz: Ikusager.
Calleja, José María (2006) *Algo habrá hecho. Odio, muerte y miedo en Euskadi*. Madrid: Espasa.
Cuesta, Cristina (2000) *Contra el olvido: Testimonios de víctimas del terrorismo*. Madrid: Temas de hoy.
Dawson, Graham (2003) 'Mobilising memories: Protestant and Unionist victims groups and the politics of victimhood in the Irish Peace Process'. In *Political Transition: Politics and Cultures*, ed. Paul Gread, 127–147. London: Pluto Press.
Dignan, Jim (2000) *Restorative Justice Options for Northern Ireland: A Comparative Review*. Belfast: Northern Ireland Office.
Etxeberria, Xabier (2007) *La participación social y política de las víctimas del terrorismo*. Bilbao: Bakeaz.
Fernández, Gaizka (2015) 'Mitos que matan, La narrativa del conflicto vasco'. *Ayer* 98: 213–240.
Flesher, Cristina and Rosemary Barberet (2012) 'Defining the victims of terrorism: Competing frames around victim compensation and commemoration post-9/11 New York City and 3/11 Madrid'. In *Violence and War in Culture and the Media: Five Disciplinary Lenses*, ed. Athina Karatzogianni, 113–130. London: Routledge.
Gilligan, Chris (2003) 'Constant crisis/permanent process: Diminished agency and weak structures in the Northern Ireland Peace Process'. *The Global Review of Ethnopolitics* 3: 22–37.

Graham, Brian and Yvonne Whelan (2007) 'The legacies of the dead: Commemorating the Troubles in Northern Ireland'. *Environment and Planning D: Society and Space* 25: 476–495.

Hamber, Brandon (2009) *Transforming Societies after Political Violence: Truth, Reconciliation, and Mental Health*. New York: Springer.

Hoffman, Bruce and Anna-Britt Kasupski (2007) *The Victims of Terrorism. An Assessment of Their Influence and Growing Role in Policy, Legislation and the Private Sector*. Santa Monica, CA: RAND.

Lawther, Cheryl (2010) 'Securing the past: Policing and the contest over truth in Northern Ireland'. *British Journal of Criminology* 50: 455–473.

Leonisio, Rafael (2013) 'Las víctimas del terrorismo en el discurso de los partidos políticos vascos: una aproximación cuantitativa (1980–2011)'. *Revista de Estudios Políticos* 161: 13–40.

Leonisio, Rafael (2015) 'Basque Patriotic Left: 50 years of political and terrorist acronyms'. *RIPS* 14: 83–104.

Letschert, Rianne, Ines Staiger and Antony Pemberton (eds) (2010) *Assisting Victims of Terrorism. Towards a European Standard of Justice*. Houten: Springer.

López, Raúl (2014) *Informe Foronda. Los contextos históricos del terrorismo en el País Vasco y la consideración social de sus víctimas 1968–2010*. Vitoria-Gasteiz: Instituto de Historia Social Valentín de Foronda.

Lynch, Orla and Javier Argomaniz (2015) 'Meeting the needs of victims of terrorism – Lessons for the international context'. In *Victims of Terrorism. A Comparative and Interdisciplinary Study*, eds Orla Lynch and Javier Argomaniz, 139–148. London: Routledge.

Lynch, Orla and Javier Argomaniz (forthcoming) 'Victims of terrorism and political violence: Identity, needs, and service delivery in Northern Ireland and Great Britain'. *Terrorism and Political Violence*.

Lynch, Orla, Javier Argomaniz, Rogelio Alonso, Cheryl Lawther, Gilbert Ramsay, Carmel Joyce, Agata Serranò and Egoitz Anton (2013) *Good Practices in the Provision of Support Initiatives to Victims of Terrorism. Lessons from the Case of the UK and Spain*. Saint Andrews: European Commission report.

Martin-Peña, Javier, Susan Opotow and Álvaro Rodríguez-Carballeira (2011) 'Amenazados y víctimas del entramado de ETA en Euskadi: un estudio desde la teoría de la exclusión moral'. *Revista de Psicología Social* 26: 177–190.

Mateo, Eduardo and José Antonio Pérez (2014) *Políticas de memoria, Qué, cómo y para qué recordar*. Proceedings XI seminario Fernando Buesa. Vitoria-Gasteiz: Fundación Fernando Buesa and Instituto Universitario de Historia Social Valentín de Foronda.

McAloney, Kareena, Parrick McCrystal, Andrew Percy and Claire McCarton (2009) 'Damaged youth: Prevalence of community violence exposure and implications for adolescent well-being in post-conflict Northern Ireland'. *Journal of Community Psychology* 37: 635–648.

Mesev, Victor, Peter Shirlow and Joni Downs (2009) 'The geography of conflict and death in Belfast, Northern Ireland'. *Annals of the Association of American Geographers* 99: 893–903.

Morrissey, Mike and Marie Smyth (2002) *Northern Ireland after the Good Friday Agreement. Victims, Grievance and Blame*. London: Pluto Press.

Muro, Diego (2015) 'Healing through action? The political mobilization of victims of Al Qaeda-inspired violence in Spain and the United Kingdom'. *Studies in Conflict and Terrorism* 38: 478–493.

Nagle, John and Mary-Alice Clancy (2012) 'Constructing a shared public identity in ethno nationally divided societies: Comparing consociational and transformationist perspectives'. *Nations and Nationalism* 18: 78–97.

Noor, Masi, Nurit Shnabel, Samer Halabi and Arie Nadler (2012) 'When suffering begets suffering: The psychology of competitive victimhood between adversarial groups in violent conflicts'. *Personality and Social Psychology Review* 16: 351–374.

Pascual, Esther (ed.) (2013) *Los ojos del otro. Encuentros restaurativos entre víctimas y ex miembros de ETA*. Santander: Sal Terrae.

Pulgar, María Belén (2004) *Víctimas del terrorismo. 1968–2004*. Madrid: Dykinson.

Mate, Reyes (2008) *Justicia de las víctimas. Terrorismo, memoria, reconciliación*. Barcelona: Anthropos.

Rodríguez, José Manuel (2013) *Las Víctimas del Terrorismo en España*. Madrid: Dykinson.

San Sebastián, Isabel (2003) *Los años de plomo, memoria en carne viva de las víctimas*. Barcelona: Temas de hoy.

Schmid, Alex P. (2012) *Strengthening the Role of Victims and Incorporating Victims in Efforts to Counter Violent Extremism and Terrorism*.The Hague: ICCT Research Paper.

Serranò, Ágata (2012) 'La lucha social contra el terrorismo: testimonios de algunas víctimas de ETA'. *Eguzkilore. Cuaderno del Instituto Vasco de Criminología* 26: 253–279.

Sutil, Lucía and Eduardo Lázaro (2007) *El dolor incomprendido. El sufrimiento en las víctimas del terrorismo*. Barcelona: Plataforma Editorial.

8 Between fear, indignation and indifference

Basque public opinion and socio-political behaviour facing terrorism

Rafael Leonisio and Raúl López[1]

Introduction

In this chapter we address one of the questions raised in the Introduction to this book: the consequences of political violence. The mark left by terrorism on the societies it affects is sometimes described as 'traumatic'. In the Basque case this has been expressed in different political and historiographical reflections (Zallo 2014; Fundación Fernando Buesa 2015) and in the Basque autonomous legislation on the memory of violence (Law 4/2014, creating the Institute of Memory, Coexistence and Human Rights).[2] Such use of the term seeks a rhetorical effect rather than conceptual precision and is related to the tendency to transplant clinical diagnoses to the analysis of social processes.

According to a report made public in 2011, Northern Ireland has the highest registered rate of post-traumatic stress in the world, related to the impact of the Troubles (Ferry *et al.* 2011). If other indicators are added to this, such as the fact that Northern Ireland is a paradigmatic example of a deeply divided society, then it is possible to speak of collective trauma without incurring an abusive use of medical metaphors. However, this affirmation should not be generalised. The main argument we set out below is that, unlike what happened in Ulster, terrorism in the Basque Country did not provoke a collective trauma but instead a series of measurable effects. These effects had an unequal impact on society, and their victims were particularly non-Basque nationalist people and organisations.

In particular, we focus on the consequences that ETA's terrorism produced in society from two perspectives. In the first place, from the point of view of public opinion, we use survey data to study ETA's image in Basque society (and in the Basque electorate) since the transition, in addition to the consequences that terrorism had for that society in terms of fear and coercion. While these data refer us to a 'private dimension' (what people think) of the consequences of terrorism, the second part is centred on the 'public dimension' (what people do). That is, we analyse the reaction of Basque society facing ETA in the form of street mobilisations from the end of Francoism to the death throes of terrorism.

In recent decades great advances have been made in understanding the causes, forms and strategies of terrorism, but there is still little knowledge of its consequences, which are normally studied in terms of its electoral impact

(McAllister 2004; Bali 2007; Berrebi and Klor 2008; García 2012). The support, both explicit and implicit, that terrorism receives from public opinion is a key element, since it can facilitate a continuation of violence as terrorists feel that there is support for their actions (Tessler and Robins 2007, 305; De la Calle and Sánchez-Cuenca 2013, 95). Such support has been analysed in Western societies (Hayes and McAllister 2001, 2005; Sánchez-Cuenca 2007) and in the rest of the world, above all in Muslim countries (Fair and Shepherd 2006; Tessler and Robins 2007; Maleckovà and Stanisic 2011). The effects that terrorist attacks have on the political attitudes of citizens, above all in terms of support for anti-terrorist measures, have also been studied (Robinson 2009; Bozzoli and Müller 2011). However, few studies have focused on how fear caused by violence creates anomalies in the form of political participation in democratic societies or how violence affects the supporters of the political groups linked to the terror-ists.[3] We deal with both issues in this chapter.

Along the same lines, Waldmann suggests that it would be interesting to enquire more deeply into the neglected relationship between terrorism and its supporters, who, through their support (in the form of votes, speeches or mobili-sations), prove to be essential for the persistence of violence (Waldmann 2008). In the Basque case there is a series of works that examine that relationship (Mata 1993; Sáez de la Fuente 2002; Muro 2007; Casquete 2009; Bullain 2011; Fern-ández and López 2012). These works reflect the mobilising nature of Basque radical nationalism, which for decades managed to dominate the streets through a profusion of collective actions. Many of the latter had an aggressive character directed against peaceful initiatives of civil society, which, together with other factors that we will mention below, dissuaded citizens from participating in such initiatives.

When it comes to explaining the development of terrorism we can refer to a combination of elements. These include: police response to protest cycles (phases of intensification and diffusion of social conflicts: Tarrow 1994), a response that can be more or less aggressive; the progressive ideological encap-sulation of the group of supporters, fed by Manichean narratives about 'Us' and the 'Others'; and the confrontation of more radical demonstrators not only with the security forces, but also with other social sectors that hold more moderate and pragmatic definitions of reality (Della Porta 2013), or who simply defend more humanitarian positions. The latter is the case of Basque pacifism and its opponents, to which we have already referred.

Evolution of the attitude towards ETA

In the Basque case, the surveys made by the Euskobarómetro Team of the Uni-versity of the Basque Country[4] provide a very precise means of evaluating support for terrorism as this is done in a direct way (interviewees are explicitly asked about their attitude towards ETA). The surveys cover almost the whole democratic phase since, with some interruptions, they provide data from 1980 to the present, making it possible to study the evolution of such support.

Specifically, seven possible answers are provided for the question '*In general, what is your opinion of, or your attitude towards, ETA at the moment?*' These answers are: (1) total support; (2) support but recognising mistakes; (3) support for its ends but not for violent methods; (4) support in the past but not in democracy; (5) fear; (6) indifference; and (7) total rejection. The evolution of this question for Basque society as a whole may be seen in Figure 8.1. In the interests of simplicity, we have grouped together the first two answers (support), the third and fourth answers (remote justification) and indifference with non-response (don't know/no reply).

The first thing that stands out is the high index of non-response up until the 1990s (indifference is always minimal and in the first years never exceeds 2 per cent), above all in 1981 and 1982, years when it is the majority response. It is surprising that in the years when terrorism was striking most forcefully, with 100 violent actions a year and several dozen deaths, nearly half of the Basques said that they had no formed opinion on a phenomenon that was so present in their everyday lives, although in the majority of cases it did not affect them directly. Without doubt fear plays a decisive role in explaining this phenomenon (Linz *et al.* 1986, 625; Llera 1992, 86). This fear (or prudence when answering such a delicate question) could also explain the lack of social mobilisation during the early 1980s, as we will see. Non-response becomes a minority from the mid-1990s onwards, exceeding 10 per cent of the answers on very few occasions.

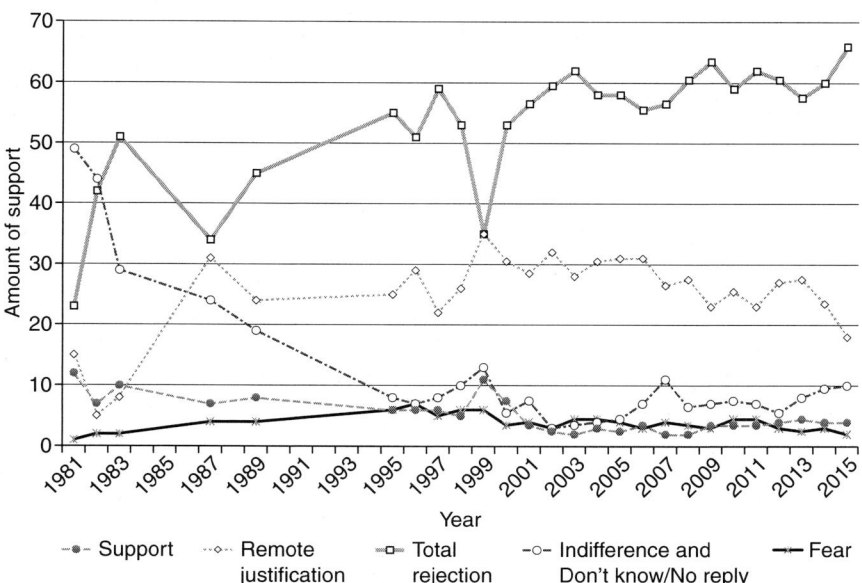

Figure 8.1 Evolution of the attitude towards ETA in the Basque Country (1981–2015) (source: Euskobarómetro, various surveys).

In the second place, it is notable that in 1983 total rejection becomes the first option of the Basques and, apart from a couple of exceptions, stands out clearly, nearly always situated at about 60 per cent of the answers.[5] What is most important, therefore, is that the Basques in general have always shown an explicit rejection of ETA's violence, at least in their consciences, since, as we will see below, this rejection was not transformed into mobilisation until some years later. Remote justification, at first a very small proportion, grows to between 20 and 30 per cent in the mid-1990s, remaining very stable. With respect to support, two stages must be clearly distinguished: the 1980s and 1990s, when it was a significant minority, between 5 and 10 per cent depending on the years; and from the start of the twenty-first century, when it becomes residual, always below 5 per cent.

In any case, the image shown in Figure 8.1 is fairly stable over time. Explicit rejection always stands out clearly, with the rest of the answers, with exceptions, far below, normally 30 points behind. Such stability, however, is not what stands out when analysing the same question but considering only the voters of the self-proclaimed Basque Patriotic Left, that is, the voters of *Herri Batasuna* (HB – Popular Unity) and the parties of radical Basque nationalism that succeeded it.

Indeed, Figure 8.2 presents a very different picture from Figure 8.1. This is not only because the answers are more unstable, but also because of *which* answers stand out most over the whole period. What is most striking is the stable support that ETA maintains among this electorate – around 50 per cent – during the 1980s and 1990s. This support reached its maximum level in 1999, during the Lizarra truce (see Chapter 2). One observation with respect to this is that we believe 50 per cent to be a minimum figure for the support ETA had among this electorate, due to the possible reluctance of many interviewees to openly support violence when facing an unknown interviewer.

In any case, it must be stressed that the support is not homogeneous, although this is not seen in Figure 8.2. While in the first two years total support (42 per cent and 35 per cent) far exceeds support but recognising mistakes (7 per cent and 16 per cent), the tendency changes in 1989 (18 per cent total support, 34 per cent critical support) and remains this way throughout the series. That is, since 1989 the support that the electorate of radical Basque nationalism (under its different names) has given to ETA has been more critical (recognising mistakes) than total. It may be possible to attribute this change of tendency to the use of car bombs, which led ETA to practise a more indiscriminant terrorism from the mid-1980s, whose zenith was the terrorist attack in a Barcelona supermarket in which 21 civilians died. In the opinion of Sánchez-Cuenca (2007, 301) the same reason was responsible for the fall in the vote for HB from 1987 onward, the moment when it reached its highest point in that year's European election.

At the other extreme, rejection of the gang has always been minimal and only grew significantly (to reach almost a quarter of the answers) from 2011 onward, the moment when ETA abandoned violence. Such increase in rejection is certainly due to the greater plurality in the radical nationalist electorate from that date onward. This is when, through a coalition, it comes to include other nationalist sectors like *Eusko Alkartasuna* (EA – Basque Solidarity), *Aralar*[6] and

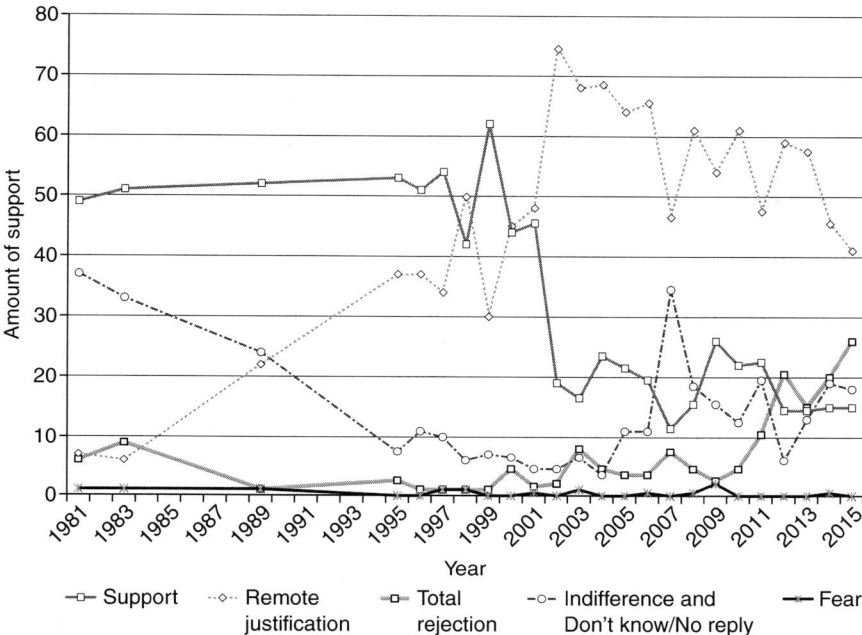

Figure 8.2 Evolution of the attitude towards ETA in the radical nationalist electorate (1981–2015) (source: Euskobarómetro, various surveys).

even *Alternatiba* (Alternative),[7] a split from the Basque branch of *Izquierda Unida* (IU – United Left), a post-communist coalition at the Spanish level. As with Basque citizens in general, non-response and indifference also seem to be of great importance in this electorate. This is the second answer in the 1980s, then falling sharply from the mid-1990s to the benefit of remote justification, which is then situated between 40 and 50 per cent. With the start of the twenty-first century the latter becomes the majority response at the expense of support, which becomes a minority answer. The evolution of remote justification is surprising. From being an absolutely minority answer (less than 10 per cent), it grows at the expense of non-response to become the second option (after support) in the mid-1990s, and from 2002 onward it becomes the majority response.

It is highly revealing to observe the change that takes place in the radical nationalist electorate from the year 2002 onward. This was the year of the illegalisation of this political force and it followed the disappointment caused in this electorate by ETA's breaking the truce it had observed in the years 1998 and 1999.[8] In the light of the data, it would seem that the circumstances of the post-Lizarra context (breaking of the truce, electoral fall,[9] subsequent illegalisation) had a very pronounced effect on (declared) support for ETA, which until then had remained stable at around 50 per cent.

In other words, since the start of the twenty-first century the majority of the radical nationalist electorate ceased to support ETA. This may partly explain the electoral decline of this option until 2011, the correlative rise of *Aralar* in the same years and finally, due to all of that, ETA's definitive abandonment of violence. An interesting proof of the decline in support for ETA among the grassroots of radical Basque nationalism lies in the different attitudes that the latter showed in the various truces that occurred over this period. Thus, while the truce of 1999 produced a rise in explicit support, which reached its zenith, the truce of 2006 to 2007 resulted in a dramatic increase of non-response at the expense of remote justification, by then the majority answer. Meanwhile, not even the definitive laying down of arms in 2011 brought a rise in support: quite the opposite. From that date onward, both support and remote justification fell, as in the previous truce, to the benefit of non-response and total rejection – the latter a novel feature that was the position of 25 per cent of the electorate of *EH Bildu* in 2015. That is, lacking greater empirical evidence, we put forward the hypothesis that the progressive decline in explicit support for the gang by the electorate of radical Basque nationalism, which was situated at around 20 per cent in 2011, had a certain influence on ETA's decision to lay down its arms in 2011.This last figure acquires further significance if we bear in mind that it is measured according to recollection of voting in the autonomous elections of 2009; that is, those who cast a null vote due to the illegalisation of electoral candidacies. Thus, in addition, that limited support was found in what could be termed the 'hard core' of voters of radical Basque nationalism.

Consequences of terrorism in political life: fear and lack of freedom

Fear is one of the consequences usually caused by terrorism in societies where it is present. Instilling fear is usually one of the main goals of terrorists (De la Calle and Sánchez-Cuenca 2011, 456) and one of the basic elements for defining the concept of terrorism itself (Weinberg *et al.* 2004, 781–785; Schmid 2013, 87). The spread of fear often gives rise to the so-called 'spiral of silence' (Noelle-Neumann 1974) and the Basque Country was no exception, since the non-nationalist sectors saw their freedom of expression coerced due to the effect of terrorist violence (Spencer and Croucher 2008). In 1986 Juan Linz and his team recognised that the answers that some Basques gave to questions they were analysing in their study on terrorism might be mediated by that lack of freedom. Specifically, they said that there was fear due to the pressure of ETA's supporters, or that those who considered themselves Spanish could not demonstrate their feelings of identity without this being perceived as a hostile act against everything Basque, all of which contributed to a spiral of silence (Linz *et al.* 1986, 625).

In spite of the complications involved in measuring the fear of a population through a survey, the Euskobarómetro Team attempted this in two different ways: measuring fear in society in general (through the individual perceptions of the interviewees); and, in an indirect way, asking the latter about their feelings of freedom to speak about politics.

Figure 8.3 is highly revealing with respect to the second question. In general, only 40 per cent of the Basques – sometimes even less than 30 per cent – felt free to speak about politics 'with everyone', while the figure for those who said they did not speak to anyone or hardly anyone was around 20 per cent. However, Figure 8.3 shows that there was a significant change following ETA's laying down of its arms in 2011. There was a significant rise in the percentage of Basques who feel free to speak about politics with everyone, a tendency that is confirmed in the data for the following years, with about half the population feeling no coercion when it comes to expressing itself politically. Indeed, the data for this answer from 2012 onward are the highest of the whole series and displace the answer 'only with some people' from the first position, which was systematically the majority response of between 40 and 50 per cent of the Basques. Moreover, while the percentage of those who say they don't talk to anyone is much more stable (around 20 per cent), it is also true that the levels registered from 2012 onward are the lowest of the whole series, remaining slightly above 10 per cent in the past two years. These figures thus indicate a progressive relaxation of political stress in Basque society and point to a decreasing influence of the terrorist phenomenon in the different electoral processes that will take place in the Basque Country in coming years.

With respect to the perception of fear of participating in politics in the interviewee's milieu, Figure 8.4 presents this indicator from 1995 to 2015. There is a clear evolution. Thus, from the mid-1990s until 2003, the existence of a lot or

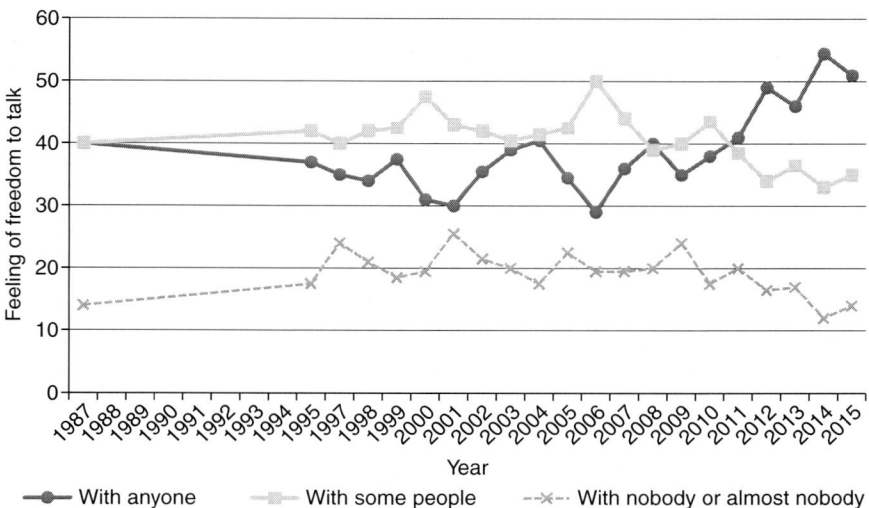

Figure 8.3 Evolution of the freedom to speak about politics among the Basques (1987–2015) (source: Euskobarómetro, various surveys).

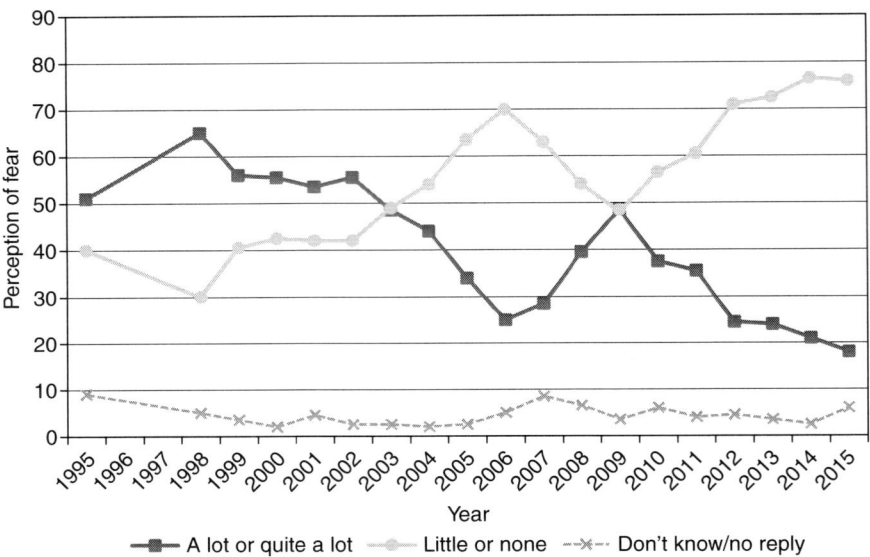

Figure 8.4 Evolution of the perception of the existence of fear of participation in politics in the Basque Country (1995–2015) (source: Euskobarómetro, various surveys).

quite a lot of fear of participating in politics is what predominates in Basque society. This was the period of the 'socialisation of the suffering', the Lizarra truce with its increase of *kale borroka* (street rioting carried out by young ETA supporters) and the harassment of non-nationalist politicians, and, finally, of the post-truce terrorist offensive, which was especially aimed at constitutionalist town councillors in small towns.[10] From 2003 there is a clear change of tendency, coinciding with the drastic fall in ETA's lethalness[11] and the ceasefire of 2006. Following the end of the ceasefire things were reversed until 2009 (with the Socialist Party assuming the presidency of the Basque government and ETA's threat to the whole Cabinet). This was a time when Basque society became divided into two equal parts – those who thought there was fear and those who did not. The final year with mortal victims in Spain was 2009 and that is also reflected in the figures. From then onward fear starts to dwindle, repeating the tendency that took place from 2003. Thus, the data for 2012 to 2015 are the lowest of the whole series, with the figure for Basques who believe that in their milieu there continues to be fear of taking part in public affairs dropping to around 20 per cent.

Table 8.1 shows two lineal regression models in which the dependent variables are fear of participating in politics (model 1) and freedom to speak about politics (model 2).[12] All the Euskobarómetro surveys (merged) that include these variables were included. The independent variables are the same for both models. With respect to the first model, it may be seen how the fact that ETA is observing a truce or is inactive (since 2011) is indeed key in explaining a greater or lesser perception of fear of participating in politics. On the other hand, the nationalism–pro-Spain scale[13] also has a major influence: the more nationalist the interviewee, the less the perception of fear he or she has. Finally, while statistically significant, other variables contribute less: living in a municipality with fewer than 4,000 inhabitants registered in the census (with respect to municipalities with between 4,000 and 20,000) and being under 35 years old (with respect to middle age) have a negative influence on the perception of fear; the left–right scale has a positive influence (the further to the right, the greater the fear); born outside the Basque Country or born in the Basque Country but to parents from outside (with respect to the natives with Basque parents); and living in the province of Gipuzkoa (with respect to Biscay). The results with regard to speaking about politics are very similar. In this case ETA's inactivity also explains the dependent variable (more freedom) but has less importance in the model, with the nationalist scale having much more weight: the less Basque nationalist the interviewee, the less the freedom to speak about politics. The rest of the variables appear to operate in the same direction: less freedom the further to the right, in those born outside the Basque Country and natives born to parents from outside; greater freedom in inhabitants of small municipalities and in those under the age of 35. There are some small differences, such as the fact that the inhabitants of large towns or those over 64 years of age have greater freedom with respect to average-sized towns or those of middle age, questions that were not significant with respect to fear. The greatest difference is found in the province of residence: if those from Gipuzkoa noted more fear than the Biscayans on this occasion, those from both Gipuzkoa and Araba feel more freedom to speak about politics than the Biscayans, and the same holds for men with respect to women.

Thus we confirmed the existence of fear and lack of freedom in the Basque Country. Far from being uniform, we insist that this is something that had geographical, ideological and chronological variations. Moving on from the sphere of public opinion to the sphere of collective action, we will now consider Basque society's attitude towards terrorism as expressed in the streets. We will examine when, how and why this attitude evolved.

A society mobilised against terror?

In recent years a current of opinion has formed which holds that the critical attitude of Basque society played an essential role in putting an end to terrorism. One of its main proponents is Jonan Fernández, Head of the Secretariat for Peace and Co-existence of the Basque Government, formed of moderate nationalists from the PNV. Fernández, who is in charge of public memory policies in this autonomous community, argues that Basque society has been one of the most active in the world in its opposition to political violence (Fernández 2006; a critique may be found in Alonso 2014). In reality, the role of one part of this society was key to the subsistence of terrorism. If there was a pacifist mobilisation, this was because a domestic form of political violence persisted in the

Table 8.1 Lineal regression analysis for fear of actively participating in politics and sense of freedom to discuss politics

	Fear of participation in politics[1]		Sense of freedom[2]	
	Beta	B (est.)	Beta	B (est.)
Habitat				
Less than 4,000	−0.125** (0.016)	−0.044	0.030* (0.015)	0.011
More than 20,000	−0.014 (0.011)	−0.007	−0.034** (0.010)	−0.019
(Between 4,000 and 20,000)				
Province of residence				
Araba	0.014 (0.013)	0.005	0.037** (0.012)	0.015
Gipuzkoa	0.153** (0.010)	0.078	0.076** (0.009)	0.042
(Biscay)				
Origin				
Basque (mixed parents)	0.001 (0.014)	0.000	−0.030* (0.013)	−0.012
Basque (not Basque parents)	0.052** (0.013)	0.021	−0.047** (0.012)	−0.020
Not Basque	0.038** (0.012)	0.017	−0.075** (0.012)	−0.038

(Basque, Basque parents)				
Left–right scale	0.038** (0.003)	0.061	-0.041** (0.003)	-0.072
Basque nationalism – Pro-Spain scale	0.104** (0.003)	0.218	-0.065** (0.002)	-0.152
Ceasefire or ETA inactive	-1.051** (0.045)	-0.547	0.094* (0.042)	0.053
Age				
Under 35	-0.039** (0.011)	-0.019	0.059** (0.010)	0.032
Over 64	-0.013 (0.012)	-0.006	-0.154** (0.011)	-0.074
(Between 35 and 64)				
Male	-0.013 (0.009)	-0.007	0.123** (0.008)	0.073
Constant	2.210** (0.031)		3.657** (0.029)	
R^2	0.169		0.081	
N	37.096		39.904	

Source: Euskobarómetro.

Notes

Standard errors in brackets.

* $p < 0.05$.

** $p < 0.01$.

Both models include controls by survey (results not shown).

1 None (1), Little (2), Quite a lot (3), A lot (4).

2 With nobody (1), With almost nobody (2), With some people (3), With anyone (4).

Basque Country – unlike nearly all of the rest of Europe – and there were numerous demonstrations extolling those who practised it (Casquete 2013).

The question of the end of terrorism is a complex one. Our interpretation for the case of the Basque Country is multifactorial and is thus in line with what may be detected on a more general level: few authors opt for mono-causal explanations (Guelke 2009, 36). Now, when it comes to hierarchising causes, we would put the police and judicial pressure on ETA and its milieu in the first place. The efficient work of these state apparatuses deprived radical Basque nationalism of the expectation of attaining political conquests by force (Domínguez 2012; see also the Introduction to this volume).

Together with the above, other aspects must be considered, such as the lack of international models to follow after the Provisional IRA laid down its arms in 2005. Moreover, incomprehension of violence reached its highest levels at the end of the period, rising substantially, as we saw, even within the electorate of Basque radical nationalism itself. This rejection was not always translated into pacifist mobilisation, and this certainly did not occur in the last-mentioned socio-political sector. However, it should also be noted that such mobilisation was appreciably broader in the second half of the 1980s and above all from the 1990s onward, when it contributed to the social de-legitimisation of violence through a routine of collective actions in the streets (Funes 1998).

We will now consider the extent to which there were social mobilisations (in the form of strikes, demonstrations or rallies) following deadly terrorist actions. Similarly, we will check whether there were variations depending on the status of the victim or the organisation responsible for the crime, and if there were cases of justification of terrorism. Given the volume of information to be dealt with, we took a sample of 154 cases of deadly terrorist actions, using the daily press as our source (*Egin, El Correo, El País, ABC*).[14] The years selected for this sample cast light on what happened during the dictatorship (1973 and 1975), transition (1979) and democracy (1984, 1992, 2000 and 2003).

Terrorism had a polarising effect under the Francoist regime. Police repression, far from affecting ETA alone, fell on broad social strata, above all during the states of exception. In the Basque Country this strengthened disaffection towards the dictatorship and towards Spain in general (Pérez-Agote 2006). ETA was not only a derivation but also a mirror of the tyrannical nature of Francoism (Fernández 2014). In fact, ETA continued to try to impose its political project by force following the death of Franco. Ninety-five per cent of the murders related to the Basque case were committed once the dictatorship had ended (López 2015, 40).

During Francoism there was a tangible exploitation of terrorism and its victims by the government to try to reinforce the continuity of the dictatorship, justifying the need for its repression, for example (Uriarte 1998). This is visible in the acts of protest held following 64 per cednt of the cases of deadly terrorist actions during this period (data for 1973 and 1975). These were mass events normally held at the entrances of churches where the funerals for the victims of terrorism were held, and were directed by the authorities in order to extol the regime. Attendance at such mobilisations in the Basque Country was small. The biggest social reactions relating to the question of terrorism in this period were the expressions of solidarity with ETA members who were victims of Francoism. In 1975 the entire opposition united to try to save the lives of ETA members Juan Paredes, Txiki and Ángel Otaegi, who were finally executed. ETA emerged from the dictatorship with a prestige and heroic aura which it progressively lost, but that was still strong during the following years.

One of the pillars of the transition was the approval of the constitution in 1978 and, within its framework, the re-establishment of Basque autonomy which included a broad range of self-government powers. In spite of the relative speed of the transition process, those were years when there was a greater concentration of politically motivated murders. The clearest effect of terrorism during this period was its causing a deterioration of the process of democratisation, above all in the Basque Country. Radical Basque nationalism was an agent of de-democratisation if we consider that the latter occurs when, among other things, participation in the political process by other agents is prevented or limited, thus causing inequality (Tilly and Wood 2009, 139). The extreme right and the regressive sectors of the army, who carried out an attempted *coup d'état* in 1981, also played a de-democratising role. But radical Basque nationalism, and ETA as its 'armed vanguard', was the only one of those agents with support in the Basque Country, and the only one with political weight that continued to have an anti-democratic nature following the transition.

ETA's violence spread fear to such an extent that, for example, the party in government in Spain between 1977 and 1982, the *Unión de Centro Democrático* (UCD – Union of the Democratic Centre), was unable to present its own list of candidates for the 1977 general election in Gipuzkoa, nor for the municipal election of 1979 in many municipalities, among them the city of San Sebastián (Fernández 2013, 176). The problem was not a lack of voters. In another Basque province, Araba, the UCD was the first political force in 1977, with 31 per cent of the votes. It was a problem of harassment, which in the most extreme cases resulted in the murder of six militants of the UCD and the *Alianza Popular* (AP – People's Alliance, Spanish right-wing party) during the transition, at the hands of the two branches of ETA and the *Comandos Autónomos Anticapitalistas* (Autonomous Anti-capitalist Cells).

Political violence generally spreads during protest cycles in which there is a concentration of the demands of different social movements – movements in which the majority of militants of terrorist organisations had previously participated (Della Porta 1995). Such was the Spanish case in 1978 when the protest cycle related to the process of democratisation ended, but one sector, radical Basque nationalism, considered that this process had not been concluded. Therefore this sector believed that it could legitimately continue carrying out attacks. The intensification of the terrorist spiral was accompanied by an increase in police reactions outside the law (see Chapter 3). English holds that the most serious danger terrorism represents for democratic societies is probably its capacity to provoke rash or counterproductive responses from the state, rather than the direct result of its actions, which represent a limited danger in statistical terms (English 2009, 119). While agreeing with the appreciation of the gravity of the state sliding towards that type of intervention, what we are emphasising here is that in the Basque case terrorism had more decisive effects, such as: an increase in the social divide; a rise of sectarianism in one part of the population; and a fear of openly participating in politics in another part.

ETA and its allied organisations were responsible for 90 per cent of the terrorist murders committed in Spain between 1976 and 1981 in relation to Basque political claims. Table 8.2 reflects how during the transition only a quarter of ETA's deadly terrorist attacks were answered in the form of protest mobilisation (data for 1979). The notable social demobilisation on the question of victims derived from several factors: fear of reprisals; confusion, shortly after emerging from a repressive dictatorship, between public rejection of ETA and support for the police; disagreement with ETA's means but support for its ends; and, at the furthest extreme, explicit support for the gang.

The figures speak for themselves: society largely distanced itself from a certain type of victim of terrorism (see Table 8.3). When such victims were policemen, mobilisations fell to 7 per cent of the cases. However, the percentage rose to 100 per cent when it was a case of victims of extreme right-wing terrorism, including ETA members. Moreover, there was invariably a justification of terrorism in the acts of tribute to the latter. This attitude was repeated following the arrest of ETA cells or the release of its militants from jail, shaping a dense routine of mobilisation that was decisive in intensifying the spiral of silence among non-Basque nationalists to which we referred above.

The polarising effect of terrorism may be clearly seen: policemen, considered as alien to the 'Us', were left without social support, while the terrorists were publicly applauded by the supporters of radical Basque nationalism. During those years the latter provided itself with a political culture characterised by hatred of the 'Other' (see Chapter 5); this was a culture that was prepared to accept the use of violence in its name during the following decades, in spite of the change of regime in Spain.

Table 8.2 Cases of deadly terrorist attacks followed by protest mobilisations, according to authorship of the murder (ETA and related organisations or extreme right-wing terrorism) (1979)

		Responsibility for attacks		
		ETA and related organisations	*Extreme right-wing*	*Total*
Mobilisations 1979	Yes	24% (14)	100% (5)	30% (19)
	No	76% (45)	0% (0)	70% (45)
	Total of deadly attacks	92% (59)	8% (5)	100% (64)

Source: elaborated by the authors.

Table 8.3 Cases of deadly terrorist attacks followed by protest mobilisations, according to the status of the victims (1979)[1]

	Members of the armed forces	Policemen	Civilian victims of ETA	Civilian victims of ERT	Terrorists
Yes	57% (4)	7% (2)	36% (9)	100% (2)	100% (3)
No	43% (3)	93% (26)	64% (16)	0% (0)	0% (0)
Total	100% (7)	100% (28)	100% (25)	100% (2)	100% (3)

Source: elaborated by the authors.

Note

1 Civilian victims of ETA: civilian victims of ETA and allied organisations. Civilian victims of ERT: Civilian victims of extreme right-wing terrorism.

In spite of the consolidation of democracy from 1982, more than three-quarters of the murders committed by ETA lacked a response in the form of social protest mobilisations during the first half of the 1980s (data for 1984; see Table 8.4). On the contrary, all the murders of ETA members by the GAL were answered with strikes and demonstrations called by radical Basque nationalism, in which there were constant slogans in favour of continuing the 'armed struggle'.

The situation changes in the second half of the 1980s, when the incipient Basque pacifist movement crystallised with the emergence of *Gesto por la Paz* (Gesture for Peace). From then onward all deadly attacks were followed by silent rallies in condemnation organised by this association, which was later joined by other groups like *Denon Artean* (Among Everyone) and *Bakea Orain* (Peace Now). On numerous occasions those rallies were held in an atmosphere of hostility, facing counter-demonstrations by radical Basque nationalists. Insults, threats and physical aggression against pacifists were common (Gómez 2013, 101; Alonso and Casquete 2014).

Radical Basque nationalism started a strategy of 'socialising the suffering' in parallel with the growing capacity to mobilise Basque pacifism, which since

Table 8.4 Cases of deadly terrorist attacks followed by protest mobilisations, according to authorship of the murder (ETA and related organisations or para-police terrorism) (1984)

		Responsibility for attacks		
		ETA and related organisations	Para-police terrorism	Total
Mobilisations 1984	Yes	18% (5)	100% (8)	36% (13)
	No	82% (23)	0% (0)	64% (23)
	Total of deadly attacks	100% (28)	100% (8)	100% (36)

Source: elaborated by the authors.

1993 had developed a significant campaign for the liberation of those kidnapped by ETA. The murders of politicians, judges and intellectuals affected social sectors that had not previously been targeted by terrorism in a very direct way. The elected representatives of half of the citizens (those who were not Basque nationalists) were persecuted. A milestone in the social mobilisation against terrorism was the kidnap and murder of the young PP town councillor Miguel Ángel Blanco in 1997. This gave rise to massive demonstrations, with millions of people calling for an end to the violence in both the Basque Country and Spain as a whole.

Conclusion

This chapter has shown how ETA and radical Basque nationalism had a clear de-democratising influence (in the sense of Tilly and Wood). We have provided empirical evidence that fear and coercion affected political participation (measured in the form of freedom to speak about political issues or to demonstrate against violence without threats) of important sectors of Basque society, above all the non-Basque nationalist sectors. One lesson of unquestionable importance is the fact that terrorism not only causes physical and/or psychological victims; it also affects the functioning of the democratic system itself, creating inequalities in the expression and defence of certain political projects. Apart from the agent cited above, other de-democratising agents functioned in the Basque Country, especially extreme right-wing terrorists. But ETA was by far the most deadly and long-lived terrorist organisation, and the only one with relevant social support in the Basque Country. Ninety-two per cent of the murders committed between 1968 and 2010 in relation to the Basque case were its work (López 2015, 149).

In deeply divided societies, a national, ethnic or religious element – or the sum of several elements – becomes a powerful line that divides citizens. At times this can take such explicit form as walls erected to separate different communities, the absence of mixed marriages or the weakness of integrated education, making democratic governance a complicated challenge (Guelke 2012, 2–12). In Northern Ireland two politico-religious communities confronted each other. The population there, unlike in the Basque Country, experienced a latent civil war and suffered a collective trauma, if by this we understand a common experience, with a very natural and very human origin, that affected the whole population to different degrees. Besides, a collective trauma is characterised by the physical and psychological damage caused to a large number of people, social repercussions such as those that occurred in Northern Ireland, the duration and intensity of the conflict, and its narrative construction in terms analogous to those of a catastrophe (Shamai 2015, 10–13).

In the Basque Country the traumatic experience of terrorism was essentially confined to its victims. The physical and emotional sequels are especially serious – generating lasting disabilities that affect quality of life – in the primary victims, those who suffered violence personally or who are relatives of those murdered

(Larizgoitia *et al.* 2011). In relation to this, we have questioned whether terrorism was a traumatic experience for the whole of Basque society, because, intentionally or not, this argument transmits a sensation of global victimisation that trivialises the specific suffering of the direct victims.

There is an ongoing debate on how to narrate the issue of terrorism. In this respect, we have discussed the narrative which holds that an attitude of active rejection towards the phenomenon predominated in the Basque Country. Such readings are not exclusively local; instead they may be found with relative frequency following violent periods, with the aim of excusing the affected populations. For example, after the Second World War countries like France and Holland highlighted the national resistance to the invaders, concealing or softening the phenomenon of collaborationism, while in West Germany the deep roots of Nazism were covered up (Judt 2005).

The need to critically discuss such watered-down views does not involve going to the opposite extreme, namely that of fomenting collective guilt. This is why in this chapter we have stressed the fact that terrorism did not have a homogeneous impact on society and that it is instead necessary to identify the existence of three major groups: perpetrators, victims and bystanders. To suggest that everyone was in some sense a victim or, on the contrary, that everyone was guilty, means proposing that nobody was really one thing or the other (Arendt 1964).

Notes

1 Prepared as part of the research project HAR2014–51956-P.
2 www.euskadi.eus/r48-bopv2/es/bopv2/datos/2014/12/1405141a.pdf (last accessed 10 November 2015).
3 There are some exceptions; for example, Criado (2011) or De la Calle and Sánchez-Cuenca (2013), who analyse such support indirectly: through the evolution of the vote received by the political wings of terrorism. In this chapter we analyse such support directly.
4 The Euskobarómetro Research Team is linked to the University of the Basque Country. It has conducted biannual public opinion polls since 1995 (www.ehu.eus/euskobarometro). It also has a broad database with surveys of previous years. In general these are surveys of 1,200 interviewees, although this number has varied on occasion depending on the context.
5 In 1981 the Basques showed a similar rate of rejection – around 60 to 65 per cent – of terrorist actions against members of the police and armed forces, and the murder of José María Ryan, an engineer from the Lemóniz nuclear power station; and in 1987 of the murder of former ETA member 'Yoyes' (Llera 1992, 95).
6 A political party that split from *Batasuna* in 2001 due to differences with respect to ETA's violence, which *Aralar* rejected.
7 For example, following the general election of 2011, 60 per cent of the electorate of the *Amaiur* coalition identified with *Sortu* (i.e. with the hard core of the so-called patriotic left) but also 16 per cent identified with *Aralar*, 6 per cent with EA and 4 per cent with *Alternatiba*, besides those who did not identify with any specific party in the coalition. These figures reveal that the electorate of the patriotic left from 2011 is considerably wider and more plural ideologically than the traditional electorate of the patriotic left linked to *Batasuna*, today's *Sortu* (figures obtained from the post-electoral study of Euskobarómetro, November to December 2011).

8 The electorate of radical Basque nationalism was the most credulous with respect to ETA's truce. Thus, 83 per cent of the voters of EH believed that ETA's readiness to lay down its arms was genuine, against 60 per cent of the electorate in general (data obtained from Euskobarómetro, first wave of the year 2000).

9 In 1998, at the height of the truce, EH obtained the best results in its history up until then (224,000 votes and 14 of the 75 seats in the Basque Parliament). Part of this increase in votes was related to the state of truce, with EH obtaining new voters from among those who believed that this political force would be the best option for leading a peace process (Criado 2011, 504). In 2001 it lost more than one-third of its votes and half of its seats.

10 Forty-four per cent of the people murdered by ETA in 2000 were politicians, a figure that falls for the year 2001, but which remained at a significant 26 per cent. In fact, almost one-third of the politicians assassinated by ETA were murdered between 2000 and 2002. Data obtained from 'The victims of ETA dataset' of the Fundación Juan March: www.march.es/ceacs/proyectos/dtv/datasets.asp#eta (last accessed 10 November 2015).

11 In 2003 ETA murdered three people and no one in 2004, 2005 and the greater part of 2006, since in that year its only lethal action (in the car park at the Madrid-Barajas Airport) took place at the end of December.

12 In spite of being ordinal variables, we preferred to use lineal regressions due to the greater ease in the interpretation of the coefficients. However, we also developed ordinal probit models (available on request) with the same models, without the results differing at all.

13 A scale of 1 to 10 where 1 means maximum Basque nationalism and 10 maximum pro-Spanish feeling.

14 This database may be consulted at the 'Valentín de Foronda' Social History Institute of the University of the Basque Country (www.ehu.eus/es/web/institutovalentindeforonda).

Bibliography

Alonso, Martín (2014) 'La sociedad vasca, el "proceso de paz" y el "tercer espacio"'. *Revista Pueblos* 63 (www.revistapueblos.org/?p=18114).

Alonso, Martín and Jesús Casquete (2014) 'ETA, el miedo domesticado y el desafío de los gestos'. *Claves de Razón Práctica* 236: 66–77.

Arendt, Hannah (1964) *Eichmann in Jerusalem. A Report on the Banality of Evil*. New York: Viking Press.

Bali, Valentina (2007) 'Terror and elections: Lesson from Spain'. *Electoral Studies* 26: 669–687.

Berrebi, Claude and Esteban F. Klor (2008) 'Are voters sensitive to terrorism? Direct evidence from the Israeli electorate'. *American Political Science Review* 102: 279–301.

Bozzoli, Carlos and Cathérine Müller (2011) 'Perceptions and attitudes following a terrorist shock: Evidence from the UK'. *European Journal of Political Economy* 27(1): s89–106.

Bullain, Iñigo (2011) *Revolucionarismo patriótico: el Movimiento de Liberación Nacional Vasco (MLNV). Origen, ideología, estrategia y organización*. Madrid: Tecnos.

Casquete, Jesús (2009) *En el nombre de Euskal Herria. La religión política del nacionalismo vasco radical*. Madrid: Tecnos.

Casquete, Jesús (2013) 'Commemorative calendar and reproduction of radical Basque nationalism'. *Politics, Religion and Ideology* 14: 21–35.

Criado, Henar (2011) 'Bullets and votes: Public opinion and terrorist strategies'. *Journal of Peace Research* 48: 497–508.

De la Calle, Luis and Ignacio Sánchez-Cuenca (2011) 'What we talk about when we talk about terrorism'. *Politics and Society* 39: 451–472.

De la Calle, Luis and Ignacio Sánchez-Cuenca (2013) 'Killing and voting in the Basque Country: An exploration of the electoral link between ETA and its political branch'. *Terrorism and Political Violence* 25: 94–112.

Della Porta, Donatella (1995) *Social Movements, Political Violence, and the State: A Comparative Analysis of Italy and Germany*. Cambridge: Cambridge University Press.

Della Porta, Donatella (2013) *Clandestine Political Violence*. Cambridge: Cambridge University Press.

Domínguez, Florencio (2012) *La agonía de ETA: una investigación inédita sobre los últimos días de la banda*. Madrid: La Esfera de los Libros.

English, Richard (2009) *Terrorism: How to Respond*. Oxford: Oxford University Press.

Fair, Christine and Bryan Shepherd (2006) 'Who supports terrorism? Evidence from fourteen Muslim countries'. *Studies in Conflict and Terrorism* 29: 51–74.

Fernández, Jonan (2006) *Ser humano en los conflictos. Reflexión ética tras una vivencia directa en el conflicto vasco*. Madrid: Alianza.

Fernández, Gaizka (2013) *Héroes, heterodoxos y traidores. Historia de Euskadiko Ezkerra (1974–1994)*. Madrid: Tecnos.

Fernández, Gaizka (2014) 'El simple arte de matar. Orígenes de la violencia terrorista en el País Vasco'. *Historia y Política* 32: 271–298.

Fernández, Gaizka and Raúl López (2012) *Sangre, votos, manifestaciones. ETA y el nacionalismo vasco radical (1958–2011)*. Madrid: Tecnos.

Ferry, Finola *et al.* (2011) *The Economic Impact of Post Traumatic Stress Disorder in Northern Ireland*. Bamford Centre for Mental Health and Wellbeing and the Northern Ireland Centre for Trauma and Transformation.

Fundación Fernando Buesa (ed.) (2015) *La sociedad vasca ante el terrorismo: pasado, presente y futuro*. Vitoria-Gasteiz: Fundación Fernando Buesa.

Funes, María Jesús (1998) 'Social responses to political violence in the Basque Country: Peace movements and their audience'. *The Journal of Conflict Resolution* 42: 493–510.

García, José (2012) 'Re-examining the evidence on the electoral impact of terrorist attacks: The Spanish election of 2004'. *Electoral Studies* 31: 96–106.

Gómez, Ana Rosa (2013) *Un gesto que hizo sonar el silencio*. Bilbao: Coordinadora Gesto por la Paz de Euskal Herria.

Guelke, Adrian (2009) *The New Age of Terrorism and the International Political System*. London: I.B. Tauris.

Guelke, Adrian (2012) *Politics in Deeply Divided Societies*. Cambridge: Polity Press.

Hayes, Bernardette C. and Ian McAllister (2001) 'Sowing dragon's teeth: Public support for political violence and paramilitarism in Northern Ireland'. *Political Studies* 49: 901–922.

Hayes, Bernardette C. and Ian McAllister (2005) 'Public support for political violence and paramilitarism in Northern Ireland and the Republic of Ireland'. *Terrorism and Political Violence* 17: 599–617.

Judt, Tony (2005) *Postwar: A History of Europe since 1945*. New York: Penguin Books.

Larizgoitia, Itziar *et al.* (2011) 'Secuelas de la violencia colectiva: hablan las víctimas del estudio ISAVIC'. *Gaceta Sanitaria* 25: 115–121.

Linz, Juan J., Manuel Gómez-Reino, Francisco Andrés Orizo and Darío Vila (1986) *Conflicto en Euskadi*. Madrid: Espasa-Calpe.

Llera, Francisco (1992) 'Violencia y opinión pública en el País Vasco'. *Revista Internacional de Sociología* 3: 83–111.

López, Raúl (2015) *Informe Foronda: los efectos del terrorismo en la sociedad vasca.* Madrid: Los Libros de la Catarata.

Maleckovà, Jitka and Dragana Stanisic (2011) 'Public opinion and terrorist acts'. *European Journal of Political Economy* 27(1): s107–s121.

Mata, José Manuel (1993) *El nacionalismo vasco radical. Discurso, organización y expresiones.* Bilbao: Universidad del País Vasco.

McAllister, Ian (2004) ' "The armalite and the ballot box": Sinn Fein's electoral strategy in Northern Ireland'. *Electoral Studies* 23: 123–142.

Muro, Diego (2007) *Ethnicity and Violence: The Case of Radical Basque Nationalism.* New York: Routledge.

Noelle-Neumann, Elisabeth (1974) 'The spiral of silence: A theory of public opinion'. *Journal of Communication* 24: 43–51.

Pérez-Agote, Alfonso (2006) *The Social Roots of Basque Nationalism.* Reno: University of Nevada Press.

Robinson, Kristopher (2009) 'Terror's true nightmare? Reevaluating the consequences of terrorism on democratic governance'. *Terrorism and Political Violence* 22: 62–86.

Sáez de la Fuente, Izaskun (2002) *El Movimiento de Liberación Nacional Vasco, una religión de sustitución.* Bilbao: Desclée de Brouwer.

Sánchez-Cuenca, Ignacio (2007) 'The dynamics of nationalist terrorism: ETA and the IRA'. *Terrorism and Political Violence* 19: 289–306.

Schmid, Alex P. (2013) 'The definition of terrorism'. In *The Routledge Handbook of Terrorism Research*, ed. Alex P. Schmid, 39–89. London: Routledge.

Shamai, Michal (2015) *Systemic Interventions for Collective and National Trauma: Theory, Practice and Evaluation.* London: Routledge.

Spencer, Anthony T. and Stephen M. Croucher (2008) 'Basque nationalism and the spiral of silence'. *The International Communication Gazette* 70: 137–153.

Tarrow, Sidney (1994) *Power in Movement: Social Movements, Collective Action, and Politics.* Cambridge: Cambridge University Press.

Tessler, Mark and Michael D.H. Robbins (2007) 'What leads some ordinary Arab men and women to approve of terrorist acts against the United States?' *Journal of Conflict Resolution* 51: 305–328.

Tilly, Charles and Lesley J. Wood (2009) *Social Movements, 1768–2008.* Boulder, CO: Paradigm Publishers.

Uriarte, Eduardo (1998) 'La manipulación de ETA por la prensa del Movimiento'. *Zer* 5: 247–261.

Waldmann, Peter (2008) 'The radical milieu: The under-investigated relationship between terrorists and sympathetic communities'. *Perspectives on Terrorism* 2: 25–27.

Weinberg, Leonard, Ami Pedahzur and Sivan Hirsch-Hoefler (2004) 'The challenges of conceptualizing terrorism'. *Terrorism and Political Violence* 16: 777–794.

Zallo, Ramón (2014) 'La Transición vista desde el País Vasco: una interpretación'. *Viento Sur* (www.vientosur.info/spip.php?article8760).

Part III
Narratives and memory

9 Historical narratives, violence and nation

Reconsidering 'the Basque conflict'

Martín Alonso and Fernando Molina

Introduction

Basque historical experience reflects how political violence always requires a discursive instrument that justifies and rationalises it and how this can end up being broadly shared not only by those who practise such violence but also by those who reject it. If this instrument includes a series of historicist and semantic components of an ideological type, it will acquire a persuasive potential that can extend beyond the community which exercises violence as a political act or adopts it as an identity referent. To demonstrate this argument we address in this chapter the principal rhetorical instrument that has channelled the public representation of terrorist violence in the Basque Country: the 'Basque conflict'.

This rhetorical figure was invented by the intellectual milieu of ETA and rapidly adopted by Basque nationalism as a whole. Its great persuasive success was largely due to its suitability as the 'narrative truth' – the canonical definition of reality – of the Basque nation. It has become the traditional way in which media discourse refers to the phenomenon of Basque political violence, its remote causes, and its past and present consequences in the form of victims, murders, imprisoned terrorists, unsatisfied nationalist claims, etc. (Alonso 2007; Montero 2014; Fernández 2015; Molina 2015).

In the political context created by ETA's declaration that the armed campaign was over in October 2011 and the debate around the memory of political violence, the 'Basque conflict' has become a performative concept that covers both the community strategies for remembering the violence and the political claims shared by broad sectors of civil society and the Basque political class. This chapter addresses the centrality of this narrative and its reasons. In the first section we set out its semantic genealogy and its imbrication in collective memory. We then show its seductive capacity, reflected in the host of actors that have taken it up as a discursive template. The third section considers the theoretical studies that try to establish the function of this type of narrative, recovering the category of the ideograph and the social problems approach. The fourth section shows its narrative anatomy, filled with rhetorical tropes and resources that explain the ease of its assimilation as a core metaphor of Basque national identity. The conclusions underscore the functionality of this rhetorical device as the canonical narrative that frames the memory of Basque terrorist violence.

Genealogy of a 'talisman word'

The 'Basque conflict' is a figure that served to give meaning to terrorism in the years when it was practised and that narratively orients the institutional and social treatment of its consequences in Basque society today. It functions as a sort of 'talisman word' that situates terrorist violence in the wake of a collective memory of suffering (Alonso 2004, 95; Montero 2014, 78). Logically, it is manufactured by the 'producers of the nation' (Molina 2013). These are politicians, artists, intellectuals, journalists and academics linked either to Basque nationalism, both moderate and radical, or to a political left that, while having Spain as its referent, has adopted the narrative of peripheral national identity (Ovejero 2014). Its content is notoriously simple, which enables it to group together heterogeneous events of the past in a storyline that confers plausibility on the interrelation between violence and nation that it proposes. Its conceptual core is as follows: there has been a secular 'dispute' or 'conflict' between the Basque people and the Spanish state, with victims on both sides, to resolve which 'it is not only necessary to equate the victims, but also to banish the idea of victors and vanquished' (Bezunartea 2013, 31).

As a political concept its semantic history dates back to the 1990s, although this feature has been blurred insofar as it has managed to feed off other previously used political concepts. Its remote origin is found in the construction of Basque autonomy in the framework of the new, decentralised Spanish state of 1978. At that time Basque nationalism, the hegemonic political movement with its two ideological versions (Marxist and Christian Democratic), promoted the construction and spread of a new narrative of the past with two political intentions. The first, which was retrospective, consisted in objectifying the historical existence of the Basque nation and explaining the phenomenon of violence accordingly. The second, which was projective, communicated a future expectation according to a teleological narrative: when correctly understood and disclosed, knowledge of the past would guide the transformation of Basque society according to the historical model of the lost nation, and this would facilitate peace (Pérez and López 2015; Molina 2015).

Two narrative figures channelled the interconnection of violence, nation and politics in the public space: the 'Basque question' and the 'Basque problem'. Both were synonyms. The first was a concept invented in the mid-nineteenth century to group together the debates on the self-government of the Basque provinces and its compatibility with the building of the national state. The second referred to the debates that took place in the 1930s on self-government in the context of the 'cultural war' between Catholics and secularists; it also alluded to Basque nationalism's position in support of the II Republic against the antirepublican role adopted by other Catholic political movements (Molina 2015, 191–193).

With the irruption of terrorist and counter-terrorist violence (see Chapter 3) in the process of democratisation and decentralisation that began in 1978, both figures were widely used by the mass media and academia as a euphemistic metaphor for this new traumatic phenomenon, which was thus provided with a historicist logic. The normalisation of the two concepts in the public space was a reflection of the progressive assimilation of Basque nationalism's memory as the narrative of the political violence that was taking place in the Basque Country. The communicative potential of the two terms does not lie in their capacity for interpreting the past according to historical parameters but in their self-serving potential for framing the debates of the present (violence, self-determination, territoriality, etc.) (Molina 2015, 193–195).

In the 1990s this terminology underwent a metamorphosis. The Basque 'problem' or 'question' began to mutate semantically into a 'historical dispute' between the 'Basque people' with sovereign aspirations and the 'Spanish state' as its necessary antagonist:

> Mention of the Basque *dispute* with the Spanish state is common in the Basque press (and not only there), as is the explanation that ETA is the expression of that confrontation. ETA is the Basque reaction to the Francoist (that is to say, Spanish?) dictatorship against Euskadi.
>
> (Corcuera 1994, 21)

Some years later, the 'dispute' was interpreted as a 'conflict': 'In recent times the 'dispute' or 'conflict' has managed to eclipse any other stellar reference in the Basque firmament. Once again switching between the ends supposedly sought and the means employed, the violence of ETA has turned the 'conflict into something transcendental, into what is most transcendental' (Aulestia 1998, 104).

The determining factor for its rapid insertion into Basque political language was the crisis experienced in ETA between 1988 and 1992 due to the unity of the Basque parties against its means and political ends (the Ajuria–Enea Pact, 1988), as well as the successful police operations that resulted in the arrest of its leadership. In this context, the organisation's new leaders decided to widen its list of victims to include non-nationalist politicians and intellectuals, and to extend its impact by means of more intensive and better organised street violence (see Chapter 2). Contrary to what had been proclaimed from the late 1970s onward, it was evident that there would be no military 'victory' of ETA that would force the state to consider the demands for sovereignty and self-determination of the 'Basque people'. This encouraged the different currents of Basque nationalism to come together to put an end to a terrorist practice that was increasingly seen as hindering rather than supporting their interests. This was the purpose of the 'Estella Pact' (or 'Lizarra Pact' as it was called by its signatories), an agreement signed in 1998 by all the nationalist political formations and the post-communist left (see Chapter 2). The base document of the agreement adopted the 'Basque conflict' as the all-encompassing explanation of the phenomenon of terrorist violence and facilitated its normalisation in Basque political language: 'The Basque dispute is a historical conflict with a political origin and nature in which the Spanish state and the French state are involved. Its resolution must necessarily be political'. This agreement had been preceded by several clandestine meetings between the *Partido Nacionalista Vasco* (PNV – Basque Nationalist Party) and ETA in which both agreed to adopt this new narrative figure as an instrument for explaining the violence and its resolution.[1]

This political *rapprochement* between terrorists and democrats, moderate and radical nationalists, was promoted by the so-called 'third space', a type of 'civil society' related to Basque nationalism and linked to the local church, nationalist trade unions and ethno-pacifist organisations (Elkarri, Lokarri, Baketik). Their characterisation as ethno-pacifist is because their public calls for an end to the terrorist violence were always accompanied by a demand that the state fulfil some of the goals of the Basque nationalist programme. A good example of that is the binary couple 'pacification–normalisation' that articulated their political discourse. This, in accordance with the discursive logic of the 'conflict', argued that the end of the violence would be linked to state concessions in the field of self-government. Peace was made conditional on the satisfaction of ethno-nationalist claims for sovereignty (Alonso 2007). Nationalist and left-wing parties, social and cultural organisations and the new intelligentsia of the PNV aligned themselves with these proposals. The narrative axis of their common political discourse was the 'Basque conflict' (Molina 2015, 198–199).

Following ETA's return to terrorist activity in 1999 and the failure of that agreement, the regional president, Juan José Ibarretxe, and his party, the PNV, promoted a new initiative which was also based on that figure: the 'Ibarretxe plan'. This sought to move beyond political autonomy in favour of a new confederal project or independence. It was rejected by the majority of the Spanish Congress and withdrawn, as it was only supported by the Basque nationalist groups (Whitfield 2014, 114–118).

A seductive polyvalent narrative

The 'Basque conflict' is a narrative used by multiple actors; for example, by media academics seduced by poststructuralist proposals concerning political reality: 'The Basque conflict exists to the extent, in the form and with the intensity that it is felt by the citizens, no more and no less' (Innerarity 2007). The media platforms of Basque nationalism have made it into an explanatory storyline for their political demands, making its historical negation by the state the cause of terrorism (Gabina 2000). It is, precisely, the indicator of a political anomaly or abnormality that must be recognised and solved (Zabalza 2000). These examples correspond to the broad spectrum of public and private mass media managed or funded by conservative nationalism, which has repeatedly controlled the regional government and exploited its institutional discourse (Casquete 2009b). The peculiar political semantics associated with this storyline have become partially normalised by the Basque public mass media.[2]

The socialisation of this concept is even more intense in the case of radical nationalism. It is not for nothing that it was invented in this milieu on the initiative of the ETA leadership (Martínez 2011, 100). This political community reproduces itself in a closed cognitive system where its militants only read, listen to and observe reality through their own communications media (Sáez de la Fuente 2002, 240–244).

The radical Basque nationalist collective has historically reproduced itself as a 'community of violence' to which terrorist activity provided identity, meaning, value and status (Casquete 2009a, 12; Molina forthcoming). Hence it contemplates this violence as a metonym for the nation and uses it as a trope of the 'conflict'. Following one of the last terrorist murders, the official newspaper of this community stated: 'The spokespersons of the government [the Basque government was then in the hands of the non-nationalist Socialist Party of Euskadi] have said that no political conflict exists in Euskal Herria (...). But they cannot deny reality'. The 'reality' was that each terrorist act reflected 'the Basque conflict in all its crudity' (*Gara*, 20 June 2009). Every terrorist action thus had a 'pedagogical' logic insofar as '[it brings] to light the essence of the conflict, the core of the problem' (Gil 1994, 21). Intellectual negation of the 'conflict' is thus unthinkable, as it is for conservative nationalism (the Basque Nationalist Party), since it would entail negating the existence of the nation (Erkizia 2015).

The 'Basque conflict' is also a constant in a very active sector of the local social scientists, which is decisive for giving it a scientific seal of approval by constituting it as an epistemological object (Idoyaga and Ramírez de la Piscina 2002; Antón 2011). Its scientific normalisation has benefited from its successful internationalisation as a subject of academic analysis, thanks to the conversion of the Basque Country into a case study in the field of conflictology. Several examples reflect this. The first is the initiative of the Peace Research Institute of Oslo (PRIO), which has funded a research project entitled 'Imagined Sovereignties: Frontiers of Statehood and Globalisation'. Pedro Ibarra, one of the main promotors of this narrative in Basque academia, participates in its 'reference group' in the capacity of 'lead researcher'.[3] The second refers to the activities of the 'Lehendakari Agirre Center', directed by the former regional president Juan José Ibarretxe. The Center receives support from the universities of Columbia (New York) and George Mason (Virginia); it is located in the Basque public university and is funded by Kutxabank, a public bank with strong historical and sociological ties to the PNV. One of its aims is to share 'the experience of the Basque political conflict with other places in the world that have similar problems' (*El País*, 4 March 2013). This Center has a proactive function in favour of the Basque nationalist cause, as its programme of activities reveals: it has organised conferences on the right to self-determination in the USA and seminars on the 'Basque conflict' in Great Britain.[4]

In the field of academic analysis, the study most oriented to inserting the Basque case into comparative conflict analysis is Whitfield (2014). This includes occasional references to the 'Basque conflict' and repeated references to an earlier figure that the latter has absorbed: the 'Basque problem'. In these analyses the key is always semantic. It could be considered normal to insert political violence into the Basque Country as a case study in the field of conflictology, given that different conflicts are interconnected within it (between the constitutional state and a terrorist organisation, between different currents of Basque nationalism, between the latter and pro-Spanish autonomy positions, etc.). The problem arises when there is a slippage in the reference of the term, from the conventional reference in the paradigm of conflict resolution to another that contains essentialist and identitarian contents that acquire particular meaning within the nationalist memory.

Internationalisation has a second, non-academic facet represented by the international mediators convened by the nationalist autonomous governments, radical nationalism and ethno-pacifism, to advocate for a resolution of terrorist violence based on dialogue (Whitfield 2014, 207–209, 256–262). In their public interventions the spokespersons of this type of para-diplomacy replicate the political language of their political sponsors (Alonso 2011, 194–197; Bezunartea 2013, 31–32; Balmaseda 2013, 32–35, 39–42). This is the reason why the 'Basque conflict' occupies a central place in the final declaration of the Aiete Conference, which prepared the way for ETA's announcement that it was laying down its weapons (Alonso 2012).

On a different level, this figure also inspires the evocation of the past of the collective memory centres. This is the case of the Peace Museum in Guernica, which deals with the problem of violence in the Basque Country and dedicates its final room to the 'Basque conflict'.[5] The initiatives of the Peace and Coexistence Plan aimed at directing the memory and reconciliation policies of the regional government led by Iñigo Urkullu are also based on this narrative figure of the past (see Chapter 10). Outstanding among them is 'Gogora', the Institute of Memory, Coexistence and Human Rights, which dissolves terrorist violence into an amalgam of types of violence occurring in a historical period that includes the civil war, the military dictatorship and the subsequent democratic regime. The chronology employed already reflects the interest in explaining the terrorist phenomenon as a continuation of past violence (Rivera 2015).

Other vehicles of memory inspired by the 'conflict' include documentary photography, for example. In 2007 the Navarrese photographer Clemente Bernard exhibited a polemical photographic series dedicated to the 'Basque conflict' in the Guggenheim Museum Bilbao. The exhibition included the documentary project 'Basque Chronicles', which was being elaborated as a book. The photos group together victims of ETA and prisoners from this organisation, terrorist actions and demonstrations by radical Basque nationalism. All are placed on the same level according to the reasoning that all those events reflect a secular 'conflict' rooted in the Middle Ages, which continued in the civil wars of the nineteenth century and is reproduced in ETA's fight against the Francoist dictatorship. On this basis, the deaths caused by terrorism are equated with the victims of 'police or para-police violence' (which include terrorists killed by the police or those who denounce police torture following their arrest).[6]

This equidistant and historicist canon is shared by films like *The Basque Ball* (2002) by the director Julio Medem. This is a documentary that presents interviews with politicians, intellectuals and victims of terrorist and counter-terrorist violence, mixed with archive images, films or idyllic landscapes of Basque nature. Thirty-four per cent of the visual discourse is dedicated to the victims of terrorism, and twenty four per cent is dedicated to commenting on the historical struggle of the 'Basque people' to preserve its identity against the Spanish state. The editing thus strengthens this narrative figure and accordingly deals with the terrorist phenomenon in a hesitant manner (Cabeza and Montero 2012, 472). This way of recounting Basque terrorist violence as the materialisation of a 'historical conflict' is shared by other filmmakers such as Pablo Malo, director of *Lasa y Zabala* (2014), Aitor Merino or Ander Iriarte, directors of *Asier ETA biok* (2013) and *Echevarriatik Etxebarriara* (2014).

The list of social actors involved in the normalisation of this narrative figure is only complete if mention is made of the perpetrators themselves, who have turned it into a central element of their 'narrative identity' (McAdams and McLean 2013). In their case this figure enables them to relieve their consciences when confronting their actions, following Troy Duster's maxim that 'the most general condition for guilt-free massacre is the denial of humanity to the victim' (Staub 1992, 61). When Asier Karrera explained the reasons why he murdered the socialist politician Fernando Buesa and his bodyguard, he declared that the former was 'directly responsible for the conflict in Euskal Herria'. The leadership of ETA had by then claimed responsibility for the murder of the writer José Luis López de Lacalle, whom it accused of '[advocating] the oppression of Euskal Herria and the perpetuation of the conflict'. In 2013 Garikoitz Azpiazu, head of the military apparatus of ETA at the time of his arrest, read out a statement before the French court that was trying him in which he said that he solely regretted 'the pain [he had] caused to those who had nothing to do with the conflict'. An MP of EH Bildu, the coalition promoted by radical Basque nationalism in its process of accepting the democratic game, stated in 2012: 'ETA has created a lot of pain and victims. And we are all also aware that this is a consequence of a conflict that has lasted for centuries'. In a contemporaneous statement this political coalition called for a truth commission entrusted with 'analysing the causes and consequences of the conflict'.[7]

An ideographic narrative

In the light of what we have seen thus far, we can describe the 'Basque conflict' as a rhetorical device that legitimises or explains the practice of political violence by conceiving it as a means at the service of a transcendental goal: the nation (Alonso 2004, 102; Fernández 2015). It may therefore be conceived as a metanarrative, a totalising narrative that groups together a multiplicity of phenomena (violence, politics, history, memory, identity) around a national meaning (Villanueva 1999, 214; Alonso 2014, 85; Molina 2015, 205–207). Following these interpretive registers, the 'Basque conflict' institutes the nation as the master frame that provides a 'continuous storyline between the nation's holy origins and the present state of the nation' (Berger and Lorenz 2011, 15). This 'continuous storyline' reflects the narrative held by every nation (Bhabha 1990; Berger 2008). It explains the violence practised in the name of the Basque nation according to a metonymic logic: by identifying Basque history with the history of the 'conflict', ETA is no more than a reflection of the existence of the Basque nation insofar as it reflects the latter's historical 'conflict' with Spain.

Myth, totalising narrative, rhetorical device or metanarrative are substantially interchangeable categories insofar as they underscore a triple condition of symbolic production, social construction and political functionality. They are situated at the theoretical crossroads of the 'cognitive revolution', the 'narrative turn', 'constitutive rhetoric' and 'symbolic politics'. The common denominator of this perspective lies in the idea that the narrative does not reflect meanings and realities but creates them, through a process of meaning attribution that rests on explicative plausibility: 'narratives, then, are a version of reality whose acceptability is governed by convention and "narrative necessity" rather than by empirical verification and logical requiredness' (Bruner 1991, 4). This plasticity may be put to use by political leaders and reflects a performative power related to self-fulfilling prophecies (Bruner 2004; Hyvärinen 2008).

Our aim is to question the naturalist interpretation of the 'Basque conflict' from the postulate that there are no 'immaculate conceptions' in social reality. However, our theoretical analysis does not proceed from a postmodern sensibility. We understand that subjective definitions are *part* of reality but *are not* the reality and that one of the functions of the social scientist is to explain how certain definitions of reality can become hegemonic. The social problems approach offers a solid theoretical basis for carrying out these tasks (Blumer 1971; Spector and Kitsuse 1987; Loseke 1999; Alonso 2015a, 46–52). This approach holds that the transformation of an issue into a problem does not proceed from objective external conditions but from social processes of collective definition that incorporate those conditions. A given assumption becomes a social problem thanks to the intervention of significant actors. The 'Basque conflict' is an example since, although 'as such ... it has only existed on paper' (Fernández 2015, 215), it has produced dramatically real consequences. To explain this imbalance between paper and reality it is worth recalling that 'in the garden of cultural identities, silk flowers quickly grow roots' (Appiah 2005, 135). Perceptions also produce consequences because it is the former and not the situation in itself that determines conduct, as Thomas' theorem establishes. A historical and social analysis must explain what conditions are favourable for certain 'silk flowers' to grow roots rather than others: 'It is the historian's business to discover them [social practices, tastes and fashions] retrospectively – but also try to understand why, in terms of changing societies in changing historical situations, such needs came to be felt' (Hobsbawm 1983, 307).

One particularity of certain rhetorical structures that support or excuse violence, such as the case which concerns us here, is that they tend to constitute closed systems that, while being resistant to scientific criticism, are, paradoxically, taken up enthusiastically by many social scientists, as we saw above when considering the adoption of this figure by academia. This particularity is an attribute of 'ideographs', which are

> one-term sums of an orientation, the species of 'God' or 'Ultimate' term that will be used to symbolize the line of argument the meanest sort of individuals *would* pursue if that individual had the dialectical skills of philosophers, as a defense of a personal stake in and commitment to the society.... [Ideographs] exist in real discourse, functioning clearly and evidently as agents of political consciousness. They are not invented by observers; they come to be as a part of the real lives of the people whose motives they articulate.
>
> (McGee 1980, 7)

For this reason they act as expressive channels of 'narrative identities' and their referents of meaning, as in the case of the nation.

The features that define ideographs reflect the qualities of the figure of the 'Basque conflict': (1) an ideograph must be a term taken from ordinary language that can prove attractive in political discourse (there is nothing more attractive than a term as banal as 'conflict', which has the support of an enormous sociological, anthropological and politological background, even resulting in the particular academic approach of conflictology); (2) it must be 'a high order abstraction representing collective commitment to a particular but equivocal and ill-defined normative goal' (McGee 1980, 15); (3) in political terms, it justifies the use of power, excuses beliefs and conducts and adapts both to behaviour that is acceptable to the community; (4) its meaning is culture-bound, but this dimension is diffused in a belief in its natural existence, one that is neither contingent nor invented; (5) it has a double functionality: diachronic in order to enter the historical discourse of a culture, and synchronic in order to adapt and respond to the circumstances of the moment (Condit and Lucaites 1993, xiii).

Ideographs provide 'the texture of reality' needed to give plausibility to seductive political narratives (Miller 2004, 470). They are thus essential tools in any process of mass institutional 'renationalisation' (Quiroga 2014, 690–691). Variants of this analytical category are 'the clash of civilizations' (Cloud 2004), the myth of 'Kosovo' (Anzulovic 1999), 'terrorism' (Winkler 2006), 'family values' (Powell 2006), etc. They can also function as historical terms that have been distanced from their objective content through use, such as the 'Shoah' (Meidani 2015) or the 'Nakba', and that in their new acceptance are condensations of current political programmes (Alonso 2006). The same is true for the Irish 'Hunger'.[8] A more immediate example is the *procés català*, a concept that refers to the practices of secessionist mobilisation taking place in Catalonia and whose meaning was made clear in a formally academic event, the historical symposium 'Spain against Catalonia' (Alonso 2015b, 262–274).

As an ideographic figure, the 'Basque conflict' is thus able to determine the subjects of the communitarian worldview that creates it: the Basque nation, its defenders and its enemies. All contingent events are a particular expression of this ontological matrix. As one prominent spokesperson of conservative Basque nationalism put it: 'there is a collision between two peoples and two sovereignties' (*El País*, 8 September 2001). The ideograph marks these positions separated by the identity divide, and these delimit the different storylines contained in this totalising narrative, which are essentially two: resistance and loss. The 'resistance' storyline associated Basque identity (the nation) with nationalism and democracy, against Spanish identity (the state), centralism and dictatorship (Francoism). The subject of this storyline is the Basque people who resist the attempts by the Spanish state to impose uniformity, which culminated in the Francoist dictatorship (Pérez and López 2015; Fernández 2015).

The storyline of loss (in reality usurpation or plundering) refers to the loss of identity of this 'people', identified with the nationalist community. This loss was the stimulus of the secular 'resistance', and the demands for identity, sovereignty and territoriality derive from it. Such claims are converted into a 'debt', a liability, which the 'state' must legally repay. The storyline places the strength of the political claim in the past: it makes use of the Endowment Effect – the high value we attribute to any object in the belief that it has belonged to us – and exploits Loss Aversion – the indignation caused by its loss. In this explanatory framework, the Basque nationalist imaginary – nourished by symbolic dates like 1839/1876 (the loss of Basque provincial self-government) or 1937 (the bombing of Guernica and the fall of the Basque autonomous government facing the Francoist troops) – feeds a successful narrative figure: 'the beneficial disaster' which 'commutes the value of negative events.... Historical wrongs ... breed historical rights' (Alonso 2009, 27–28, 37, 44–47). 'Credible narratives of loss, blame, and threat are ubiquitous' (Brubaker 1998, 283): the defeat of Kosovo for Serb nationalism, the *caiguda* (fall) of Barcelona in 1714 for Catalan nationalism, the loss of Cuba and the Philippines for Spanish nationalism, the Treaty of Versailles for German nationalism, the *année terrible* of the French defeat of 1870 for French nationalism, the *conquête* of Quebec in 1760 for Quebecois nationalism, are suppositions that mix together tropes in different proportions – lost cause, stolen destiny, chosen trauma – which Schivelbusch (2004) baptised as 'the culture of defeat'.

The qualitative formula of the 'conflict'

The narrative generating this ideograph, which interweaves politics and identity, presents a repertoire of seductive features. First, this is a narrative grounded in a tautological logic, as every sub-state nationalism is constituted in permanent confrontation ('conflict') with the state from which it wishes to separate (Molina 2015, 207–208). This feature was present at the very beginnings of this concept:

> The conflict has come to replace identity, the homeland itself. The radical [Basque nationalist] realises him or herself in the conflict, the existence of the conflict becomes the definitive proof of the very existence of Euskal

Herria [the nation]. Maintaining the climate of conflict, recreating it, constitutes the guarantee of its survival. The conflict is the driving force of this
history.... The conflict has become an object. And the object called conflict
has penetrated nationalism as a whole.

(Aulestia 1998, 106)

A second feature is historicity; the storyline is formed by having recourse to an
imaginary past to trace the identity frontier and give meaning to the confrontational
formula. The distinction between perpetrators and victims is thus distorted by a
historical illusion of depth (Molina 2015, 192, 207). Aulestia (1998, 106) recalls
what an older radical nationalist said to him: 'The conflict didn't start yesterday
(...) we have been in conflict for centuries, and it doesn't look like it's going to
end'. The premises of the 'conflict' establish fixed historical routes along which
events must necessarily or inevitably develop, hence its condition as a narrative of
inevitability (Clark 2013, 76–77; Molina 2015, 187). An example of this second
feature is provided by the statements of the interviewed perpetrator Koldo Azpiazu,
an ancient member of ETA (*El País*, 14 August 2001):

How did you become a murderer?
I am not a murderer.
You have killed.
Out of historical necessity, out of responsibility to the Basque people.

This ideograph makes terrorist violence into a further experience in a secular
tradition which brings together other episodes of past violence that are selected
because they are in tune with the national saga: the conquest of Navarre in the
sixteenth century, the civil wars of the nineteenth century, the Civil War of 1936
to 1939 or the violence of Franco's dictatorship. In 2002, Batasuna, a political
coalition on the point of being illegalised because of its relations with ETA, published a document stating that: 'Our People has not known a scenario of stable
peace for approximately 200 years.... This reality is what gives a historical,
political and tragic character to the conflict we are experiencing' (Fernández
2015, 235–236). In 2007 three academics evoked several Francoist bombings
during the Civil War, describing them as 'bloody expressions of the Basque
political conflict' (Ibarra, Irujo and Castells 2007). In 2013 a spokesperson for
Sortu, the party that currently represents radical Basque nationalism politically,
argued before a French lawcourt in defence of two perpetrators charged with
murdering two policemen that their crime 'is inscribed in an armed conflict with
a political origin'. In 2015 Arnaldo Otegi, one of the charismatic leaders of this
political community, declared that 'there has not been a single generation in our
country in the last two centuries that has not experienced and suffered the buffet-
ings of the armed confrontation' (*El Mundo*, 18 April 2013).

Tautology and historicity give plausibility to this ideograph. Hence the third
feature: its pieces are always adjusted to the narrative mould of Basque nationalism. The latter has been established since more than a century ago through a

series of stories structured according to triadic schemas of biblical reminiscences. All of them speak of an immemorial nation, which saw its Golden Age (foundation) cut short by Spanish invaders (deviation), a historical course that nationalism tries to redirect (restoration or resurrection). This historical confrontation is reflected in a succession of violent phenomena (civil wars) that preceded the foundation of the Basque Nationalist Party (the first nationalist organisation, founded in 1895) or ETA, in 1958. The goal that both organisations set themselves in accordance with this narrative is the same: the recovery of the stolen (national) destiny. Political violence is presented through this ideograph as the central piece of the third restorative moment (Alonso 2009, 23–25; Muro 2008, 19–38; Coakley 2012, 103–107; Fernández 2015, 221–227). This teleological storyline of inevitability explains the exoneration of the perpetrators, accomplices and consenters to the terrorist violence and the euphemisation of their actions. The young director of the film *Asier ETA biok*, which evokes his friendship with an ETA activist in order to 'humanise' him, stated recently: 'I do not share his decision to join ETA, but it results from … a political situation that was also inherited'.[9]

A fourth feature of this narrative is simplicity, which gives it a powerful persuasive strength. The emotional irredentism of the stolen destiny, of the impeded nation, is psychologically explosive. The deprivation is not material but moral, a usurpation of identity that motivates a violent action to re-establish justice. Hence this type of narrative (as in the case of the Shoah, the Nakba, the Greater Serbia, the Islamist melancholy of Al-Andalus, the loss of Catalan 'sovereignty' in 1714, etc.) acts as a factory of resentment. To activate this primary emotional circuit the identity message is oversimplified through a mono-causal and dichotomous explanation, which converts the other into the scapegoat and shows frustration as resulting from past violence and as the cause of present or future violence (Alonso 2009, 37, 45–48). The cases indicated above all serve here. As Stern (1961, 290, 295) notes, referring to National Socialism:

> By heightening the dissatisfaction of many men, theirs had been a self-fulfilling prophecy…. [T]he success of national socialism convinces us that this particular translation of resentment and discontent into political myth offered hope to those who … craved the certainty of a spiritual redemption.

The semantics surrounding this ideograph are not innocuous. The narrative subjects are not terrorism, its victims and the democratic state but 'human rights violations' and 'all the victims' of 'various types of violence' generated by the 'conflict'. The plurality of victims is a consequence of the plurality of 'violences' (see Chapter 10).[10] The victims and the perpetrators disappear as protagonists of the history of violence and are replaced in academic studies and cinematographic discourses by euphemistic descriptions: people who 'suffer the violence of the conflict' or who 'suffer in their own flesh and soul the violence related to the Basque conflict (on one side and the other)' (Molina 2015, 213). In this way, those who decided on and perpetrated the [terrorist] actions are exculpated, as they have done no more than fulfil their historical obligations. The victims, for the same reason, acquire connotations of co-responsibility. In short, all are victims of the same conflict.

(Montero 2011)

The phenomenon of Basque nationalist terrorism is thus radically distorted as a historical experience.

Establishing an equivalence amongst all the cases of extreme injustice that have occurred since the establishment of the Francoist regime until today not only constitutes a historical absurdity.... Because while the personal suffering of illegitimate violence might merge the individual spaces of very different people in very different circumstances, the merged result would strip each victim and enable the perpetrator to take refuge in that kind of collective guilt that describes each terrorist action as the inexorable fatality of a 'secular conflict'.

(Aulestia 2011)

All of this is in order to diffuse the terrorist nature (and the nationalising aims) of ETA's violence:

What was behind that terrorism, that is, the attempt to impose a very concrete political project on the rest of the citizens by means of crime, the intellectual and human complicity of many others, the generalised, docile, social acceptance of the role of spectator, all of that will be erased and suppressed, as if it had never happened in history.

(Ruiz 2013)

Conclusion

In view of what we have said thus far, we could agree that political violence has its particular narrative consequences which interact with processes of building territorial identities and with the forms in which the past is represented according to memory or history. The practice of political violence tends to favour a public reinterpretation of the past in accordance with the identity patterns of the perpetrators. Psychosocial processes like the Endowment Effect explain why violence tends to be represented according to communitarian patterns that relieve those who practise it of the weight of having taken the final decision to exterminate. The act of violence strengthens the beliefs of its perpetrators and gives these beliefs plausibility. Meanwhile, rationalisation of the violent fact tends to generate in the intellectuals, politicians or academics who elaborate such rationalisation a certain desire to understand the perpetrators' reasons, especially if the latter can count on a solid community that supports, extols and excuses them. Political violence strengthens community ties – the identity divide – and is thus a powerful instrument of homogenisation and conformity. Meanwhile, from a psychological viewpoint it facilitates self-justification among perpetrators and the community from which they emerge, with the aim of safeguarding collective self-esteem. Both aspects are complementary; hence ETA's interest in maintaining control of the prisoners and preventing individual responses.

In the 'battle for the past' being waged in the Basque Country there is not only debate about the events that took place but also about how these should be recounted (see Chapter 10). It will be on this basis that the violence will be provided with, or deprived of, logical plausibility, and greater or less honour will be conferred on the nationalising objectives it pursued. Hegemony over language is the necessary step to control the past through establishing a canonical narrative about traumatic events that have marked the present of the Basques, because this control of the past is what will make it possible to control the future, according to George Orwell's famous assertion. With the end of the terrorist violence, the ideograph of the 'conflict' appears as a comfortable resource for a society that has coexisted with traumatic episodes that include hundreds of necessary perpetrators, accomplices and collaborators, as well as thousands of fellow citizens who chose to look the other way. The 'Basque conflict' diverts the attribution of responsibility, something that is very common in contexts generated by massive political violence. As a narrative of collective victimhood it strengthens the idea of a people that is both chosen and suffering, which is in line with the sensibility of the influential local Catholicism that has lent Basque nationalism a large part of its rhetorical arsenal.

The comparative advantage of this narrative formula in the market of ideas is due to two intersecting motives: one indebted to the field of rhetoric and the other to sociology. We have explained how the master frame of the 'Basque conflict' is a rhetorical artefact with an ideographic character. It thus incorporates all the strength provided by its mythical foundation: 'A myth cannot be refuted, since it is, at bottom, identical with the convictions of the group' (Sorel 1972, 38, 152). From the other angle, the social problems approach accounts for the functionality of this type of formulation for a society that, coexisting with terrorist violence, needed to justify its hesitant behaviour while that violence existed by attributing the latter to a historical process represented with essentialist and teleological materials. Once the violence ended, it is logical that the society that sheltered and observed it – at times in fascination, at others with indifference – should try to construct a soft memory that ensures its psychological comfort by ignoring disturbing questions about the past, as the next chapter tells us. One necessary element for this soft formulation of the traumatic past to achieve social success is the infrastructure available for giving it public resonance. That is, once this foundational narrative (the 'Basque conflict') has been made into the canonical definition of reality during the cycle of violence, it is essential that there should be sufficient resources for it to be circulated massively and obtain prestigious supporters among international personalities and respected academic centres. That is the current state of the debate whose outlines we have sketched.

Apart from that, we have highlighted that the use of the concept of the 'Basque conflict' is far from being innocuous. It was the legitimising narrative of terrorist practice in the past and drives the implantation of an equidistant and apologetic memory in the present. We will conclude with a crucial and recurring question: How is it possible to discredit the closed worldview of an ideograph if there is not a common, shared ground of accepting the protocols of intellectual discussion? The answer does not provide much reason for hope. In his attempt to dismantle revisionist imposture, Pierre Vidal Naquet was able to verify the advantage held by myth-makers over those who try to dismantle myths. Is it possible to validate a discursive formation that has served to justify hundreds of deaths, the violence involved in the persecution of thousands of people and the acquiescence of hundreds of thousands of bystanders over four decades?

Judging from what has been set out in these pages, it seems that it is indeed possible. The problem lies in the fact that this validation can count on support from social and historical science, which should not be exempt from the following ethical requirement: 'we must resist the formation of national, ethnic and other myths', because 'bad history is not harmless history. It is dangerous. The sentences typed on apparently innocuous keyboards may be sentences of death' (Hobsbawm 1997, 9, 277). In short, '[d]decommissioning minds is therefore as important as decommissioning weapons' (Kemp 2000, 305).

Notes

1 The text of the declaration may be found at: www.edualter.org/material/euskadi/lizarra.html. The clandestine negotiations in 'Quince años de un pacto imposible', *Diario Vasco*, 12 September 2013.
2 *Marcos interpretativos difundidos por la izquierda abertzale, una amenaza para las políticas públicas de seguridad, Observatorio Internacional de Estudios sobre Terrorismo*, Vitoria, 9 October 2015, 40–47, available at: http://observatorioterrorismo.com/wp-content/uploads/2015/10/marcos-interpretativos.pdf.
3 www.prio.org/Events/Event/?x=8166 (last accessed 28 August 2015). The work of Ibarra in Molina (2015).
4 *El Correo* and *El Mundo*, 21 July 2015; Seminar, 'An End to the Basque Conflict?', March 2015, consulted at: http://nationalismsinspain.com/page/2/ (last accessed 9 September 2015).
5 www.museodelapaz.org/es/expo_desarrollo.php?idexposicion=2 (last accessed 11 November 2015).
6 https://basquechronicles1esp.wordpress.com/portfolio/financiacion/ (last accessed 4 November 2015).
7 References taken from *El Diario Vasco*, 14 June 2002, 2 January 2012, 18 February 2013; *El Correo*, 26 February 2012 and Bezunartea (2013, 147–148).
8 An Irish person could explain a murder by the IRA in the 1970s by using the argument that 'it wouldn't have happened if it wasn't for the Hunger', as heard by the Reverend Nicholas Frayling, available at: Bishop Teaching Day07.pdf, www.chichestercathedral.org.uk (last accessed 25 September 2015).
9 Interview with Aitor Merino, 10 January 2014, available at: www.eldiario.es/politica/Asier-ETA-pelicula-amistad-violencia_0_216628652.html (last accessed 25 October 2015).
10 Whitfield (2014, 280–286) explains the public debate about the plural condition of victimhood in the period following the end of ETA.

Bibliography

Alonso, Martín (2004) *Universales del odio. Creencias, emociones y violencia.* Bilbao: Bakeaz.

Alonso, Martín (2006) 'Relatos exclusivos, políticas excluyentes. El patrón de Oriente Medio'. *Cuadernos Bakeaz* 74: 1–16.

Alonso, Martín (2007) '¿Sifones o vasos comunicantes? La problemática empresa de negar legitimidad a la violencia desde la aserción del 'conflicto vasco'. *Cuadernos Bakeaz* 80: 1–12.

Alonso, Martín (2009) 'El Síndrome de Al-Andalus: relatos de expoliación y violencia política'. In *Comunidades de Muerte*, ed. Jesús Casquete, 19–54. Barcelona: Anthropos.

Alonso, Martín (2010) 'Estructuras retóricas de la violencia política'. In *Violencia política. Historia, memoria y víctimas*, eds Antonio Rivera and Carlos Carnicero, 118–148. Madrid: Maia.

Alonso, Martín (2011) 'Collective identity as a rhetorical device'. *Synthesis Philosophica* 51: 7–24.

Alonso, Martín (2012) *La Conferencia de Ayete. Una coreografía para la impunidad*, available at: www.yumpu.com/es/document/view/14780690/alonsoayete121230-inf-efaber.

Alonso, Martín (2014) 'Memoria para ser, memorias para estar'. In *Políticas de la Memoria*, XI Seminario Fundación Fernando Buesa, 70–91. Vitoria: Fundación Fernando Buesa.

Alonso, Martín (2015a) *El catalanismo, del éxito al éxtasis.1. La génesis de un problema social.* Barcelona: Viejo Topo.

Alonso, Martín (2015b) *El catalanismo, del éxito al éxtasis.2. La intelectualidad del 'proceso.* Barcelona: Viejo Topo.

Alonso, Rogelio (2011) 'The international dimension of ETA's terrorism and the internationalization of the conflict in the Basque Country'. *Democracy and Security* 7: 184–204.

Antón, Egoitz (2011) *The impact of peace movements on a society immersed in conflict. An analysis of the framing processes of the Basque peace movement.* Doctoral thesis defended in the Department of Peace Movements of the University of Bradford.

Anzulovic, Branimir (1999) *Heavenly Serbia: From Myth to Genocide.* New York: New York University Press.

Appiah. Kwame A. (2005) *The Ethics of Identity.* Princeton, NJ: Princeton University Press.

Aulestia, Kepa (1998) *HB. Crónica de un delirio.* Madrid: Temas de Hoy.

Aulestia, Kepa (2011) 'Derrota triunfal'. *El Correo*, 22 October.

Balmaseda, Javier (2013) *ETA's international makeover. A study of the campaign that is reframing the history and the political project of a terrorist organization.* Submitted for the degree of MA in Political Communications, Goldsmiths College, University of London.

Berger, Stefan (2008) 'Narrating the nation. Historiography and other genres'. In *Narrating the Nation. Representations in History, Media and the Arts*, eds Stefan Berger, Linas Eriksonas and Andrew Mycock, 1–16. New York: Bergham Books.

Berger, Stefan and Chris Lorenz (2011) 'Introduction. National history writing in Europe in a global age'. In *The Contested Nation. Ethnicity, Class, Religion and Gender in National Histories*, eds Stefan Berger and Chris Lorenz, 1–23. Basingstoke: Palgrave.

Bezunartea, Ofa (2013) *Memorias de la violencia. Profesores, periodistas y jueces que ETA mandó al exilio.* Córdoba: Almuzara.

Bhabha, Homi (1990) 'Introduction: Narrating the nation'. In *Nation and Narration*, ed. Homi Bhabha, 1–7. London: Routledge.

Blumer, Herbert (1971) 'Social problems as collective behavior'. *Social Problems* 18: 298–306.

Brubaker, Rogers (1998) 'Myths and misconceptions in the study of nationalism'. In *The State of the Nation: Ernest Gellner and the Theory of Nationalism*, ed. John Hall, 272–305. Cambridge: Cambridge University Press.

Bruner, Jerome (1991) 'The narrative construction of reality'. *Critical Inquiry* 18: 1–21.

Bruner, Jerome (2004) 'Life as narrative'. *Social Research* 71: 691–710.

Cabeza, José and Javier Montero (2012) 'El terrorismo de ETA en el cine documental. Dos ejemplos del uso de los recursos narrativos en la representación de las víctimas'. *Palabra Clave* 15: 461–481.

Casquete, Jesús (2009a) 'Comunidades de muerte o los claroscuros de la comunidad'. In *Comunidades de muerte*, ed. Jesús Casquete, 7–17. Barcelona: Anthropos.

Casquete, Jesús (2009b) 'Nacionalismo y medios de comunicación'. *El Correo*, 13 September.

Clark, Christopher (2013) *The Sleepwalkers. How Europe Went to War in 1914*. London: Penguin Books.

Cloud, Dana L. (2004) 'To veil the threat of terror: Afghan women and the "clash of civilizations" in the imagery of the U.S. war on terrorism'. *Quarterly Journal of Speech* 90: 285–306.

Coakley, John (2012) *Nationalism, Ethnicity and the State*. London: Sage.

Condit, Celeste and John Lucaites (1993), *Crafting Equality: America's Anglo-African Word*. Chicago, IL: University of Chicago Press.

Corcuera, Javier (1994) 'De Guernica a Sarajevo pasando por Burgos'. In *Auto de Terminación*, eds Juan Aranzadi, Jon Juaristi and Patxo Unzueta, 11–24. Madrid: El País-Aguilar.

Erkizia, Tasio (2015) '¿Cuál es el camino de la convivencia?' *Gara*, 27 August.

Fernández, Gaizka (2015) 'Mitos que matan. La narrativa del "conflicto vasco"'. *Ayer* 98: 213–240.

Gabina, Jon (2000) 'El conflicto vasco tiene solución'. *Deia*, 23 November.

Gil, Iñaki (1994) '¿Opinión pública o concienciación abertzale? Crítica constructiva de la práctica comunicativa del MLNV,' available at: www.matxingunea.org/dokumentua/opinion-publica-o-concienciacion-abertzale/ (last accessed 9 June 2015).

Hobsbawm, Eric J. (1983) 'Mass-producing traditions: Europe, 1870–1914'. In *The Invention of Tradition*, eds Eric Hobsbawm and Terence Ranger, 263–307. Cambridge: Cambridge University Press.

Hobsbawm, Eric J. (1997) *On History*. New York: The New Press.

Hyvärinen, Matti (2008) 'Life as narrative revisited'. *Partial Answers* 6: 261–277.

Ibarra, Pedro, Xabier Irujo and José María Castells (2007) '70 años después'. *El Correo*, 26 April.

Idoyaga, Petxo and Txema Ramírez de la Piscina (2002) *Al filo de la incomunicación. Prensa y conflicto vasco*. Madrid: Fundamentos.

Innerarity, Daniel (2007) '¿Qué conflicto?' *El Correo*, 7 September.

Kemp, Walter (2000) 'Book reviews'. *Nations and Nationalism* 6: 295–316.

Loseke, Donileen R. (1999) *Thinking About Social Problems. An Introduction to Constructionist Perspectives*. New York: Aldine de Gruyter.

Martínez, Regina (2011) *El lenguaje en la política vasca: tres corrientes, tres lenguajes (1996–2004)*. Doctoral thesis defended in the UPV-EHU.

McAdams, Dan P. and Kate C. Mclean (2013) 'Narrative identity'. *Current Directions in Psychological Science* 22(3): 233–238.

McGee, Michael C. (1980) 'The "ideograph": A link between rhetoric and ideology'. *Quarterly Journal of Speech* 66: 1–16.

Medem, Julio (2003) *La pelota vasca, la piel contra la piedra*. Madrid: Aguilar.

Meidani, Mahdiyeh (2015) 'Holocaust cartoons as ideographs,' available at: http://sgo.sagepub.com/content/5/3/2158244015597727 (last accessed 4 October 2015).

Miller, Hugh T. (2004) 'The ideographic individual'. *Administrative Theory and Praxis* 26: 469–488.

Molina, Fernando (2013) 'La nación desde abajo. Nacionalización, individuo e identidad nacional'. *Ayer* 90(2): 39–63.

Molina, Fernando (2015) 'El conflicto vasco. Relatos de historia, memoria y nación'. In *El peso de la identidad. Mitos y ritos de la historia vasca*, eds Fernando Molina and José Antonio Pérez, 181–223. Madrid: Marcial Pons.

Molina, Fernando (forthcoming) 'Violencia en comunidad. El terrorismo nacionalista y la política del miedo, 1976–1982'. In *Euskadi: Transición y democracia*, eds José Antonio Pérez and Juan Pablo Fusi. Madrid: Biblioteca Nueva.

Montero, Manuel (2011) 'Víctimas del conflicto vasco'. *El Diario Vasco*, 28 August.

Montero, Manuel (2014) *Voces vascas. Diccionario de uso*. Madrid: Tecnos.

Muro, Diego (2008) *Ethnicity and Violence. The Case of Radical Basque Nationalism*. London: Routledge.

Ovejero, Félix (2014) 'La izquierda, el nacionalismo y el guindo'. *Revista de Libros* 3: 1–19.

Pérez, José Antonio and Raúl López (2015) 'La memoria histórica del Franquismo y la Transición: un eterno presente'. In *El peso de la identidad. Mitos y ritos de la historia vasca*, eds Fernando Molina and José Antonio Pérez, 225–263. Madrid: Marcial Pons.

Powell, Elizabeth C. (2006) *The political use of family values rhetoric*. Thesis, Georgia State University, available at: http://scholarworks.gsu.edu/communication_theses/17 (accessed 4 October 2015).

Quiroga, Alejandro (2014) 'The three spheres. A theoretical model of mass nationalisation: The case of Spain'. *Nations and Nationalism* 20: 683–700.

Rivera, Antonio (2015) 'La historización del terrorismo. El informe Foronda'. *Revista de Libros* 5.

Ruiz, José María (2013) 'Privatizar las víctimas'. *El País*, 11 November.

Sáez de la Fuente, Izaskun (2002) *El Movimiento de Liberación Nacional Vasco, una religión de sustitución*. Bilbao: Desclée de Brower.

Schivelbusch, Wolfgang (2004) *The Culture of Defeat: On National Trauma, Mourning, and Recovery*. London: Granta.

Sorel, Georges (1972) *Réflexions sur la violence*. Paris: Marcel Rivière.

Spector, Malcolm and John I. Kitsuse (1987) *Constructing Social Problems*. New York: Aldine de Gruyter.

Staub, Ervin (1992) *The Roots of Evil. The Origins of Genocide and Other Group Violence*. Cambridge: Cambridge University Press.

Stern, Fritz (1961) *The Politics of Cultural Despair. A Study in the Rise of the Germanic Ideology*. Berkeley: University of California Press.

Villanueva, Javier (1999) 'Apuntes para una nueva cartografía del 'contencioso' vasco'. In *La cuestión vasca. Claves de un conflicto cultural y político*, ed. Josetxo Beriain and Roger Fernández, 211–221. Barcelona: Proyecto A.

Whitfield, Teresa (2014) *Endgame for ETA. Elusive Peace in the Basque Country.* London: Hurst & Company.

Winkler, Carol K. (2006) *In the Name of Terrorism: Presidents on Political Violence in the Post-World War II Era.* Albany: State University of New York Press.

Zabalza, Iñigo (2000) 'Reconocimiento de la naturaleza política del conflicto vasco'. *Deia*, 31 August.

10 The battle for the past

Community, forgetting, democracy

Luis Castells and Antonio Rivera

Nationalist terrorism in a nationalist society

From 1968 to 2010 terrorism related to the Basque Country caused 914 mortal victims. Ninety-two per cent of them were the responsibility of ETA. Only 5 per cent of these crimes were committed in the years of the dictatorship. The most lethal years occurred between the death of Franco in 1975 and the end of the transition to democracy: 96 murders took place in 1980, the year of the formation of the first Basque Parliament and government. With the coming of democracy ETA's revolutionary project proved to be more aggressive, efficient and influential than ever. During those years its political design to bring about a rupture clashed intensely and violently with the democratic and institutional course followed by the rest of the parties. It was a true 'battle of legitimacies' (Ardanza 1993; López 2015, 45). The leading role in Basque terrorism was played by the different brands of ETA following the split in this organisation (see Chapter 1) and by related groups (particularly the autonomous anti-capitalist cells). Besides being responsible for nine out of every ten victims, during this period only ETA maintained its continuity, its constant criminal capacity and, above all, its ethno-nationalist political project, which was defended using violence and supported by the civil fabric formed of radical Basque nationalism.

The 'other' terrorism – that carried out by the extreme right-wing and para-police groups – was responsible for 7 per cent of the murders. This refutes the existence of two symmetrical types of violence corresponding to the two communities of a broken society, the traditional view defended by Basque nationalism and reflected in the concept of the 'Basque conflict' (see Chapter 9). This is a reality very different from Northern Ireland, where the murders were carried out by armed groups representing the opposing communities: 68 per cent by the republicans, especially by the PIRA (Provisional Irish Republican Army) and 32 per cent by the unionist paramilitaries (De la Calle and Sánchez-Cuenca 2011, 26). In Euskadi only the radical nationalist community legitimised violence through ETA, which emerged as the nucleus of terror, seeking to intimidate those who disagreed with its political project.[1] ETA's centrality derives not only from quantitative considerations – the number of murders it committed – but also from qualitative ones. It managed to spread a sort of 'ethnic cleansing' based on fear among those who disagreed, converting them into a 'foreign' collective, alien to what was understood to be the Basque community. Hence that moral indifference with which Basque society regarded many of the murders. The victims were not people, they were 'Spaniards' (Simmel 1950; Zulaika 1988, ch. 4; Zubero 2012).

Moreover, this activity took place in a society that increasingly identified with Basque nationalism. This process accelerated with the end of Francoism until a situation of nationalist hegemony was reached in the 1980s, thanks in part to its control of the regional autonomous institutions (this was not the case in the Navarrese institutions). With democracy and self-government the Basque Country was not a state, 'but without doubt it was much more than a region' (Fusi 2003, 302). And while the majority of its citizens did not declare themselves to be Basque nationalists, they did support parties of that political colour with their votes (Euskobarómetro 2015a: 81–93).

The markedly nationalist political purpose of a terrorist organisation that was acting within a clearly nationalist society explains its continuity and why social reaction was limited and late (López 2015, 88–93). The fact that a large part of Basque society acted as 'spectators' in the face of terrorism explains the difficulties and current requirements when it comes to elaborating a shared narrative on that past that could serve as a basis for reconstituting a fragmented community. For its own comfort, Basque society needs to conceal or at least dilute ETA's centrality in that violence, its ideological character, its concrete political intentions, as well as that society's responsibility for its late retaliation against ETA (Arregi 2015, 189–193).

In this appetite for a comfortable memory, the desire of the majority of Basque society to distance itself from any trace of responsibility for what happened in the past coincides with the strategy of reconciliation and the public memory policies of the nationalist Basque regional government. By following different paths – party interests and the social will of the majority – a policy tending to blur the past has become hegemonic today. This blurring is achieved by turning a gaze on the recent past that is above all moral – although the word 'ethical' is used more in the texts – and consists in a generic rejection of violence. This is an attempt to once again regroup the divided community, regardless of the position of each citizen or group during the years of terrorism. In this way the old nationalist utopia of erecting a cohesive and virtuous community is revived.[2] In that context the myth of the suffering Basque people, portrayed as a secular victim, is reiterated as a unifying device that should bind all the Basques together. A second intention of representing the past in this way is to reduce the political dimension of what happened, concealing the intentions of the perpetrators, principally ETA. The delegitimation of nationalism as a political project is thus avoided (Arregi 2015, 206–207), and the need to recover democratic social practices eroded by terrorism and its rhetorical justifications loses importance.

The post-trauma social reaction: a tradition of forgetting

However, what Basque society is experiencing in relation to the treatment of its immediate past is neither exceptional nor unprecedented. On the contrary, it reproduces situations and behaviours for which there are already diverse precedents that reflect the logical consequences of terrorist violence in liberal and democratic societies. It is a commonplace to point to the difficulties that memory faces following traumatic periods: a detailed evocation of stages dominated by terror and violence is almost unbearable. Hence the normal social reaction is to forget, to omit the most painful parts of the past, which in addition place society in front of a mirror that interrogates it about its behaviour, about what it did facing the injustices that were committed. The task of remembrance is even more complex in cases where a significant sector of the population participated in those criminal policies, either actively or as bystanders.

Historiography has emphasised that responsibility in such situations falls not only on political leaders but also on passive subjects, who did nothing and were prepared to accept those aberrant situations, making their existence possible (Voegelin 1999). Of course nothing is clear-cut: Levi spoke of *grey areas*, those hazy frontiers that blur categorical good and evil. But this did not prevent him from blaming the Germans for the Nazi horror through their indifference and passivity (Levi 1989, 42ff.; Todorov 2002, 223). In all cases that ominous, shared past makes remembrance difficult because it evokes the responsibility of broad groups of the population and spreads an uncomfortable and disquieting sensation of guilt, even if this is only *moral* guilt (Jaspers 1998, 53).

But before such self-perception is reached, the mechanisms of forgetting come into operation, because when one speaks of traumatic pasts *the truth* tends to be *bitter*, and hearing it proves uncomfortable. That is why it is usually omitted (Boraine 1999, 10): 'Truth is good, but not all truth is good to say' (Ignatieff 1999, 162). These are social reactions that have occurred in very different contexts. In Chile it occurred with the arrival of democracy in 1990, when society initially expressed indifference facing the 'discovery' of the barbarity that had been experienced (Stabili 2012, 132–133). Or in Spain itself it occurred at the start of the transition period, when there was a majority tendency in favour of sidestepping what had happened during the Francoist regime and marginalising the most controversial aspects of that stage (Aguilar 2008, 401 and 415).

An even more eloquent expression is found in several European societies following the Second World War, when they coincided in a reaction of 'memory blockage'. The most striking cases were, on one side, France, which generated an exculpatory version by which the Vichy government's collaborationism was marginalised in favour of the myth of the French resistance (Rousso 1987, 1992). The other referent is post-war Germany, which was reluctant to analyse Nazism and the involvement of a large part of the population in the regime. While former Nazis recovered prominent positions in administration and education, many Germans felt uncomfortable facing the presence of the concentration camp survivors because it was a reminder that more could have been done against Hitler (Groppo 2002, 27).

Although Germany and a large part of the occupied countries of Europe initially developed their own *Vichy syndrome* (Judt 2006, 1.153), the necessary memory gradually emerged and the way was opened to history. It took more or less time – in Germany the process of critical remembrance began in the 1960s – but it was a requirement that finally materialised. Memory, and its historicisation, is not only a question of knowledge, of the following generations knowing about the past and why they are what they are; nor is it solely of a practical order in order to avoid reproducing mistakes. It is also an ethical and moral question, of reparation for those who have suffered unjustly. On this issue the German case has been exemplary, fomenting a rigorous reflection on its history during Nazism, assuming its guilt and giving it a public projection so that it might serve as a lesson that must be present in the lives of Germans. Since the *Historians' Quarrel* in 1986, that embarrassing past has been the subject of lively debates (e.g. the *Goldhagen controversy* ten years later) that have helped keep the Nazi regime present in the collective memory; so much so that memory as a moral exercise is a substantive item in German life and is considered an obligatory reference for building a democratic order (Bernecker 2015). As against this case there are others where collective memories take different routes with respect to an ominous past. Such is that of Japan where the choice has been a refusal to make a critical review of its pre-war stage in favour of an attitude holding that 'we are all guilty' (Buruma 1994).

It is precisely the Japanese case, as well as the revitalised use of history to feed nationalist narratives, which alerts us to a revisionist current that is especially tangible in Europe. This makes it possible to contextualise the public memory policies that are being developed today in the Basque Country. It is a post-totalitarian logic that marginalises the active resister to fascism while pardoning and exonerating individuals in that *grey area*, the neutral mass that did not take a position against violence and crime. In this way political reason is subordinated to humanitarian reason and when observing the past the accent is placed on suffering and not on the ideologies that resorted to violence. Put in graphic terms: Schindler dethrones Manouchian (Traverso 2009, 14).

That turn may be seen in Italy, which is abandoning the paradigm of antifascism as the core of its identity in the recent past and where historical interpretations abound that stress a unified history. Such interpretations make no ideological distinctions between the partisans and the fascists of Salo: they were Italians. This is an exercise that attempts to arrive at a shared memory where there is room for eulogising those who were in the *grey area* (Tabet 2015, 227). But also in the public use of history in Germany explanatory approaches are appearing that once again emphasise the idea of the Germans as victims and not as persecutors. This is done by placing the spotlight on the suffering of the Germans, with narratives on the Allied bombings of Dresden and Hamburg or the ethnic displacements following the defeat, events that are becoming the nucleus around which memory is cemented. The tendency is for Auschwitz to no longer be the *symbol/name*; rather Dresden or Stalingrad instead (Robin 2009, 243). Such positions are being questioned in these countries (Focardi 2009; Faulenbach 2009) and denounced by historians from abroad who draw attention to this *latest* turn which suggests that 'all forms of collective victimhood are essentially comparable, even interchangeable, and should thus be accorded equal remembrance' (Judt 2006, 1.181). This is what Snyder described in his interview with Judt as the shift from *historicisation* to *victimhood* as central concerns of Western politics and historiography (Judt 2012, 55). These turns and references help us situate on a more international level the type of narrative that is being introduced in the Basque Country and the social reception it may expect to find.

Government policy: a narrative without history

The Euskobarómetro survey for May 2015[3] asked the Basques about 'the most suitable decision for reconciliation between the sectors' divided over terrorism. Public opinion was split: 44 per cent were in favour of 'turning the page', forgetting the past; while 36 per cent favoured preserving the memory of the victims. The former was the majority option among Basque nationalists and the latter among non-nationalists, although it is not possible to speak of univocal positions in each bloc (Euskobarómetro 2015b, 64–69).

The present Basque government represents and skilfully manages that state of opinion, even encouraging it through its policies. In the spring of 2013 the regional president established peace as one of the three goals of the legislative term. To that end, in January Jonan Fernández was appointed Director of the Secretariat of Peace and Coexistence attached to the presidential Cabinet. The entire policy of memory, victims and promotion of human rights was grouped in this Secretariat, in order to seek 'a critical review of the past to consolidate peace and strengthen coexistence'. Aintzane Ezenarro was soon appointed adviser to the Secretariat and two years later she was made Director of the Institute of Memory, Coexistence and Human Rights created by the Basque government. Both Fernández and Ezenarro are from pacifist bodies created in the milieu of radical Basque nationalism, although they distanced themselves from the official sector after holding relevant positions in the so-called 'third space'. The latter was a sort of civil society related to Basque nationalism that initiated different strategies in the late 1990s aimed at promoting a peaceful solution to the violence (see Chapter 9). This 'third space' generated a framework of reflection that helped radical Basque nationalism to eventually distance itself from terrorism, but its activity was not restricted to this work. Through organisations like Elkarri it promoted three aims linked to pacification from that political perspective: questioning the police and judicial action against ETA; affording respectability to the thesis of the 'Basque conflict' (see Chapter 9); and replacing the idea of terrorism's defeat with the concept of a so-called 'peace process' (or 'orderly end to the violence') (Alonso 2014; Pérez 2015).

The instrument of this government policy is the Peace and Coexistence Plan, approved in late 2013. It pivots around reconciliation and human rights.

Outstanding among its initiatives are the setting up of an Institute of Memory; elaborating a report on 'the verification of human rights violations' since 1960; promoting policies of support, recognition and reparation for victims of terrorism; and investigating cases of torture. Those initiatives form a policy of 'managing the past' that has generated broad controversy among the Basque political forces and is considered 'the most delicate part following a period of violence' (Secretaría 2013b, 25). Semantics proves to be of capital importance in this plan. The meanings of words are essential and, on this point, the terminology is striking due to its ambiguity, its search for imprecision: words like 'terrorism' or 'history' barely appear and are replaced by 'violence and violation of human rights' and 'memory', respectively (Secretaría 2013, 2013b; Instituto 2013: 2). It is not amiss to recall that the recurrent use of euphemisms in history is a form of masking reality, of eliminating all traces of the past, or of recalling the latter in a watered-down fashion (Todorov 2000, 141).

In the presentation of the draft of the Plan, Fernández stated his hope that it would serve for the four Basque political cultures (democratic nationalism, the non-nationalist left, the pro-Spanish right and radical Basque nationalism) to share the same institutional framework in the future, unlike what had happened in the transition period (Secretaría 2013a). This endeavour omitted the fact that it was the latter sector that had not participated in the democratisation project, to which it had opposed its own particular political project, supported by terrorism. This is a detail of great importance. The intention to establish a shared recognition of the past by all Basque political sectors lies at the basis of the constant contradictions of government policy on matters of public memory and meaning regarding both terrorism and its victims. It could be summed up by saying that the intentions are laudable, but the difficulty of bringing together those who still hold opposing views of the past gives rise to a practice that is criticised from all socio-political spheres, except for that supporting the nationalist government.

As noted above, the strategy is based on the intentional marginalisation of both history and terrorism. In spite of repeated government declarations that ETA was chiefly responsible for the terrorist violence, the role of that organisation was only included in the final version of the Plan at the suggestion of an external body (the 'Valentín de Foronda' Institute of Social History).[4] It is worth emphasising that the final document of the Plan thus recovered the term 'ethical ground' as the central axis of the policies of the past, an important concept that the Basque Parliament agreed upon in March 2013 (Secretaría 2013b, 84–85).

Neutral language and public statements about ETA's bearing the main responsibility coexist with political decisions which blur that organisation's centrality. There are repeated statements about the will to attend to the victims, taking their different conditions of victimhood into account. However, government reports on the 'violation of human rights' mix together all types of victims and activities. In practice, these reports establish an equivalence between cases investigated by the courts and other generic accusations of abuse of power by the police in the years of the dictatorship and those of democracy, without such cases being suitably studied and resolved. One example is the 'Municipal

Portraits of Violations of the Right to Life in the Basque Case', an official document presented by this Secretariat to the city and town councils in 2015 which ends up comparing the victims of terrorism with terrorists who had died in action. Similarly, the reports on torture elaborated by this Secretariat speak of thousands of documented alleged cases – exactly 3,587 (Instituto Vasco de Criminología 2014, 60) – when few were in fact presented to the research committee created for that purpose. The tendency to inflate figures and relax scientific rigour already had its origin in the first works on the civil war and the Francoist repression; these works were sponsored with public funds by *partisan* historians more interested in myth-making than empirical verification. Finally, the sequence of violence over the course of 80 years means that the ensemble of very different victims and contexts of violence – civil war, totalitarian violence, terrorism, counter-terrorism, maltreatment, police excesses – ends up being compared in a hurtful and incomprehensible way. In this interpretation terrorism is just one more among a number of forms of violence. The idea of victim is thus diluted by the aggregation of very different kinds of cases. What is lost in the process is the importance and meaning of what Bauman (2010, 79–82) called the *categorial victim* or the *categorial murder*, understood as the death of those people who were deprived of life because they were relegated to a specific category ('enemies of the Basque people' in our case), without any proof being required for this purpose. This was the *modus operandi* of ETA.

If terrorism becomes blurred and loses its meaning, the same thing happens with history. In this case, a clear choice is made for memory, and there is a complete rejection, even contempt, for history. The Basque government's Peace Plan and policy of the past give privilege to subjective memories. In itself this is positive for the victims, but it needs to be contextualised historically so as to measure the dimension and reasons of the suffering. In light of the difficulty encountered in establishing agreements on that past, one may conclude that the contribution of historiographical methodology and rigour is neither relevant nor necessary; and that, like memory, each person has their own history of what happened and need aspire to nothing more. Only one limit is set on that 'freedom of memory': it should not be used to legitimise the violation of human rights, violence or war.

Faced with that tendency, different voices have been raised in academia, history and the social sciences (Castells 2013; Arregi 2015, 29–48; López 2015; Rivera 2015). This refusal to understand the situation in a methodical and rationalised way results in two consequences. On one side, it blurs the political character of the victims as it conceals the causes and setting of their victimhood, starting with the political intentions of the perpetrator. The government's Peace Plan insists on not comparing victims, in rejecting a supposed equivalence of types of violence; but if no effort is made to reach an historical understanding, its objective is impossible. Thus the victims become synthesised in a number and their aetiology refers to a generic evil: the violation of human rights, which completely dilutes the key role of ETA and terrorism. Preference is given to the suffering of the victims, and their political status, derived from the political reasons pursued by the perpetrator, is erased. We know that there are victims, but not why and who caused them to be those victims. As a result, the responsibility for what Basque society did and did not do in the time of terrorism becomes blurred and its citizens can only express regret. Ethical rejection of the use of political violence may thus be claimed by anyone so long as no questions are asked about their political motivations at the time and their current position. The same thing happened in Northern Ireland, where the private and personal spheres were given priority over political reflection, and the narrative of the past was approached from a quasi-psychological perspective (McGrattan 2012, 172).

A blank piece of paper: the strategy of radical Basque nationalism

On 2 October 2011, a few days before ETA announced 'the definitive cessation of its armed activity', an editorial in the radical nationalist newspaper *Gara* gave advance notice of the importance this sector awarded to the so-called 'battle for the narrative':

> Those who seek a narrative with victors and vanquished are mistaken. To paraphrase Unamuno, in Euskal Herria the one who convinces his own side and then the rest will win. The pro-independence leaders have already achieved the first and have made great advances in the second. The unionists have done neither one thing nor the other.

Two things were understood clearly in that political culture: first, Basque society would finally forge a criterion on what terrorism had been and its treatment in collective memory; second, that social perception would result from a confrontation – of narratives in this case. Consequently there was total rejection of a version in which ETA (and the cause it violently defended) appeared as defeated; they were already committed to a reading they presented as 'inclusive' – in reality exculpatory of what had happened and the role of that organisation. Four years later, the radical nationalist Mayor of Rentería argued for 'a blank piece of paper' on which to write 'the roadmap of institutional collaboration in matters of pacification and coexistence'.

The narrative of the past is of central importance in the strategy of radical Basque nationalism after ETA. This is the political sector that understands this most clearly. Radical nationalism needs it in the short term because it continues to harbour 400 prisoners who are calling for a position to be adopted that does not refute the reasons that led them to act violently and to prison. Any statement by the leaders of EH Bildu or Sortu (the electoral coalition and the party that represent radical Basque nationalism today), recognising the harm caused by ETA, is accompanied by multiple references to those prisoners and their situation. In the second place, one must recall the centrality of ETA and political violence in radical Basque nationalism, a factor that articulated and energised the latter. Any criticism of that organisation in the past would be to criticise the whole of this political space (and its possibilities of future action). The weight of the past is overwhelming here, but, in addition, the unilateral end of the gang may be read as capitulation and must therefore be framed in a narrative of greater scope. But, at the same time and in the opposite direction, radical Basque nationalism must take steps towards recognising its responsibilities in the terrorist past if it wants to obtain a certain social legitimacy and the votes needed for access to power.

For all of these reasons, this sector bears a contradiction: it must be sensitive to current public opinion and oppose violence, but in relation to its social base it must continue to defend the strategies pursued in the past, which includes justifying the resort to terrorism. For that purpose it distinguishes between two channels of communication, although common arguments always appear in both, such as: the primacy of the future over the past; its vision of the latter as a history of collective victimhood that forced it to take unwanted decisions;[5] the centrality of the historical conflict between the Basque Country and Spain (see Chapter 9); its generic regret over the pain suffered and caused; the rejection of any rigorous contextualisation of its past; and its distancing from political violence in the present, compatible with its rejection of a historical critique of ETA. All of this is summed up in the phrase 'killing was wrong', but without condemning the trajectory and goals of those who killed and fought against democracy. Violence is renounced today and in the future, but there is no condemnation of its use in the past and much less of ETA. This is the key to the so-called 'ethical ground'. That gaze fixed on the future so as not to have to look back is the equivalent of the Northern Irish policies of 'moving on' (McGrattan 2012, 125).

This form of reasoning is transmitted, as we said, along two channels of communication. One channel uses conventional media to try to reach a broad public: above all its own media, but it also uses its influence in the nationalist private and public media (the public broadcasting corporation), and even in other nonnationalist media. The discourse of radical Basque nationalism has penetrated far beyond the spaces where it has a direct influence. It has clearly asserted itself in the battle for the language (Montero 2014). Miralles (2016) supports this theory by showing how the central argument of the existence of a historical conflict between the Basque Country and Spain is reflected in 40 per cent of political information referring to these issues published in the Basque (non-nationalist) newspaper with the highest circulation (*El Correo*) and in about 30 per cent of the political information in the two most widely read Spanish newspapers (*El País* and *El Mundo*). In the case of conservative nationalism's newspaper (*Deia*) the level is 77 per cent, and it reaches 83 per cent in the text of the Peace Plan.[6] In this field radical Basque nationalism transmits a discourse on its past that is softer and more moderate, in order to connect with that broad stratum of the population which, without explicitly supporting ETA's terrorism, may feel itself emotionally linked to what this organisation represented or have an ethnicnationalist affinity.

The other communication channel is aimed at its highly active and mobilised militant core, using clearer and more assertive language. Here, a constellation of media and resources, led by the newspaper *Gara*, may be appreciated historically. Radical Basque nationalism also has a prolific publishing company, *Txalaparta*, which contributes to establishing its narratives, myths, martyrology and even history. In 2009 an association of historians, 'Euskal Memoria', was set up, which is aimed at its 'hard core'. Its documentation centre, for example, provides information on a heterogeneous conglomerate of some 500 individuals, grouping together people who died for very different reasons (terrorists killed in confrontations with the security forces, but also those who died of natural causes, in traffic accidents, by drowning, on demonstrations, in police stations, etc.). All of them are presented as 'victims of the conflict and the repression'.[7] The important thing is number, not rigour. The idea is that the higher the number of people counted as victims of the state, the greater the endorsement of its argument that there was an equivalence between ETA's violence and state violence, and that terrorism was no more than a necessary response to the oppression of the Basque people. These commemorative instruments provide material that is propagated throughout the Basque Country (and beyond) thanks to a dense, active, specialised and complex framework.

The policy of the past in the Basque case is more alive than ever and changes every day due to variations in public opinion and the movements of the political agents. It is a policy that is 'under construction', both due to its actuality and to the fact that, as historian Manu Montero ironically observed, in the Basque Country the past is the only thing that is unpredictable. At present, the litmus test is the so-called 'ethical ground', an agreement in relation to the violent past that must be reached by all the political forces with the aim of showing their distance from this violence or its clear rejection. But even that term and its content are subjected to the turbulence of party convenience. Resulting from a broad parliamentary agreement, its obscure language tries to satisfy the diverse political families of the Basque Country. However, that transversal character does not hide its nationalist ideological paternity. The subject to be reflected upon is not ETA or terrorism, but *violence* and the *violation of human rights* – where there is space for very different phenomena and, once again, the centrality of ETA is dissolved. In spite of not having approved it at the time, radical Basque nationalism feels no discomfort with the premises of that 'ethical ground'. For their part, the non-nationalists insist on the demand of 'determining and recognising the responsibility of each in the past and the consequences' deriving from those events. Sixty-seven per cent of Basques consider that 'ETA and its activists should recognise the error of their history of violence' (Euskobarómetro 2013, 63). At first sight it would seem that society is ahead of the political formations on this issue and that the cost of attracting radical Basque nationalism would be too high. But putting that recommendation into effect is highly complex and can take different forms. Managing the past and the 'battle for the narrative' respond respectively to those two points of view: blurring or specifying the principal responsibility of ETA in the terrorism of the past 50 years.

Ethics and reconciliation vs. politics and democracy

In the words of Arregi (2015, 24): 'There have been many classes of violence, but terror, basically that of ETA'. Like Arregi, other intellectuals and academics have insisted on the same idea. They radically reject the theory of the 'Basque conflict' and give more importance to the fact that terrorism resulted from a decision; that is, it was a choice made by certain individuals in a specific political situation, influenced by particular conditioning factors (see Chapters 1 and 6). This approach helps us understand the meanings of that violence at each moment and the type of evil represented by the perpetrators.[8]

From this understanding these intellectuals and academics interpret the management of the past on the basis of premises such as: the need and possibility of knowing what happened; the assertion of the political character of the victims of terrorism (due to the political intention of its perpetrators); the need to recover the life history of each of those victims so as not to diffuse them in numbers; equality of treatment for all the victims but the distinction of each case and context (a rejection of mixing all the victims of all the periods); the importance of terrorism's attack on democracy and, therefore, the usefulness of addressing the question of freedom rather than that of peace in itself; the resulting insistence on the full recovery of freedoms and democratic values; and the need for democratic nationalism to carry out a self-criticism of its past activity. Many of these premises are contained in this book and explain why Basque nationalist terrorism must be studied in historical terms.

On analysing the first draft of the Peace Plan, the historian Antonio Elorza concluded that reconciliation, from the perspective of the nationalist regional government, was placed 'above knowledge of reality'. Traditionally, post-trauma societies face the situation of trying simultaneously to achieve peace and truth. This combination is a difficult one to articulate, since a true knowledge of the past creates difficulties for the reconstitution of society, the goal pursued in all cases. Memory (and we believe that history even more so) is 'unsettling', it 'opens wounds and makes coexistence complicated' (Mate 2009, 151); hence the temptation of amnesia or of presenting a 'stylised' past.

As we have observed, public memory policies in the Basque case opt for this second path, for an empty narrative, one that shows the community in a kinder light. In short, they opt for a 'neutral closure of the past' which can satisfy both radicalised Basque nationalism that supported the perpetrators and society in general (Ruiz 2011, 7). With these premises, history is given a subordinate role: its use can be accepted on condition that it serves the higher aim of reconciliation, presented as a totem – a common good – to which any public discourse, whether political or academic, must be adapted. Reconciliation appears as the imperative and the latent discourse is that of elaborating the past to serve the present. The public policies put into practice in Northern Ireland also follow this direction in a more or less unconscious way (McGrattan 2013, 13).

Nonetheless, there are variants. The nationalist Mayor of San Sebastián recently stated that 'ETA had a strategy of attacking those who did not think like them'. This statement would support the argument that there was a totalitarian intention behind the violence, an exclusive and exclusionary political design sustained with terrorism. Should that assertion become established as the analysis of what happened and be accepted by the majority, it would then be possible in future to elaborate processes of recovering democracy, of affirming and restoring its principles and values in everyday life. On the contrary, the understanding that it was a bad choice, or a justified reaction facing a secular conflict, would imply a more complacent memory policy, less interested in analysis and historical detail, more favourable to once again integrating the divided community around the idea of multiple and shared pain. Taken to its extreme, the choice would be for coexistence without memory, the 'blank page' on the past that enables any future project to be constructed, abstracting from and forgetting what happened. This would mean dispensing with a rigorous narrative and the duty to truth, and seeking by default 'a minimum ethic for coexistence'. In that case, the necessary narrative would be one that omitted the centrality of ETA in this whole history and the principal responsibility of this organisation for the lack of democracy experienced by the Basques (Mata 2005). This is the thesis shared by the two major currents of Basque nationalism (the more moderate current of the PNV and the more radical one of Bildu): neither of them feels comfortable about its past trajectory in relation to terrorism (Aizpeolea 2015; Santarén 2015). Facing that temptation we may recall the memorable speech of the German president in 1985: '[A]nyone who closes his eyes to the past is blind to the present. Whoever refuses to remember the inhumanity is prone to new risks of infection' (Von Weizsäcker 1985, 5).

The fact is that this 'soft' or masked memory, besides being ethically reproachable, proves to be unviable. It requires a broad social consensus, as occurred in South Africa, for example, that is able to silence dissonant opinions. Where such consensus is absent, as in the Basque case, the voice of the victims – the narrative of the suffering they experienced – becomes stronger and makes it impossible to close the past; at the same time it clashes with the narrative promoted by the official version. This is an experience that has also occurred in Northern Ireland (Hackett and Rolston 2009). False closure results in memory resurfacing time and again. The past becomes a persistent voice that returns insistently like a haunting echo. But there is more besides. When we speak of traumatic events, the frontier between the past and the present becomes blurred so that those events, due to their very importance, their 'irrevocable' nature, form part of our present; they are not closed until they have been suitably resolved in memory (Bevernage and Aerts 2009). The Mothers of the Plaza de Mayo in Argentina could serve as an example. In the Basque Country and Spain, the commemorative role played by the associations of victims proves important so that the memory of the terror and the traumas it caused continue to be present. Because, as Roth (2011, 85) points out, 'acknowledgement of the past in the present is a necessary ingredient of modern historical consciousness'.

Conclusion

Throughout the chapter we have been addressing and replying to two questions posed in the Introduction to the book: 'Does terrorism work in liberal societies?' and 'What are the consequences of political violence?' Both questions find expression in the context of managing the past in a narrative moulded to social taste, one that is adapted and 'comfortable' in the face of the bitter truth (Levi 1989, 30). Basque society has opted for the 'ethical thesis', centred on the will to recompose a political community fragmented by terrorism, without developing a deeper understanding of what happened in the past. The result would be the absence of a democratic memory and the formal coexistence of those who previously opposed each other. That would enable memory and responsibilities to fade with time; the history of terrorism in this last half-century would become one more 'cycle of violence' among those suffered by the Basque Country (basically the same as in any other place in Western Europe). Indeed, there would be neither narrative, nor victors, nor vanquished, nor 'flesh-and-blood' victims. Nor history, nor the will that this latter should serve to build a different future on the basis of the recognition and knowledge of what happened as something that was not fatal but meaningful. The urgency of the desire for a consolidated peace could lead Basque society to make that choice. The significance would lie in the principles accepted, more than in the play of words. Nor would it be the only society to have had recourse to burying or forgetting the past. Its community vocation forces it to adopt a uniform attitude towards what happened. It is the only way of being singular. Hence the temptation to renounce a narrative of the past that reminds it of what it is not.

The constant references to Northern Ireland that appear in the text also enable us to see the existing parallels regarding the policies of managing the past. Although terrorism developed on a very different basis in the two places, in both Basque Country and Northern Ireland the experience affected broad sectors of the population, either as active agents or as bystanders. In this respect, the differences with other contemporary European terrorisms are evident and influence the question of the various after-effects in society. At the end of the 1960s, Western Europe was the scenario for the emergence and revitalisation of terrorism. But while in some cases these were movements without great social depth, others did indeed have such depth. The former would include the Red Brigades in Italy or the Baader-Meinhof in Germany, while the latter would include ETA in Spain or the different types of terrorism in Northern Ireland. This has given rise to different historiographical and commemorative treatments. Where there was no social support, a narrative has been made of this phenomenon without need for reconciliation, a truthful narrative as there was no need for social consolation. On the contrary, where there was an active or passive involvement of the population in terrorism, as in the second case, the narrative has been conditioned by an ahistorical demand that places social reunion before confronting the past in all its crudity.

But facing that temptation of a 'soft' narrative, which in the Basque Country involves diluting the importance of ETA into an amalgam of different classes of violence, there is the testimony of the victims. With their experiences the victims remind us of what happened. They ask that this should not be forgotten, that what happened, their trauma, should serve as a moral lesson and also as history. That is why they are uncomfortable for the public powers. The voice of the victims of terrorism is an ethical responsibility for society and also for historians, who should ensure that there is no forgetting (Spiegel 2014, 175). If not, what Primo Levi warned us about will occur:

> It is not licit to forget, nor is it licit to be silent. If we are silent, who will speak? Certainly not those responsible and their accomplices. If our testimony is lacking, in the near future the feats of Nazi bestiality, due to their very enormity, might be relegated to the world of legends. It is, therefore, necessary to speak.
>
> (Levi 2010, 30)

Notes

1 Police violence in the transition served to 'balance' the perception of ETA's terrorism. From 1969 to 1986 it was responsible for 73 deaths in the Basque Country (at checkpoints, repression of demonstrations, altercations, excesses, etc.). The worst years were from 1975 to 1979 (Pérez and Carnicero 2008, 15). Other sources raise the figure to 94 between 1960 and 2013 (Carmena 2013, 14).
2 According to Novick (2007, 44), 'The use of the word "community" has become standard in recent decades, but it is a term of art – of aspiration or of exhortation, not of description'.
3 A research team from the Basque public university that conducts referential periodical surveys on Basque society.
4   Due to its prolongation in time, its goal of political imposition, its perpetuating itself after the Transition and the general amnesty, due to the sociopolitical accompaniment on which it could count and, above all, due to the gravity and intensity of the balance of human and irreparable damage caused, the violence of ETA requires an express evaluation of its injustice, especially the unjust damage caused to victims and their families. This is the position that is called for by the ethical ground on the basis of the principle of responsibility in questions of critically reviewing the past.

       (Secretaría 2013b, 10)

5 Zabarte, 17 murders, a 30-year prison sentence: 'I have not murdered anyone; I have executed. For me the state is the terrorist, it is what forced ETA to take a series of decisions' (*El Mundo*, 21 October 2014).
6 The report of the International Observatory of Studies on Terrorism reached the same conclusion for the public media corporation (9 October 2015).
7 'Nabarralde' and 'Korapiloa' are other similar websites.
8 A summary of the justifying contexts, in Arregi (2015, ch. II); a former terrorist refers to them in Ventura (2015, 255). The rejection of the theory of conflict does not question that there is a historical issue concerning the Basque Country's integration in Spain, but denies that this is the only one and that, in itself, it justifies recourse to violence. On the importance of the decisions of individuals over and above the conditioning factors of their setting, see Juliá (2010); on the 'Basque conflict', see Chapter 9 (this volume) and Molina (2015).
9 The references in the text are to Spanish editions of the works when such editions are available.

Bibliography[9]

Aguilar, Paloma (2008) *Políticas de la memoria y memorias de la política*. Madrid: Alianza.

Aizpeolea, Luis R. (2015) 'En Euskadi se convive sin compartir la memoria'. *El País*, 13 October.

Alonso, Martín (2014) 'La sociedad vasca, el "proceso de paz" y el "tercer espacio"'. *Pueblos. Revista de información y debate* 63, available at: www.revistapueblos.org/?p=18114.

Ardanza, José Antonio (1993) *Conferencias pronunciadas por el lehendakari José Antonio Ardanza: Pacificación y Democracia, Euskadi en el Estado de las autonomías*. Vitoria: Gobierno Vasco.

Arregi, Joseba (2015) *El terror de ETA. La narrativa de las víctimas*. Madrid: Tecnos.

Bauman, Zygmunt (2008) *Does Ethics Have a Chance in a World of Consumers?* Cambridge, MA: Harvard University Press [Spanish edition, Barcelona: Paidós, 2010].

Bernecker, Walter (2015) 'Alemania y su pasado dictatorial. Culturas de la memoria en un país dividido y reunificado'. In *La sociedad vasca ante el terrorismo. Pasado, presente y futuro*, eds Eduardo Mateo and Antonio Rivera, 41–63. Vitoria: Fundación Fernando Buesa.

Bevernage, Berber and Koen Aerts (2009) 'Haunting pasts: Time and historicity as constructed by the Argentine *Madres de Plaza de Mayo* and radical Flemish nationalists'. *Social History* 34: 391–408.

Boraine, Alex (1999) *All Truth is Bitter. A Report of the Visit of Doctor Alex Boraine, Deputy Chairman of the South African Truth and Reconciliation Commission, to Northern Ireland*, available at: http://cain.ulst.ac.uk/issues/victims/docs/alltruthisbitter99.pdf.

Buruma, Ian (1994) *The Wages of Guilt: Memories of War in Germany and Japan*. New York: Plume.

Castells, Luis (2013) 'La historia del terrorismo en Euskadi: ¿entre la necesidad y el apremio?' In *Construyendo memorias. Relatos históricos para Euskadi después del terrorismo*, eds José María Ortiz de Orruño and José Antonio Pérez, 210–244. Madrid: Los Libros de la Catarata.

De la Calle, Luis and Ignacio Sánchez-Cuenca (2011) 'The quantity and quality of terrorism. The DTV dataset', available at: www.march.es/ceacs/proyectos/dtv/.

Euskobarómetro (2013) *November 2013*, avaiable at: www.ehu.eus/euskobarometro.

Euskobarómetro (2015a) *Series temporales, May 2015*, available at: www.ehu.eus/euskobarometro.

Euskobarómetro (2015b) *May 2015*, available at: www.ehu.eus/euskobarometro.

Faulenbach, Bernd (2009) 'La difícil asimilación de las dos Alemanias'. In *La cultura de la memoria. La memoria histórica en España y Alemania*, eds Ignacio Olmos and Nikky Keilholz-Rühl, 147–159. Madrid: Iberoamericana.

Focardi, Filippo (2009) 'El debate sobre la resistencia en Italia: legitimación política y memoria histórica de la primera a la segunda República'. In *El Estado y la memoria. Gobiernos y ciudadanos frente a los traumas de la historia*, ed. Ricard Vinyes, 249–291. Barcelona: RBA.

Fusi, Juan Pablo (2003) *La patria lejana. El nacionalismo en el siglo XX*. Madrid: Taurus.

Groppo, Bruno (2002) 'Memoria y olvido del pasado nazista en la Alemania de la segunda posguerra'. *Memoria. Revista Mensual de Política y Cultura* 164: 26–32.

Hackett, Claire and Bill Rolston (2009) 'The burden of memory: Victims, storytelling and resistance in Northern Ireland'. *Memory Studies* 2: 355–376.

Ignatieff, Michael (1998) *The Warrior's Honour. Ethnic War and the Modern Conscience.* New York: Metropolitan Books [Spanish edition, Madrid: Taurus, 1999].

Instituto de Historia Social 'Valentín de Foronda' (2013) *Aportaciones a la propuesta de Plan de Paz y Convivencia 2013–16.* Vitoria, available at: www.ehu.eus/documents/ 1687243/2126107/Aportaciones+Plan+de+Paz+2+0.pdf.

Instituto Vasco de Criminología (2014) *Proyecto de investigación de la tortura en Euskadi entre 1960 y 2010. Informe preliminar.* Vitoria, available at: www.parlamento. euskadi.net/irud/10/00/026964.pdf.

Jaspers, Karl (2012) *Die Schuldfrage. Von der Politischen Hoffnung Deustchlands.* München: Piper [Spanish edition, Barcelona: Paidós, 1998].

Judt, Tony (2005) *Postwar. A History of Europe since 1945.* New York: Penguin Books [Spanish edition, Madrid: Taurus, 2006].

Judt, Tony (2012) *Thinking the Twentieth Century.* New York: Penguin Books [Spanish edition, Madrid: Taurus, 2012].

Juliá, Santos (2010) '¿Culturas o estrategias? Notas sobre la violencia política en la España reciente'. In *Violencia política. Historia, memoria y víctimas*, eds Antonio Rivera and Carlos Carnicero, 167–190. Madrid: Maia.

Levi, Primo (1989) *I sommersi e i salvati.* Torino: Einaudi [Spanish edition, Barcelona: El Aleph, 2006].

Levi, Primo (2010) *Vivir para contar. Escribir tras Auschwitz.* Barcelona: Alpha.

López, Raúl (2015) *Informe Foronda. Los efectos del terrorismo en la sociedad vasca.* Madrid: Los Libros de la Catarata.

Mata, José M. (2005) 'Terrorism and nationalist conflict. The weakeness of democracy in the Basque Country'. In *The Politics of Contemporary Spain*, ed. Sebastian Balfour, 81–105. New York and London: Routledge.

Mate, Reyes (2009) *La herencia del olvido. Ensayos en torno a la razón compasiva.* Madrid: Errata Naturae.

McGrattan, Cillian (2012) 'Moving on: The politics of shared society in Northern Ireland'. *Studies in Ethnicity and Nationalism* 12: 172–189.

McGrattan, Cillian (2013) *Memory, Politics and Identity. Haunted by History.* London: Palgrave.

Miralles, José (2016) *Los discursos sobre el final del terrorismo de ETA en el País Vasco. Aplicación de los modelos de Entman y Cohen al análisis de prensa escrita entre 2011 y 2014.* Doctoral thesis, Universidad del País Vasco.

Molina, Fernando (2015) 'El conflicto vasco. Relatos de historia, memoria y nación'. In *El peso de la identidad. Mitos y ritos de la historia vasca*, eds Fernando Molina and José Antonio Pérez, 181–223. Madrid: Marcial Pons.

Montero, Manuel (2014) *Voces vascas. Diccionario de uso.* Madrid: Tecnos.

Novick, Peter (1999) *The Holocaust in American Life.* Boston, MA: Houghton Mifflin [Spanish edition, Madrid: Marcial Pons, 2007].

Pérez, José Antonio (2015) 'El incómodo pasado del País Vasco. Historia, memoria e imposturas'. *Anatomía de la Historia*, available at: http://anatomiadelahistoria. com/2015/10/el-incomodo-pasado-del-pais-vasco-historia-memoria-e-imposturas/.

Pérez, José Antonio and Carlos Carnicero (2008) 'La radicalización de la violencia política durante la Transición en el País Vasco. Los años de plomo'. *Historia del Presente* 12: 111–128.

Rivera, Antonio (2015) 'La historización del terrorismo: el *Informe Foronda*'. *Revista de Libros*, October, available at: www.revistadelibros.com/discusion/la-historizacion-del-terrorismo-el-informe-foronda.

Robin, Régine (2009) 'El nuevo devenir victimario de Alemania'. In *El Estado y la memoria*, ed. Ricard Vinyes, 211–248. Barcelona: RBA.

Roth, Michael S. (2011) *Memory, Trauma, and History. Essays on Living with the Past.* New York: Columbia University Press.

Rousso, Henry (1987) *Le síndrome de Vichy, 1944–1987.* Paris: Seuil.

Rousso, Henry (1992) *Vichy. L'événement, la mémoire, l'histoire.* Paris: Gallimard.

Ruiz, José María (2011) *La sociedad vasca ante el final de ETA.* Bilbao: Hika Ateneo.

Santarén, Enrique (2015) 'La memoria, el nuevo "conflicto"'. *Deia*, 11 January.

Secretaría General para la Paz y la Convivencia (2013a) *Propuesta Plan de Paz y Convivencia 2013–16. Un objetivo de encuentro social.* Vitoria: Gobierno Vasco.

Secretaría General para la Paz y la Convivencia (2013b) *Plan de Paz y Convivencia 2013–16. Un objetivo de encuentro social.* Vitoria: Gobierno Vasco.

Simmel, Georg (1950) 'The stranger'. In *The Sociology of Georg Simmel*, ed. Kurt Wolff, 402–408. New York: the Free Press.

Snyder, Timothy (2015) *Black Earth: The Holocaust as History and Warning.* New York: Tim Duggan Books.

Spiegel, Gabrielle (2014) 'The future of the past. History, memory and the ethical imperatives of writing history'. *Journal of the Philosophy of History* 8: 149–179.

Stabili, María Rosaria (2012) 'El pasado incómodo en Latinoamérica: guerra, persecución, reconciliación. Tratamiento histórico-comparativo. El caso chileno'. In *Memoria de guerra y cultura de paz en el siglo XX. De España a América, debates para una historiografía*, ed. Lourdes Fernández Prieto, 129–137. Gijón: Trea.

Tabet, Xavier (2015) 'Resistencia y revisionismo en Italia'. In *El pasado en construcción, Revisionismos históricos en la historiografía contemporánea*, eds Carlos Forcadell, Ignacio Peiró and Mercedes Yusta, 207–230. Zaragoza: Institución Fernando el Católico.

Todorov, Tzvetan (2000) *Mémoire du mal, tentation du bien.* Paris: Robert Laffont [Spanish edition, Barcelona: Península, 2002].

Traverso, Enzo (2007) *À feu et à sang. De la guerre civile européene 1914–1945.* Paris: Éditions Stock [Spanish edition, Valencia: PUV, 2009].

Ventura, Borja (2015) *Guztiak.* Libros.com, online.

Voegelin, Eric (1999) *Hitler and the Germans.* Columbia: University of Missouri Press.

Von Weizsäcker, Richard (1985) *Speech in the Bundestag on 8 May 1985 during the Ceremony Commemorating the 40th Anniversary of the End of War in Europe and of National-Socialist Tyranny.* Office of the Bundespräsident (ret.) Richard von Weizsäcker.

Zubero, Imanol (2012) 'Violencia, Política e Identidad'. *Constelaciones. Revista de Teoría Crítica* 4: 325–341.

Zulaika, Joseba (1988) *Basque Violence: Metaphor and Sacrament.* Reno: University of Nevada Press.

11 Basque violence in the international academy[1]

Francisco Javier Caspistegui

Introduction

On my way home from Oxford, in 2003, the few pounds left in my pocket led me to a book stand in Heathrow. Browsing through the bestsellers, I found *The Basque History of the World* by Mark Kurlansky, and decided this was a good way to use up the pounds. Reading it showed me an idealised vision of the Basque world and led me to reflect on how what has occurred in the Basque Country since the 1950s had been dealt with, with special emphasis on violence and its consequences in the academic and intellectual world. In fact, Kurlansky himself, when asked why Basque history might be of interest to Americans, replied:

> Because assimilation is one of the most important subjects in America. Basque country is the reverse melting pot – let's all be together, work together, but let's not melt. The great lesson of the Basques is that if you preserve your culture, you are a people.
>
> (Adams 1999, 207)

On the one hand, Basqueness worked like an inverted mirror and, on the other, its peculiarity made it an example of familiar exoticism.

Although the vision of the other has been a deep-rooted means of analysis in the social sciences, particularly since the development of culturalism, its continuing interest demonstrates the importance given to other people's perspectives as a means of constructing one's own identity. In the case of Spain there have been many authors who have analysed, for example, the British presence in Iberia, emphasising the changing attitudes during the Peninsular War, which broke with the stereotypes linked to the age-old conflict between the two monarchies. The nineteenth century opened the gates of the Pyrenees to some 'impertinent curious' travellers during their journeys in Spain, confirmed some clichés and created others. In this way they wished to see themselves reflected in an inverted mirror, as their highly prejudiced observation of Spain simply confirmed the extravagance of others and their own normality. This was quite a common attitude for the time, and they sought to confirm pre-existing visions as a means of strengthening their own positions. Even more so as Spain in the nineteenth and part of the twentieth centuries still offered accessible exoticism, within reach of observations forged in the erudition of the century of history and nationalism. Thus were created the tools for the comprehension of these 'others' who were moving closer thanks to the advances of technology and had an evident political value as they represented both the friend and the enemy.

This is also the case for the Basque Country, because, as Leoné and MacClancy state (2008, 10), 'it is partly (but still precisely) because foreigners have perceived and underlined the supposed differences and peculiarities of the Basques that they can claim to exist'. Observations of what being Basque is have tended to emphasise its singularity, both inside and outside Spain, and pointed out variable perceptions which have depended as much on the circumstances in which they were seen as on the moments when they were useful. And although the central core of the observations on the Basque territory has continued to be relatively stable, the perspective from which they were seen has varied in accordance with the circumstances and the moment, but without affecting this essential core. Indeed, in the description which the North made of the South as a geographical position, but above all as a global characterisation, one of the omnipresent elements was violence. Most of the travellers who visited Spain in the nineteenth century, and even in the first few decades of the twentieth century, confirmed at every step that the South represented by the Peninsula contained such oriental characteristics as cruelty and fanaticism. The Basque Country was the North of this peninsular South, but just the same it was still the South for the British.

In a nineteenth-century context which attempted to define what was shared by all those who fit into the designation of a nation, the collective psychology and the specific idiosyncrasies were part of the object of attention of the ever more numerous disciples of the social sciences, but with one distinctive feature: that of fossilising the characters at the time of observation. A timeless way of looking at the stereotype was established, tending towards the essential and fully operational, particularly in the area of the new political sciences, as in every case they attempted to refine scientific, supposedly objective, study. The more or less poetic definitions of the profile of each country attempted to enclose the essence of a whole by avoiding the universal in order to stress the particular. But leaving aside their contradictions, these formulas spread and showed a lasting efficiency, offering arguments that were the basis for the comprehension of peoples and nations.

The Basque nineteenth century offered arguments for those who sought particular characteristics in this geographical area, and awakened growing attention towards everything to do with language and customs, following the tradition of the Romantics towards what is different. Considering Basqueness as an exotic trait within a greater exotic world increased interest in it and in its singularities. However, except for some specific studies, the difference soon became included within the characteristics of a prototypical South in which Basqueness was limited to a few nuances. When Norman Lewis reached the frontier at Irun in 1934, what he saw, despite his critical attitude, matched an image in which the distinguishing component barely appeared. When speaking about the food, the baggage porters or the frontier taxis, he said: 'If it is Oriental Sensations that you have come in search of, you are by this time sated' (Lewis 1935, 50). Along with the global stereotypes about Spain, affirmations were added about the ancestral pacifism of the Basques, who were condemned to a fatalism that was imposed and eternally present. Thus, the post-war Basque nationalists 'are the children of a century and a half of civil wars and symbolic violence' (Llera *et al.* 1993, 106), and Cameron Watson (2003, 320) stated that ETA 'emerged as the product of historical experience in Euskal Herria'. With even greater certainty, John Hollyman (1976, 231–232) stated:

> The war and the destruction of Guernika [*sic*], the repression of the early years of the Franco régime and the continued oppression of legitimate national aspirations have all served to politicize an already socially responsive Basque nation. In the search for new and effective ideas after years of such oppression, it is not surprising that a young movement should have gradually been drawn towards violence via direct action and rejection of the State apparatus.... ETA was inevitable; but the question remains, does it serve a purpose, can it survive, is it good for the Basques as a whole? It has served and continues to serve a purpose in Spain as a means of drawing attention to the perennial problem of Basque nationalism, so easily forgotten. In the process, it helps to underline Franco's rule throughout Spain as oppressive and reactionary. ETA has inspired an admiration for its Robin Hood tactics and the way it has dealt directly with problems that normally would have taken years to resolve, a surgical solution that can only improve a malignant political situation.

Not only did he establish continuity in time, but also full justification of ETA's action against the dictatorship on the basis of its roots in the past. This teleology of violence, in its most academic reading, seemed to be the only possible outcome within a situation of permanent conflict, leading to an unfathomable pessimism, to the inevitability of violence as a distinguishing mark, as the inevitable identification of the essential otherness. Recognising the existence of a Basque problem was used to show a failed model for national construction to those who sought to strengthen their own routes for the integration of the nation-state, particularly when we take into account that, in the English-speaking world, the fundamental interest in what is Basque appeared primordially in the 1970s. In short, are we looking at an interpretation in a presentist key of the inevitability of the violence in the Basque Country? How did violence become the distinguishing mark of Basque political culture? A primary response would deal with the process of cultural construction in English-speaking academia, particularly in the 1980s and 1990s, beginning with foundations which date back to the nineteenth century at least, which, with the passage of time, changed and adapted to the diverse circumstances of their time.[2]

Foundations of a construction

Although the love of all things Basque dates back to the nineteenth century, it was merely one page in the discovery of distinctive features which Romanticism encouraged; an example of this is the sonnet penned by Wordsworth in 1810 in honour of the Tree of Guernica, within the context of the struggle against Napoleon, who, for the British writer, was the incarnation of all dictators. Within this framework, Guernica was one of the symbols of tyrannised freedom:

> Those lofty-minded Lawgivers shall meet,
> Peasant and lord, in their appointed seat,
> Guardians of Biscay's ancient liberty.

(Wordsworth 1837, 229)

Shortly afterwards, British public opinion was split regarding the two sides at war in Spain: the Whigs with the Liberals and the Tories supporting the Carlists – basically focusing on the Basque provinces:

> Supporters of Don Carlos [Carlists] identified him as a chieftain of a lost race whose relatively small population and confined geography belied the debt Europe owed to a primitive people. It was a reversion to Robert Southey's emotional bond with a savage but still pure Spain.

(Howarth 2007, 52–53)

It was easy to find parallels between the Carlists in the Basque Country and the British members of certain international Celtic groups, thus contributing to a local interpretation of external events. An anonymous pamphlet from that time stated: 'The Carlistas were the descendants of free forefathers, who under the hallowed oak of Guernica, first taught to enslaved Europe the lesson of liberty' (Howarth 2007, 53). Zumalacárregui's followers in the islands saw him as a leader supported by warriors who advanced to the tune of olden national ballads ('whose bravery was legendary', which was still being repeated in 1939: The unknown diplomat 1939, 60); they were defenders of ancient liberties, which both the Whigs and the Tories accepted as their own.

As the century passed, this exhilarating curiosity about the discovery became an ever more important object for science and analysis, the medium for the creation or consolidation of the social sciences. However, the uncertain definition of many of the objectives meant that these fledgling disciplines became an area for apparently scientific inventive confabulation, such as racism cloaked by the *fin-de-siècle* dominant positivism. By then, within Spanish liberal nationalism, Basque was the paradigm for the unwillingness to accept nationalisation, the exception to the general itinerary, the atavism which, in the early years of the Second Republic, made people refer to going back to the caverns or a Vatican-style Gibraltar, although it was also described as an oasis (as by Mañé i Flaquer), which lent strength to the idea of isolation and exceptionality.

In 1908, a classic of the description of the other, *The Soul of Spain* by Havelock Ellis, spoke of the Basques as

> the primitive Iberians of Berber affinity.... Their isolation on the flanks of the Pyrenees has enabled the Basques to retain their ancient language and

some of their primitive institutions ... but the Iberians still, it is probable, form the fundamental material in the population all over Spain.

(Ellis 1937, 31)

In these words he expressed the Basque-Iberian theory which was still in fashion when it was written, according to which the Basques were the first inhabitants of the Peninsula, and were later uprooted and moved to the place where they were described. Despite the differences, Ellis offered an image of what is Basque with similarities with what is Spanish. He reminisced about his first journey to Spain towards the end of the nineteenth century, and compared it to virgin territory:

here was a land that, in spite of a taste for various modern devices, had yet in fundamentals escaped modernity and preserved a medieval aspect. The ravages of the capitalistic industrial system were scarcely visible, which meant that here we were free from the vulgarisation of modern life.

(Ellis 1937, vii)

He presented this general image of Spain when speaking of the Basques, and more specifically of Bilbao:

The Basques are honest, serious, industrious, humane, home-loving people ... but they lack the sense for the external side of life, and tenacious as they are of their ancient rights and privileges, they seem to possess no strong impulse to assert themselves in the visible splendour or urban life. The Basque is the man of the mountain village, and Bilbao is nothing more than an overgrown mountain village.... [I]n Bilbao all the signs of a vigorous urban community's collective social life – great parks and splendid churches, markets, town-halls, museums, theatres, music-halls, cafés – all the things in which Barcelona reveals her abounding splendour and vitality, are either so insignificant that they scarcely catch out attention.

(Ellis 1937, 275–276)

Peculiar, different, but at the same time part of a context which, even in their most industrial city, showed an essence on the edges of the modernity that was the distinctive characteristic of the soul of Spain. Opinions like this are what forged the image that is such a good summary of the work by Rodney Gallop (1930, 283):

The Basques are infinitely precious, not as some inexplicable exception among races, but as a living museum of human history where one may study all that is left of an older Europe, vanished elsewhere, but lingering yet awhile in this quiet corner of the Pyrenees.

The British expert in Basque studies was in no doubt about the exoticism of a stronghold which had been preserved to bear witness to times that no longer existed. The overwhelming modern world still allowed for the survival of a certain primordial golden age, an orient with all its exotic features, including a consubstantial fanatical violence. It was the inverted mirror for reality, the search for nearby paradises in which to escape from the heartaches of a place where one did not belong, as did Gerald Brenan in the Granada village, Yegen. The ethnicist tone of these approaches to Basque gave strength to the idea of the search for radical otherness and the idealisation of travel and discovery, even though texts like those of Gallop searched not so much for the science as for the description of what was discovered and confronted it with what was already known, as when the above-mentioned Norman Lewis arrived in San Sebastian during the VIII Basque Week in 1934 and decided to capitalise on it: 'We felt that we owed it to ourselves to take this opportunity of getting to know something about the Basques' (1935, 69).

Basque individuality was established in the English-speaking world through a considerable tradition of knowledge, which emphasised above all the linguistic, folklore and ethnic characteristics. Implicitly, this image gave recognition to the existence of this European singularity which had been achieved through resistance to the imposition of the innovations of liberalism, either political – thus including Carlism – or economic, with the arrival of industrialisation and the resulting immigration and loss of cultural references; in short, the loss of authenticity. There was an additional important element in this perception: the peaceful character of the Basques allowed for the adoption of violence as a form of defence when facing the challenge of said innovations; this recourse was not at all exceptional, as it was part of the Basque ethnic essence. Although it was considered a form of resistance, from an English-speaking perspective violence was an integral part of the essential characteristics of the South, and the Basque Country was a natural part of this.

The Spanish Civil War (1936–1939) helped strengthen these perceptions and became one of the central definers in the appraisal of the Basques outside the Peninsula, an event that strengthened many images which had existed since the early nineteenth century. The British were biased towards the Basques: 'The view was expressed, at the highest level in government, that the Basques were a moderate, pious and hard-working people who had managed to avoid the excesses of the rest of Spain and wanted only to be left alone' (Buchanan 2007, 6). This early profile, solidly established, was reinforced by the journalist George Steer who was very involved with the autonomous Basque government of José Antonio Aguirre and managed to create an intense feeling of solidarity with the Basques by means of his chronicles on the bombing of Guernica (which Picasso converted into a universal reference point), and on other episodes from the northern front (Steer 1938). A clear reflection of this school of thought is the poem by Cecil Day Lewis, *The Nabara*, dedicated to the battle between several armed Basque fishing boats – including the *Nabarra* – and the rebel cruiser *Canarias*, which takes its details from Steer's book:

> Of simple lives: they coveted never an epic part;
> But history's hand was upon them and hewed an everlasting

Image of freedom out of their rude and stubborn heart.
... the men, descendants
Of those Iberian fathers, the inquiring ones who would go
Wherever the sea-ways lead: a pacific people, slow
To feel ambition, loving their laws and their independence –
Men of the Basque country, the Mar Cantabrico.

(Lewis 2006, 99–100)[3]

The image of the Basques is summed up in their simplicity, freedom, independence and love for law, their peaceful character and even the above-mentioned Basque-Iberian theory, although, as Roger Collins (1986, 2) pointed out, this latter point would mean establishing links with all the peninsular peoples, a fact that the nationalist sectors would find it difficult to accept. But it could also be interpreted as treachery by Spain against its Basque ancestors, even though this theory had already been defeated and was the reflection of British opinion on the whole of the Spanish peoples which had existed since the Napoleonic wars. Epic tales, resistance and freedom (characteristics which were so habitual in the description of Spaniards between 1808 and 1814), in the 1937 context were presented as a model for the British themselves, and a wake-up call regarding the future:

Men of the Basque country, the Mar Cantabrico.
Simple men who asked of their life no mythical splendour,
The loved its familiar ways so well that they preferred
In the rudeness of their heart to die rather than to surrender.

(Lewis 2006, 109)

The successive images and the use made of them reflected an interest in the Basques originating in the starting point of the observers and destined, in many cases, to respond to internal questions and concerns. The orientalist perspective, applied to the inhabitants of the extreme west of the Pyrenees, embodied a distancing which, thanks to its contraposition, emphasised the virtues of the observer and his superiority. But simultaneously it was used as a tool for observation and analysis, given the academic aspirations that guided it, and as an instrument of power, as it even justified intervention as a means of leading those who abandoned civilisation back to it.

Spanish leviathan and violence

The observation of the Basques in the nineteenth century proved their otherness, especially in the reiteration of violence. The interpretation might vary, depending on the interests of the observation; it might even change the justification or the morality of the struggle undertaken. It almost always dealt with faraway events, the cruel tale of customs and actions which were understood to be an integral part of a way of being. The search for the spirit of the people turned into the analysis of the collective psychology, but in every case what was sought was what was distinctive and characteristic, the soul, according to Ellis' title. And within the soul, some traits were as inevitable as the geography. In the South or Orient represented by Spain, Basque might have its own nuances; however, for English-speakers it was still part of the same grouping. And one of the most notable characteristics of the oriental genre, whether Spanish or Basque, was violence. An approach to Basque reality meant accepting the normality of this, although it might be qualified depending on the emphasis given to the exoticism of the Basques or the Spaniards.[4] In the twentieth century then, particularly after the Civil War, this vision became academic, in an attempt to formalise the representation of the other in a firm and neutral scientific manner (Molina 2014).

Moreover, the vision of the Basques after 1939 was indelibly marked by the Franco dictatorship which, to foreign eyes, became the quintessential other. In the poem quoted above, the Basques were fishing in freedom 'until the morning they found the leviathan in their net' (Lewis 2006, 100). This radical otherness was used to recover the models which, in the nineteenth century, told tales of idyllic freedoms in contrast with the modernity that was prospering in much of Western Europe.[5] The Cantabrian *Orientals* were most clearly defined in the English-speaking mirror, and were easily recognisable against the background of a dictatorship repudiated due to its proximity to the loathsome fascist systems, although this recovery of the Basque image as a synonym for freedom appeared much later in reference to a most serious occurrence: the trial in Burgos in December 1970 of 16 ETA members, the starting point for public and also academic interest in Basque matters (Sullivan 1988, 91, 111–134).

The majority of the analyses and attention to the Basque world began with the trial and the arguments of those who were being prosecuted, which were publicised by the international media, and with the curiosity brought about by the general situation reflected in the window opened by the trial. A good example is Robert Clark, who visited the Basque Country shortly before Franco died and stated: 'I returned from that stay convinced that there was much about the Basque struggle that needed to be related and explained to an American public largely ignorant of developments there' (Clark 1984, xiii). Moreover, the existence of simultaneous processes of independence and the conflicts deriving from ethnic assertions and their political consequences added an extra element of attraction to the Basque case. At the peak of the modernization theory, the Basque situation offered special features that made its study attractive; one example was the absence of underdevelopment which claimed the need for economic progress as a precondition for any later political option. The prime movers of the academic perspective on the Basque situation were, above all, political scientists and sociologists, those who had also developed the theory of modernisation as a global explanation. The important point is that modernisation was not only an economic process but also included a clear political component. The final result was a liberal democratic system with a free market economy based on industrialisation and urbanisation. Basque society towards the end of the 1960s and into the early 1970s had reached high levels of industrialisation and its intense urbanisation was accompanied by considerable immigration which had occurred in the final quarter of the nineteenth and mid-twentieth centuries. In this context the need arose to interpret the increase in violence, which was particularly evident within the framework of the above-mentioned trial in 1970.[6]

For the analysts to a certain extent, the problem was that the subject was new. In the English-speaking bibliography on Basque matters, the main object of attention was the rural, traditional world, unconnected to the modern industrial and urban world. Predictably, many of the texts begin by situating the Basques in a historical perspective and, on this basis, identify their distinguishing features, particularly the language, with, in general, references to their ethnicity, and go on to describe the situation mainly after the end of the Civil War (Woodworth 2008, 171–188). Until well into the 1970s, French sources of information were used, and their interest in the Basque situation reflected their own national singularity; other resources were mainly the few authors who, in the absence of a Basque university with social and human disciplines, had reflected on the past generally from a more or less Basque nationalist perspective, as is the case of *Ortzi* (Francisco Letamendia, *Historia de Euskadi: el nacionalismo vasco y ETA*, 1975) or *Beltza* (Emilio López Adán, *Nacionalismo vasco y clases sociales*, 1976; *El nacionalismo vasco: 1876–1936*, 1976) (Heiberg 1989, x).

One of the first analysis was by the political scientist Kenneth Medhurst for the London Minority Rights Group in 1972; this institution wished to publicise the problems affecting minorities and solve them, thus avoiding their degeneration into intense conflict and, finally, to improve international understanding of human rights. Medhurst focused on the reality of the moment, although the persistence of well-rooted older images was clear, as proven by the cover of the report which showed a photograph of an old Basque peasant against a rural background. There was a clear paradox between the coexistence of an inherited image and a very different reality:

> many Basques feel that they are living in an occupied country with the security forces as their enemies and the local upper classes cast in the role of quislings.... [C]ontinuous attacks on the local culture and the very visible police presence give many Basques a real sense of forming an oppressed minority.
>
> (Medhurst 1972, 21)

Barbara Probst spoke in the same vein when she wrote the Prologue for the English edition of *Operación Ogro* by Eva Forest, dedicated to the assassination of the president of the government and Franco's right-hand man, Luis Carrero Blanco, in December 1973: 'The repression of the Basques by Franco and the Civil Guard had been brutal; there was a constant cycle of attack, resistance, torture, and murder' (Probst 1983, 92).[7]

Although the violence was part of the background, in practice it was limited almost exclusively to government repression. We must not forget that the dictatorial character (or authoritarian character, according to the political scientist

Juan José Linz, who also considers the Basque case from the American academic world), and the link with fascism, were an essential part of the set of exclusions by the new left in the 1960s and 1970s.[8] In the novel by Margaret Shedd against the backdrop of the Burgos trial, the police were called the 'gristapo', presumably a mixture between the grey uniforms of the Armed Police and the frightening German Gestapo. Moreover, this police force laid part of the blame for the Basque situation on the Jews (Shedd 1974, 30–31). In the plot of the novel, a connection was established between the Basques in the Battle of Roncesvalles – where they defeated the army of Charlemagne in the year 778 – and the ETA members, including the *gudaris* (Basque nationalist soldiers) in the Civil War, all of whom were guided by the defence of liberty against oppression. The violence was defensive, although in the more academic texts it implicitly appears as a reaction against the snares of modernisation, including the not always successful national integration process of states. The very image on the cover of Medhurst's text showed the reaction against modern threats, the peace and freedom of the rural world challenged by a wide range of innovations against which a reaction was comprehensible and justifiable. Although this explanation was the object of diverse criticism (as in Zirakzadeh 1991), it was part of a generalised interpretation which, at least until the end of Francoism in 1975, made the actions of ETA more acceptable. A good example of this is the text which Margaret Shedd (1974, 114) attributes to the diary of one of the ETA characters in her novel:

> Violent action has two contradictory sides. What is a terrorist? Is it the man who believes in violent action in order to instill the terror which will force his will or his program? If this is so then Franco and all those who support him are terrorists.
>
> But that is not the way it is in this hypocritical world. Suppose a man has made armed resistance in the name of a high patriotic ideal, and in this war (because we are in war) suppose that man kills a civil guard. He is immediately called a cowardly assassin and a terrorist. But let us imagine that he is leading a group and in a bold coup he defeats and destroys 1,000 civil guards. The next day the world press will be talking about an army of liberation and about a general, the same terrorist who in the beginning killed one civil guard.

The explanation of Basqueness revealed the difficulty of integrating it into the prevailing theories and the need for the provision of new forms of understanding for a case that showed such complexity even at an interpretive level. The political scientist Milton Da Silva began his 1975 article by stating the need to overcome previous proposals; for example, that the ethnic conflict could be explained in terms of economic inequality or class structure, or that the increase in mobilisation and communication had an integrating effect on societies which were ethnically heterogeneous. He added, '[i]t would indeed be difficult to attribute the rise of Basque nationalism simply to the lack of democratic freedoms or to political oppression' (Da Silva 1975, 228 and 248), given that it had emerged during a period of some democracy like the Restoration, and had reached its peak during the democratic regime of the Second Republic. All of this showed that there was a high level of specificity in the Basque case which required particular comprehension, increasing the pre-existing particularist perception, legitimising much of the prior perspectives and granting them scientific legitimacy. Da Silva referred to a phrase by Clifford Geertz which insisted on this need to particularise analysis: 'political modernization "does not do away with ethnocentrism, it merely modernizes it"' (Da Silva 1975, 251). In fact, although the American historian Stanley Payne accepted the idea that reaction to the threat of modernity was the reason for the emergence of a 'discontent and proto-revolutionary class' which came together in ETA, he also stated that modernisation might exacerbate the national consciousness (Payne 1974, 281, 293). Indeed, in an earlier article dedicated to the Catalan and Basque nationalisms, he pointed out, '[e]conomic development alone does not necessarily blunt nationalist sentiment' (Payne 1971, 51). For this reason he considered that the virulence of Basque nationalism owed more to the fear of losing their identity than to the strength of political nationalism, an idea with which other authors agree (Payne 1974, 293; González 1974, 356; Hollyman 1976, 215; Medhurst 1982, 257; Collins 1986, 261).

But in addition, a moral sense, either positive or negative, had to be provided for the presence of violence. In general, and not only in political or news media but also in academia – although the tone was evidently different – condemnation of state violence combined with the legitimacy of the violent action carried out by ETA. John Hollyman (1976, 213) echoed the same sentiment: 'Having suffered a repression of both nationality and class, the Basque people had struck back in the name of freedom through ETA to re-assert the independent spirit of the ancient Basque nation, Euskadi, against the Franco regime'.

These viewpoints changed once the Franco regime had ended. The arrival of a democracy in Spain, which accepted the concession of self-government as a necessity, meant that people were hopeful about the finalisation of the conflictive situation which had defined Basque reality since the end of the 1960s. This prospect could also be found in academia, but with considerable reservations during the latter half of the 1970s and even in the 1980s. It is significant that the pre-Civil War anthropological perspective returned to the study of the roots of the violence, particularly as it was at this point that the highest number of victims occurred, thus bringing about a certain amount of rejection towards the dominant political science perspective of earlier years. The apparent paradox of more intense violent action in a democratic regime led to increased attempts to understand a phenomenon for which the anthropological and historical perspective seemed the most suitable, even when both sociology and political science quickly made a recovery. In all of this, as was pointed out by MacClancy (1988, 19), there were vested interests for the observer: 'an attempt to understand Basque nationalism could conceivably make people cast a fresh eye on other problems even closer "to home"'.

Whatever the case, it began with elements which were solidly rooted in visions of what being Basque meant, such as the consubstantial unity between geography and the human community and the 1,000-year continuity of this link

(Woodworth 2002, 17–32, 2008, 1–37). Roger Collins, a specialist in the history of Antiquity and the Middle Ages, stated that its study

> is as much about a region as about a people, but uniquely in Europe this is a case in which the two cannot be separated one from another. The Basques as a people are known in no other geographical context than that of the western Pyrenees, where also they have no clearly discernible predecessors as the human occupants of the region. Thus the study of the land and of its inhabitants is at the same time the study of the continuity of a culture.
>
> (Collins 1986, xi)

This, he recognised, implied political consequences for the present which probably did not occur in any other country. Somewhat contradictorily, given the ethnicity of his argument, he complains about the excesses that may arise from this use of the past (Collins 1986, xi, xii, 1 and 261; see also Ray and Bieter 2015, 243–244). Based on this argument, any power which is broader than the territory itself would appear to be an imposition. In fact, Collins himself pointed out that 'the national historiographical traditions of both Spain and France are often reluctant to consider' Basque singularity (Collins 1986, xi). This is because history was becoming an extremely useful tool, even though its adaptation to the objectives of the present were sought, as it created identity and shaped a sense of belonging, a role in which the media had great influence:

> The nationalist project creates the notion of Basqueness as a relic of the past to be bottled, shelved, tagged and placed in a museum. This creation of ethnicity does not reflect how culture is dynamic and ever changing. Dogmatic adherence to this self-reflective imagery makes the past too precious, by appealing to the emotions and thereby harking back to a period of time when an ideal culture supposedly existed. This creation of a mythical past unifies people in believing in their folk-ness and in turn in a nationalist vision.
>
> (Linstroth 2002, 215)

As a British anthropologist explained when analysing the political culture of the radical Basque nationalist world: 'The culture they manufacture is a modern mix of the present and the past in the present, a continuing construction. Here, marked "cultural" events are appropriated by ideology which, in turn, is judged by political effectiveness' (MacClancy 1988, 18), and part of this was an everyday violence, such as the demonstrations and police charges in the Basque streets in the 1970s and 1980s, or the increase of the *kale borroka* beginning in the 1990s (Ferret 2014), which were interpreted as part of a politically significant reality that showed an anti-model with which to compare the realities of other consolidated democracies, apparently free of such problems.

Outstanding on this point is the work of Robert P. Clark, who, since 1979, has published several books on the Basque Country based on direct observation of the reality, with a first stay in 1973. As it was for travellers in other centuries, contact with reality became a requirement for knowledge and, to a certain extent, knowledge created reality or, at least, allowed the readers to understand it, or, above all, to recognise it in contrast with their own experience and reality. Clark accepted that he had links with Basque nationalism and focused his analysis fundamentally on ETA. Regarding this organisation, he drew attention to the legitimacy it had in confronting the Franco dictatorship, given its violence: 'heroic counter-measures are needed simply in order to survive' (Clark 1979, xii, 1984, xv). Although in his first book he considered that the violence made less sense, in later works he asked if 'the change in regime after Franco's death was sufficient to erode the moral justification for ETA's use of violence', particularly when he declared that 'not a lot has changed since Franco's days' (1984, xv). When asked whether ETA was or was not a terrorist organisation, his answer was that it was not. In his opinion, ETA

> used what some might call terrorist tactics sparingly, perhaps fewer than half a dozen times in its entire history. The record will show that ETA has not killed innocent bystanders indiscriminately but rather has kept its use of violence restrained and under control.
>
> (Clark 1984, xvi)

Although he did not defend violence or terrorism, he did understand that the young Basque people who were referred to as revolutionaries, guerrillas, rebels or insurgents, and given the pressures to which he believed they were subject, said: 'I could not then, and I do not now, condemn the members of ETA for feeling themselves compelled to follow the path of armed struggle, even though I could not approve of some of their acts of indiscriminate violence' (1990, 5). What is of consequence is that it was Clark's works which became the reference point for English-speaking scholars when approaching the Basque question in general and violence in particular.[9]

In any case, by the 1990s, English-speaking feelings towards the ETA actions were changing (Alexander *et al.* 2001; Quiroga 2009); understanding of the resistance against the dictatorship was more distant, although events like the dirty war launched by sectors close to the authorities kept the most radical nationalist arguments alive (Woodworth 2002), as did the images of a Hispanic Orient which strengthened the prejudices of inflexible fanaticism (Clark 1990, 88–92). Academia accepted the existence of a plurality within Basque society which went beyond idyllic visions of a people united in the defence of their freedom (Heiberg 1989, 61), and new theories to explain the violence were outlined, such as the already-mentioned rejection of Cyrus Zirakzadeh's modernisation thesis. Daniele Conversi considered that 'the two most relevant factors for explaining Basque violence are respectively anthropological and political: a lack of shared core values and the repressive action by the part of the state's military forces' (Conversi 1997, 222 and 226–227). The lack of an established culture would lead to the development of violence as an element of cohesion in the absence of other models. We could again wonder if the lack of components, in this case cultural components, could be a reflection of the difference when compared to normalised models, which, for this reason, do not suffer violent conflict, as is the case of Catalonia with which the Basque Country is compared.[10]

As may be seen in the press coverage of the violence in the Basque Country, the references to it as terrorism in certain international media were growing. This was so in the *New York Times* between 1970 and 1985, reaching 64.3 per cent of all references. This figure rose as high as 90.9 per cent between 1986 and 1996, when the ETA activity began to decrease significantly (Zabaleta 1999, 79). Likewise, in *The Economist*, out of a total of 127 references to the Basque Country between 1997 and 2014, a stage with a marked descent in ETA activity prior to the 2011 treaty, and also with a profound change in sensitivity towards terrorist activity following the 2001 and 2004 attacks, the references to the violence still made up 48.8 per cent of the total. The association between what is Basque and violence, after 50 years of being closely related, continued to exist and survived in an age-old image. Indeed, even recently it has been said that, 'the Basque people have struggled for centuries against domination by the Spanish and French governments. Since the 19th century, the Basques have had uniform resistance to that domination' (Spencer and Croucher 2008, 137). Perhaps the innovation is that, since the 1980s, when the involvement of the different French governments against ETA increased, references to oppression by France began to be added.

Conclusion

The explicit violence of ETA disappeared in 2011 and, since then, this past has become not only the object of analysis but of argument. It is a question of establishing the memory of what happened, of constructing a story (Whitfield 2014, 280–292). And in this debate the use of foreign perspectives is of outstanding importance, as may be seen in the report requested from Scensei and Columbia University for *Gure Esku Dago* (2015). What matters in Basque political violence is that the past has played a considerable role in the shaping of the English-speaking perspective on the issue, together with an extremely subjective ethnicist construction. Both of these are soaked in images with roots in a perspective weighed down with the prejudices of a global orientalism adapted to the needs of the culture of origin. Although justified during the Franco regime as a struggle against fascism and the oppression of freedom, the establishment of a democratic system seemed to be a reason for a farewell to arms. However, the strength of the image of a struggle for liberty which had existed at least since the nineteenth century meant that, for decades, a favourable or at least tolerant vision of this violence continued in the press and academic literature in English, thus invalidating the theoretical incompatibility of terrorism and democracy. With a certain simplification of a complex reality, it was apparently accepted that only the full attainment of the nationalist objectives would permit an end to violence; that is, the normalisation of the Basque situation by overcoming the orientalising stereotype which described it. Independence would thus permit the disappearance of a pattern of understanding of Basqueness which had, for a long time, been placed at the same level as Spanish exoticism.

Despite this, the reflections on the Basque case from the perspective of the social sciences have evolved towards the recognition of the worthlessness of violence and the need to appeal to dialogue and the recognition of a plurality far from any unanimity on identity as a means to find solutions, and towards completely banishing a violence which is increasingly seen as a threat even for the attainment of its initial objectives. Continuing with it means the survival of a vision reflected in a statement from Kurlansky's bestseller: 'Everything seemed a little exciting and mysterious in Basqueland' (2000, 2). Maintaining the singularity, outside the context, preserved in the formaldehyde of history, made the Basques 'a mythical people, almost an imagined people' (Kurlansky 2000, 18), and an ideal space for curious visitors eager for authentically different experiences, a theme park for the strange and exotic, a territory in which to uphold ancient struggles against enemies from other times.

Notes

1 This text is part of the project 'Representaciones de la historia en la España contemporánea: políticas del pasado y narrativas de la nación (1808–2012)' (HAR2012–31926).
2 See www.fsancho-sabio.es/html/History.html (accessed 30 October 2015).
3 In line with Steer, the American Robert Clark used the case of the *Nabarra*, and stated, 'reflect in microcosm the refusal of the Basques to give in to the overwhelming pressures of military force, coercion and numbers' (1979, xvi–xvii).
4 For Clark (1979, 125–127), Basque violence was as different as its protagonists, which differentiated it from the 'bloodthirsty character of their neighbours of the south'.
5 This vision has its epitome in the documentary made by Orson Wells in 1955, *The Basque Country*:

> Reflecting the idea of the Basque Country as an oasis that harks back to a simpler time, a conception that formed such a fundamental part of the nationalist vision, this documentary depicts a society that time had left behind and that lived in an idylic bubble, with Basque pelota as the most prominent symbol of this most ancient of European peoples.... This vision resulted in part from the particular image that the Basque nationalists projected of their people and their land as a kind of unspoiled throwback to the Middle Ages.
>
> (De Pablo 2012, 56)

6 A set of reflections on what is modern and its implications in Dipper and Pombeni (2014).
7 See also Conversi (1997, 233).
8 Davydd J. Greenwood stated:

> The actions of the separatists in particular are often reported in the French- and English-language press and are generally given favorable treatment because of the strength of antifascist sentiment in Europe and in the United States. The Basque protest is compared to the Breton and Irish situations and is concerned to be one of the classic cases of ethnic militancy.
>
> (Greenwood 1977, 85)

9 See the harsh review by Louis L. Snyder (1981) of the first of Clark's books, in which he asked him to maintain a certain distance and objectivity.
10 See Miley (2007).

Bibliography

Adams, Susan (1999) 'The wealth of a nation'. *Forbes* 164: 206–207.

Alexander, Yonah, Michael S. Swetnam and Herbert M. Levine (2001) *ETA: Profile of a Terrorist Group*. Ardsley: Transnational Publishers.

Buchanan, Tom (2007) *The Impact of the Spanish Civil War on Britain. War, Loss and Memory*. Brighton: Sussex Academic Press.

Clark, Robert P. (1979) *The Basques: The Franco Years and Beyond*. Reno: University of Nevada Press.

Clark, Robert P. (1984) *The Basque Insurgents. ETA, 1952–1980*. Madison: The University of Wisconsin Press.

Clark, Robert P. (1990) *Negotiating with ETA. Obstacles to Peace in the Basque Country, 1975–1988*. Reno: University of Nevada Press.

Collins, Roger (1986) *The Basques*. Oxford: Blackwell.

Conversi, Daniele (1997) *The Basques, the Catalans and Spain: Alternative Routes to Nationalist Mobilisation*. London: Hurst.

Da Silva, Milton M. (1975) 'Modernization and ethnic conflict: The case of the Basques'. *Comparative Politics* 7: 227–251.

De Pablo, Santiago (2012) *The Basque Nation On-screen. Cinema, Nationalism, and Political Violence*. Reno: University of Nevada Press.

Dipper, Christof and Paolo Pombeni (eds) (2014) *Le ragioni del moderno*. Bolonia: Il Mulino.

Ellis, Havelock (1937) *The Soul of Spain*. London: Constable and Co. (1st edn 1908).

Ferret, Jérôme (2014) 'Young radical nationalists: Prisoners of their own myth? The case of the *Kale Borroka* in the Spanish Basque Country'. *Current Sociology* 62: 1017–1035.

Gallop, Rodney (1930) *A Book of the Basques*. London: Macmillan.

González, Pedro (1974) 'Modern nationalism in old nations as a consequence of earlier state-building: The case of Basque-Spain'. In *Ethnicity and Nation-building: Comparative, International, and Historical Perspectives*, eds Wendell Bell and Walter E. Freeman, 341–373. Beverly Hills, CA: Sage.

Greenwood, Davydd J. (1977) 'Continuity in change: Spanish Basque ethnicity as a historical process'. In *Ethnic Conflict in Western World*, ed. Milton Esman, 81–102. Ithaca, NY: Cornell University Press.

Gure Esku Dago and the Right to Decide. Viewpoints, Challenges and Ways Forward (2015) Scensei and Columbia University, 22 September, available at: www.euskoikaskuntza.org/upload/docs/ged_en.pdf (accessed 16 October 2015).

Heiberg, Marianne (1989) *The Making of the Basque Nation*. Cambridge: Cambridge University Press.

Hollyman, John L. (1976) 'Basque revolutionary separatism: ETA'. In *Spain in Crisis: The Evolution and Decline of the Franco Régime*, ed. Paul Preston, 212–233. New York: Barnes & Noble.

Howarth, David (2007) *The Invention of Spain. Cultural Relations between Britain and Spain 1770–1870*. Manchester: Manchester University Press.

Kurlansky, Mark (2000) *The Basque History of the World*. London: Vintage (1st edn 1999).

Leoné, Santiago and Jeremy MacClancy (eds) (2008) *Imaging the Basques: Foreign Views on the Basque Country*. Donostia: Eusko Ikaskuntza.

Lewis, Cecil D. (2006) *El Nabarra*. Vitoria-Gasteiz: Basarai.

Lewis, Norman (1935) *Spanish Adventure*. New York: Henry Holt.

Linstroth, J.P. (2002) 'The Basque conflict globally speaking: Material culture, media and Basque identity in the wider world'. *Oxford Development Studies* 30: 205–222.

Llera, Francisco, José Manuel Mata and Cynthia L. Irvin (1993) 'ETA: From secret army to social movement: The post-Franco schism of the Basque Nationalist Movement'. *Terrorism and Political Violence* 5: 106–134.

MacClancy, Jeremy (1988) 'The culture of radical Basque nationalism'. *Anthropology Today* 4: 17–19.

Medhurst, Kenneth (1972) *The Basques.* London: Minority Rights Group.

Medhurst, Kenneth (1982) 'Basques and Basque nationalism'. In *National Separatism*, ed. Colin Williams, 235–261. Cardiff: University of Wales Press.

Miley, Thomas J. (2007) 'Against the thesis of the "civic nation": The case of Catalonia in contemporary Spain'. *Nationalism and Ethnic Politics* 13: 1–37.

Molina, Fernando (2014) 'Lies of our fathers: Memory and politics in the Basque Country under the Franco Dictatorship, 1936–68'. *Journal of Contemporary History* 49: 296–319.

Payne, Stanley G. (1971) 'Catalan and Basque nationalism'. *Journal of Contemporary History* 6: 15–51.

Payne, Stanley G. (1974) *El nacionalismo vasco. De sus orígenes a la ETA.* Madrid: Dopesa.

Probst, Barbara (1983) *Short Flights.* New York: Viking Press.

Quiroga, Alejandro (2009) 'The death of the tribe: New studies on the Basque Country'. *European History Quarterly* 39: 503–511.

Ray, Nina M. and John P. Bieter (2015) '"It broadens your view of being Basque": Identity through history, branding, and cultural policy'. *International Journal of Cultural Policy* 21: 241–257.

Shedd, Margaret (1974) *A Silence in Bilbao.* New York: Doubleday.

Snyder, Louis L. (1981) 'Review of Clark, Robert P. (1979) *The Basques: The Franco Years and Beyond*'. *Canadian Review of Studies in Nationalism* 8: 371–372.

Spencer, Anthony T. and Stephen M. Croucher (2008) 'Basque nationalism and the spiral of silence: An analysis of public perceptions of ETA in Spain and France'. *The International Communication Gazette* 70: 137–153.

Steer, George L. (1938) *The Tree of Gernika: A Field Study of Modern War.* London: Hodder & Stoughton.

Sullivan, John (1988) *El nacionalismo vasco radical 1959–1986.* Madrid: Alianza (1st edn 1986).

The unknown diplomat (1939) *Britain in Spain. A Study of the National Government's Spanish Policy.* London: Hamish Hamilton.

Watson, Cameron (2003). *Basque History. Eighteenth Century to the Present.* Reno: University of Nevada.

Whitfield, Teresa (2014) *Endgame for ETA: Elusive Peace in the Basque Country.* Oxford: Oxford University Press.

Woodworth, Paddy (2002) *Dirty War, Clean Hands. ETA, the GAL and Spanish Democracy.* New Haven, CT: Yale University Press.

Woodworth, Paddy (2008) *The Basque Country: A Cultural History.* Oxford: Oxford University Press.

Wordsworth, William (1837) *The Poetical Works of William Wordsworth*, III. London: Edward Moxon.

Zabaleta, Iñaki (1999) 'The Basques in the international press: Coverage by the *New York Times* (1950–1996)'. In *Basque Politics and Nationalism on the Eve of the Millennium*, eds William Douglass, Carmelo Urza, Linda White and Joseba Zulaika (eds.), 68–93. Reno: University of Nevada Press.

Zirakzadeh, Cyrus E. (1991) *A Rebellious People. Basques, Protests, and Politics.* Reno: University of Nevada Press.

Conclusion

Rafael Leonisio, Fernando Molina and Diego Muro

This book analyses ethno-nationalist terrorism in the Basque country and explores how the phenomenon of political violence is remembered. Although ETA appears as the principal historical subject of analysis it is not the only one, as these chapters also deal with the Spanish state and its counter-terrorist strategies, both legal and illegal, as well as Basque society and its complex assimilation of the terrorist experience.

The book is based on the abundant literature published on the Basque case. International scholarship has contributed to this literature by focusing on a series of topics. On the one hand, it has placed the Basque experience of violence in the history of European terrorism and counter-terrorism (Wieviorka 1997; Waldmann 1997; Burleigh 2008) but on the other hand, it has addressed the role played by the processes of political negotiation, typically seeing them as central in the dissolution of terrorist phenomena (Mees 2003; Whitfield 2014). Likewise, scholars have examined radical Basque nationalism as the principal source of support for the terrorist violence that has become strong in a particular 'geography of terror' located in the rural Basque Country (Mansvelt Beck 2005). They have also delved into the causes of the violence, either situating it in the particular history of Basque nationalism and its political conflict with the Spanish state (Sullivan 1988), or rejecting this approach from postmodern perspectives that highlight factors of cultural intimacy (Aretxaga 2005). Finally, some have compared this case of violence with that of Northern Ireland (Irvin 1999): a classic comparison in international studies that typically takes an abstract view of its theoretical and historical limits (Sánchez-Cuenca 2007; Alonso 2011) and which tends to highlight the images of other peninsular nationalisms such as that of Catalonia. The latter is traditionally represented as civic and peaceful while Basque nationalism is perceived as ethnic and violent (Miley 2007, 2–3, 24–25).

These studies have given rise to interpretive proposals that attempt to account for the causes of the violence and its long-lasting presence in Basque territory. Ludger Mees (2001) points out their shortcomings when it comes to suggesting a plausible interpretation of the phenomenon of violence, as most theories simply do not accommodate the complexity of contemporary Basque history.

Logically, it is the Spanish academia that has most intensely studied terrorist violence in the Basque country, in various branches of research. The oldest interpretation, established in the 1980s and 1990s, focused on the causes leading to the emergence of terrorist violence. Anthropological explanations were often noted, thus making the analyses into rather historicist narratives. Some books made reference to the Millenarian ideology (Aranzadi 2001) of the Basque people or their neo-pagan traditions that include the creation of sacrificial victims (Zulaika 1988). The European context of the 1990s gave way to a more cultural understanding of terrorist violence. It coincided with a new terrorist strategy that unleashed violence onto large sections of the civilian population while Basque radical nationalist youths increased their practice of social terror in the streets.

The academic analysis of those years was sensitive to the new nationalist and genocidal violence of the Balkans, affected by the debate about the responsibilities of the German people in the Holocaust (the 'Goldhagen debate'), and influenced by the theories that dissected nationalism according to moral parameters ('good' civic nationalism and 'bad' ethnic nationalism), all of which impacted upon local analyses of Basque violence. Antonio Elorza (2001) linked terrorist practice to the founding culture of Basque nationalism which was based on a racist and dehumanising interpretation of politics. Mikel Azurmendi (2000) traced this founding culture back to the ethno-Catholic tradition that described the common identity of the Basque people during the sixteenth to eighteenth centuries which was prone to practising 'ethnic' cleansing of heretics, Jews and Gypsies. This culture has come to be compared with that of German Nazism (Varela 2001). At the same time, a local revision of the Irish experience inspired by the works of Connor Cruise O'Brien gave way to successful essays like those of Jon Juaristi (1997, 1999), who discussed the biographical stories that feed Basque nationalism and its practice of violence, as well as the central role of certain emotions, such as melancholy, in their conversion into nationalist discourse.

In addition to studying the causes of violence, academic focus turned in this first phase to the characteristics of the organisations that exercised violence and their strategic evolution. This led academics to unify multiple groups as a single organisation (ETA), when in certain periods (particularly 1974 to 1984) at least two organisations were fighting for this acronym (Garmendia 1979; Jáuregui 1981; Ibarra 1989; Domínguez 1998; Elorza 2001). From a more sociological perspective, researchers have studied the strategic rationale of this violence and its evolution in the face of political disputes with the state and with the autonomous institutions that were eroding its legitimacy as an organisation (Sánchez-Cuenca 2009, 2001). Meanwhile, in the past decade, the field of political science has produced various studies of the strategies of ETA from a quantitative point of view (Argomaniz and Vidal-Díez 2015; De la Calle 2007; Pestana *et al.* 2006; Sánchez-Cuenca 2007). They have also examined the relationship between Basque public opinion and terrorism (Criado 2011; De la Calle and Sánchez-Cuenca 2013; Martínez-Herrera 2009).

A second phase of studies emerged in the 1990s and focused fundamentally on the 'radical milieu' that was encouraged sociologically, discursively and emotionally by terrorist practice. It is an area that has received little attention from the social theory of terrorism, as Peter Waldmann (2008) points out, and falls within the 'radicalisation studies' that examine the 'root causes' of terrorism. These studies were also very much conditioned by the new cycle of violence which began in the 1990s. They studied the organisation and strategy of the conglomerate of associations, parties and groups that made up the 'Basque Movement for National Liberation' led by ETA (Mata 1993). They located the political action of this movement and its terrorist practice in the classical revolutionary repertoire of the European ultra-left following May 1968 (Bullain 2011) and synthesised the historical trajectory of this radicalised community and the formation of its warlike and sacralising political discourse (Muro 2008).

Certain interpretations also questioned the social discourse of this violence by suggesting that the perpetrators came from middle-class backgrounds and the towns, which barely suffered from social conflict or from an unequal distribution of work and capital, as demonstrated by Jan Mansvelt Beck (2005). An authentic 'welfare terrorism' was practised by well-off social sectors ideally positioned for the distribution of resources and goods generated by the social state (Aulestia 1993, 1998). In contrast, Gaizka Fernández (2013) developed a novel political history of the minority branch of this nationalism (represented by Euskadiko Ezkerra and its armed side, ETA-PM) and how it implemented a democratic system to address the complexity of this world from the beginning.

More recently these studies have been complemented by cultural interpretations that highlight the significance of religion and secularisation, as pointed out by Joseba Zulaika (1988) in a ground-breaking manner. Izaskun Sáez de la Fuente (2002) has underlined the importance of this secularising phenomenon at the end of the twentieth century and its consequences for local sectors of the ultra-left coming from ultra-Catholic family backgrounds (Catholic traditionalism and Basque nationalism). Her theory is that secularisation drove the transformation of radical Basque nationalism into a substitute religion. Jesus Casquete (2009a) placed the religious variable in more political terrain, taking the long debate on fascism as a political religion and applying it to the 'radical milieu' of ETA. From there he formed his interpretation of radical Basque nationalism as a political religion fed by the mournful and warlike worship of its martyrs (dead or imprisoned terrorists) and by a commemorative ritual that exalts violence in the name of the nation. The canonisation of the dead terrorist had been underlined by Begoña Aretxaga (1988) and the importance of 'war memories' had also been underlined by Diego Muro (2009). This interaction between politics, social movements, totalitarianism and patriotic consecration of violence has been examined by Raúl López and Gaizka Fernández (2012) and by Raúl López (2013). The role that the practice of violence has played in this community has led some to refer to an authentic 'community of violence' (Molina forthcoming) or a 'community of death' (Casquete 2009b).

A third line of research has gradually formed in the past few years regarding the victims of terrorism, figures who were unknown until recently and whose role has been emphasised in parallel with their public visibility and growing political influence centred on the institutions to which they belong (Pérez 2010).

Progress has been made in defining many things; who these victims were and what identity they were assigned by their killers (Alonso *et al.* 2010; De la Calle and Sánchez-Cuenca 2004; Sánchez-Cuenca and Calleja 2006; Fernández and López 2012; Llera and Leonisio 2015); the individual and collective trauma brought on by the terrorist act and its difficult palliative treatment by the rule of law (Baca *et al.* 2012; Martín-Peña *et al.* 2015); the victimising framework generated by the social discourses and practices of radical Basque nationalism, which normalised practices of violence like the 'spiral of silence' and the transfer of guilt from the perpetrators to the victims (Domínguez 2003; Spencer and Croucher 2008; Martínez de Murguia 2001); the stigmatisation of the victims and their exclusion as moral subjects (Prieto 2011; Martín-Peña *et al.* 2011); social fear and indifference to the suffering experienced by a large part of Basque society (Calleja 2006; Santos 2009; Arteta 2010); the legitimising discourses and narratives of violence, fundamentally linked to references to national identity and presented by various social and political figures (Alonso 2009, 2010; Varela-Rey *et al.* 2013; Molina 2015); and the reflection of the normalisation of violence in civil society and later pacifist responses (Funes 1998).

Another emerging area of research in the wake of the increasing visibility of this collective, as shown by the work of Rafael Leonisio (2013), has been the examination of the collective memory of terrorism in the Basque country, its treatment of the victims, and the social function of reflecting upon the traumatic past. This issue has been pushed forward as a result of the end of terrorist violence in 2011 and subsequent political strategies that mostly favoured the construction of 'inclusive' memories, thus blurring the responsibilities for terrorist violence and of those who practised or sympathised with it (Mate 2008; Etxeberria 2010; Castells 2013; Castells and Molina 2013; Arregui 2015).

An interesting initiative has been the launch of the only database specialising in the Basque terrorist phenomenon and its literature in Spanish and Basque (with an upcoming version in English), led by historian Raúl López and the Instituto de Historia Social Valentín de Foronda of the UPV-EHU: www.arovite. com. Notable gaps in knowledge may be noted which have also been indicated in the pioneering historiographical review by Raúl López (2015). First, in the area of comparison, there is a lack of empirical analyses that place Basque terrorism in an international context beyond the recurrent comparison with the case of Northern Ireland. Second, in the quantitative sense, the total number of deceased victims is still under discussion and varies substantially across different statistical studies and databases. Added to all of this is the absence of a clear assessment of the number of those who were injured or mutilated. The same situation applies to the economic dimension of the terrorist phenomenon, where there is a lack of studies on the systematic practice of blackmailing businesspeople, athletes and professionals, and studies of the havoc wreaked on public and private property. When it comes to quantifying, the number of individuals who were forced into exile to escape blackmail or other threats is also unknown. It varies between several hundred and several thousand people, as José M. Calleja (2009) points out. Finally, a third gap is the study of the perpetrators of violence. While the victims have been coming to light as subjects of research, the identity of those who caused their suffering, the perpetrators, still remains obscure. This is typical of terrorism research at a general level and even more understandable in the Basque case, due to the normalisation of discourses and narratives that celebrate the perpetrators. One exception is Fernando Reinares (2001, 2004) and another, from a gender perspective, is Carry Hamilton (2007), as well as the no less scholarly study by Miren Alcedo (1996).

The research compiled in this book brings together the most representative of the studies listed while also covering some of the remaining analytical gaps. It presents the first English-language synthesis of Basque nationalist terrorism, its causes, historical circumstances, evolution and consequences. Furthermore, the book fulfils another critical purpose: to place this phenomenon within international debate. International contributions have repeatedly taken refuge in a very clichéd reading of Basque violence based on an ethno-historicist narrative symbolised by the reiterated introductory excursus to the ancient roots of the Basque people and their language. These narratives are fed by a romantic image updated during the Spanish Civil War of 1936 to 1939, as Francisco J. Caspistegui (Chapter 11) demonstrates. Here, we have tried to distance ourselves from this type of 'exercises in style' that tend to insert ethnic fiction into scientific analysis (there is nothing more fictitious than a primordial people and an ancient language claiming to symbolise it). In the face of these narratives 'captivated by the romance of the Basques' (Tremlett 2008, 259), this book provides more complex keys in accordance with four research questions listed in the introduction, which we believe facilitate the placement of the phenomenon of Basque political violence within an international theoretical and historical context: (1) Are democracies more able to deal with terrorism than are autocracies? (2) Does terrorism work in liberal societies? (3) When do terrorist groups end? and (4) What are the consequences of political violence?

The first three questions inform the chapters of the book contained in Part I and II. These contributions suggest that terrorism emerged in the Basque Country as the political response of a new generation of nationalists, who were searching for their place in a new society transformed by a social change that they perceived as a nationalist attack. Faced with the aforementioned ethno-historicist narratives of a secular problem or conflict between the Basque people and the Spanish state, Gaizka Fernández (Chapter 1) and Javier Gómez (Chapter 6) suggest that violence was (and has been) an option freely chosen by a minority of radicalised youth, with whom a substantial part of Basque society sympathised due to their particular identity and ideology. Neither the state violence of the Francoist dictatorship nor its centralist cultural policies solely explain the insurgent violence and its consequent murders since 1968. Fernández and Gómez indicate that the particular circumstances of the Basque nationalist community explain how a new generation opted for political violence. These circumstances are: the memory of victimisation in the Civil War and the narrative of identity which it fed, prone to resentment and to all-encompassing dichotomised approaches (us/them); interest in downplaying any benevolent treatment received from the dictatorship (relative to other losers of the Spanish Civil War such as left-wing workers or liberals); the seduction of a new generation of nationalists born after the Spanish Civil War through revolutionary and anti-colonialist messages in the 1960s and 1970s; and the apocalyptic perception generated by social change in this community, adding to an anguished identity and an aggressive view of General Franco's autocratic regime.

The origin of the insurgent violence is multifaceted. The most plausible explanation of its continuity during the transition to democracy in the late 1970s lies in a weakened dictatorship and its repressive response. The fact that terrorism became more established during this political process and acquired an operational ability and social backing that were stronger than that of the autocratic period allows for a negative answer to the question of whether democracies are more able than dictatorships to combat terrorism, and a positive answer to the second question: terrorism can work and survive in liberal systems. The Spanish case shows that democracy is not, in itself, a political system better equipped to combat terrorist insurgency than autocracy. In fact, the political stability of a democracy may be more affected than that of an autocracy (the assassination of Carrero Blanco in 1973 did not lead to any sort of crisis in Franco's dictatorship, whereas in the attempted military coup of 1981 against the new democratic regime the influence of Basque terrorism was fundamental). As a result, terrorism can flourish and reproduce itself more easily in liberal open societies than in autocratic closed ones. Such findings are confirmed by Diego Muro (Chapter 2), José A. Pérez (Chapter 3) and Óscar Jaime-Jiménez (Chapter 4), who discuss how the diverse and occasionally illegitimate responses of the state reinforced its delegitimisation among broad sectors of Basque society. At the same time, these responses facilitated the competitive legitimacy of terrorist violence, which resonated with features of identity that fitted the discourse and imagery of Basque nationalism.

Pérez and Muro also show how vigilante violence, state terrorism and the generalised practice of torturing detainees strengthened the 'radical milieu' that in the 1970s and 1980s provided personnel and resources to various terrorist organisations and, from the mid-1980s, to the reunified ETA. Added to this was the conversion of terrorist violence into a provider of meaning for this political community through the ritual and mobilising repertoire unravelled by Jesús Casquete (Chapter 5). A state undergoing a process of democratisation ended up tolerating and normalising these ritual demonstrations as legitimate, which led to great difficulty in stopping them later on, as Muro and Jaime-Jiménez suggest.

The first four chapters aim to provide an answer to the first two questions raised in the analysis of this book: that a democracy may have more difficulty than an autocracy in combating insurgent challenges of a terrorist nature, and that terrorism reproduces itself easily in a democracy. Terrorism can feed off of the contradictions and weaknesses of an open society which, when still under construction, is not experienced enough to select a balanced response. But the factor of social ties is also essential to the survival of terrorism. Basque nationalist terrorism was turned into a legitimate political arrangement in the eyes of a large percentage of Basque society, for reasons of ideological agreement or iden-tification with those who practised it. Terrorist violence sets off a tautological discursive mechanism, very characteristic of nationalism, which provides logic to the narratives of the nation. These narratives, in turn, give justification for the violence. Out of these circumstances in the 1980s and 1990s came the myth of ETA's 'invincibility', addressed by Muro and Jaime-Jiménez in their chapters.

This mythologising of ETA gave way to simplistic political interpretations, like the systematic claim in the 1980s and 1990s of Basque self-governing institutions that a horizon of 'peace' could be reached through a 'political negotiation' between the state and the ETA organisation. The 'pacification–normalisation' juxtaposition prevailed during these years through a view of what terrorism really meant in regard to the destruction of democratic culture and of civic and pluralistic liberal principles. The political debate generated by violence moved to spheres in which the nationalism that drove such violence was accepted, because this violence was interpreted as the consequence of a long-standing conflict between the Basque people and the state resulting from the denial of the identity (and sovereign rights) of the former by the latter.

The chapters by Muro and Jaime-Jiménez in Part I of the book also show that the capacity for resistance to terrorism in an open society like that of Spain in the 1980s and 1990s has its limits. The contributions of both authors address the third question on the decline of violence by showing how Basque terrorism began to be defused (and defeated) when the state started to purge its authorit-arian legacy and found ways to neutralise terrorist action without needing to resort to extreme methods. This led to the state questioning the legitimacy of its own counter-terrorist action, even in sensitive areas such as the political and judicial. Both chapters reflect this slow process of ideological rearmament by the liberal state in its struggle against terrorism, especially in the 1990s and at the start of the twenty-first century. Part of this process was accompanied by tougher laws, the separation of terrorist prisoners from each other, and the expulsion from parliamentary politics of parties linked to ETA, along with improvements in the police's technical capabilities and international collaboration. Successive blows to the terrorist network, enumerated by Jaime-Jiménez, undermined the narrative of invincibility that fuelled their charismatic power. But the focal point of the final struggle was the destruction of the 'radical milieu' that supported the violence by a shrewd and daring chain of police, judicial and political actions. These actions managed to put outside of the law political parties backed by close to 200,000 Basque voters, who unexpectedly found themselves deprived of polit-ical representation with no ability to communicate through the mass media.

Curiously, this process took place in a very precise context: one which ETA marked when it extended its selection of victims to the world of politics, the intelligentsia and the judiciary at the beginning of the 1990s. As long as the victims were military or police, the state felt no urge to reconsider its anti-terrorist policy, broaden it to include other more controversial fields like the political or the social, or provide itself with sufficient ideological legitimacy. The way terrorism affected the civil and political fringes of society was essential to it being tackled in an increasingly effective way. A complementary response to the third question is that insurgent terrorism is more adequately combated to the extent that it exceeds its own military imagery, or puts the whole responsibility for its actions on uniformed victims. That is when the political class develops real awareness of its danger and acts together to draw on the multiple resources of the rule of law to fight back. But as long as the political class perceives such terrorism as a distant or localised phenomenon, and assimilates it according to overall narratives that appeal to identity or social factors, its actions are less effective.

The previously mentioned chapters by Pérez, Muro and Gómez, along with the rest of the contributions that make up Parts II and III, help answer the fourth and last question by listing consequences of terrorist violence that go far beyond the assassinations, the devastation, and the political debate on how to fight and defeat terrorism. They touch on hazier areas: illegitimate counter-terrorism, or the temptation to employ methods contrary to the law, along with the political crisis that this generates; the exploitation of violence to obtain political advantages, in which all Basque political groups took part but especially the nationalists; the creation of a climate of opinion and public discourses prone to legitimising the violence and normalising it as part of democratic life; and the creation of a national narrative that values violence as meaningful, resulting in an abstract placing of perpetrators and victims in historicist frames or as victimised representations of the Basque people.

With regard to the fourth question on the consequences of violence, we have already mentioned that in the 1970s and 1980s terrorism drove a weak state suffering from low symbolic self-esteem to resort to answers typical of autocracies (state terrorism, denial of prisoners' rights, torture, etc.). This contributed to the strengthening of the social base of ETA and to undermining further the legitimacy of the security response of the state. In reaction to this dubious and on occasions brutal response by the state, a sense of social awareness spread through the Basque Country that was sympathetic to or at least understanding of this violence. Rafael Leonisio and Raúl López (Chapter 8) delve into the social acceptance of this violence and its reflection in studies of public opinion. At the same time, they point out that one of its most palpable consequences is the establishment of an ingrained social fear of showing disagreement with the nationalist discourse and imagery that drove this violence. Another consequence of terrorism when it is supported by a broad social base is the demobilisation of the society that experiences it, as reflected in the late social reaction to ETA's violent crimes.

The understanding of terrorist violence and its political exploitation has its roots in a very widespread discourse based on the story of two historically violent forces allegedly in conflict: Spain and the Basque Country. This is the general notion that fed ideographic meta-narratives like the 'Basque problem' or later the 'Basque conflict', as outlined by Martín Alonso and Fernando Molina (Chapter 9). With these metanarratives, violence gave meaning to the whole of the nationalist community (not just its radical sector) by providing veracity to its stories of identity and its national narrative. This acceptance has generated, as

Luis Castells and Antonio Rivera (Chapter 10) reflect, a collective memory in which a systematic attempt is made to blur the terrorist nature of this violence and to put its victims on a par with those of the other 'violence' considered to be its equivalent: that of the state terrorism, and has, with respect to this question about the consequences of violence, a perverse effect on how the media, the political class and academia interpret it.

The contributions of Leonisio and López, Alonso and Molina, and Castells and Rivera confirm that terrorist practice constitutes, in line with what was stated in the introduction, an 'act of communication' that facilitates the social assimilation of the perceived identity of the perpetrators by granting it the significance supplied by killing in its name. This act of communication favours a blurring of the perpetrator as a social subject and obscures any interpretation of his actions according to 'decision-making' variables in order to hide his personal identity in the narrative of a victimised people, as Gómez shows of the democratic period. This 'act' also motivates a blurring of the material consequences of his action, his victims, who lose any identity other than the one assigned by the perpetrator according to his 'categorical killing' (Bauman 1995, 203). The victim's individual experience is replaced with the experience attributed to the national collective in whose name the murder has been committed. Hence the slowness with which the victims of Basque nationalist terrorism were identified, as well as the change of direction that this process of public visibility has generated in the social and political treatment of the terrorist phenomenon. This is in contrast to the Northern Irish case, as Javier Argomaniz explains in Chapter 7.

As a result, terrorism generates very subtle consequences that affect how a society names its actions and dissects its subjects and objects. Societies that experience terrorism of a communal nature, based on an identity shared by a substantial part of its population, are driven to normalise the violence in order to integrate the citizens that perpetrated it or protected its perpetrators (relatives, neighbours, friends or work colleagues), according to strategies of public and political behaviour examined by Leonisio and López.

This normalisation leads to the public promotion of a comfortable memory and of a narrative that integrates it into the national fabric. The contributions of Alonso and Molina, and Castells and Rivera, show that both memory and the narrative of identity which it establishes are based on a political language that blurs individual responsibilities and favours the inclusion of the violent phenomenon in the suffering of the people in whose name it had been committed (once again, linking violence with nation). The media and the political establishment then agree on a single way of remembering, founded in language that appeals to the multiple aspects of the violence and, consequently, of its victims and their suffering. This allows for the perpetuation of a representation that takes responsibility away from terrorism by equating it with other types of violence such as illegitimate state violence.

As a result, terrorism does not end once the organisation that practises it drops its weapons, but continues through its consequences into the realm of narrative identity. Terrorism continues to exist through its transformation into collective memory, which is established according to the usual hegemonic social framework (defined by Basque nationalism), making it a political tool that is just as effective in remembrance as when it was a political practice. It is then that violence, existing side by side with politics, is dissolved into the latter like a memory manipulated by each political figure, and runs its course as the ultimate consequence of that primal moment when a group of citizens made a conscious decision to kill in the name of the homeland.

Bibliography

Alcedo, Miren (1996) *Militar en ETA. Historias de vida y muerte*. San Sebastián: Haramburu.

Alonso, Martín (2009) 'El Síndrome de Al-Andalus: relatos de expoliación y violencia política'. In *Comunidades de Muerte*, ed. Jesús Casquete, 19–54. Barcelona: Anthropos.

Alonso, Martín (2010) 'Estructuras retóricas de la violencia política'. In *Violencia política. Historia, memoria y víctimas*, eds Antonio Rivera and Carlos Carnicero, 118–148. Madrid: Maia.

Alonso, Rogelio (2011) 'The international dimension of ETA's terrorism and the internationalization of the conflict of the Basque Country'. *Democracy and Security* 7: 184–204.

Alonso, Rogelio, Florencio Domínguez and Marcos García (2010) *Vidas rotas. Historia de los hombres, mujeres y niños víctimas de ETA*. Madrid: Espasa.

Aranzadi, Juan (2001) *El escudo de Arquíloco. Sobre mesías, mártires y terroristas*. Vol. I, *Sangre vasca*. Madrid: Antonio Machado.

Aretxaga, Begoña (1988) *Los funerales en el nacionalismo radical vasco. Ensayo antropológico*. San Sebastián: Baroja.

Aretxaga, Begoña (2005) *States of Terror*. Reno: Center for Basque Studies.

Argomaniz, Javier and Alberto Vidal-Díez (2015) 'Examining deterrence and backlash effects in counter-terrorism: The case of ETA'. *Terrorism and Political Violence* 27: 160–181.

Arregui, Joseba (2015) *El terror de ETA. La narrativa de las víctimas*. Madrid: Tecnos.

Arteta, Aurelio (2010) *Mal consentido. La complicidad del espectador indiferente*. Madrid: Alianza.

Aulestia, Kepa (1993) *Días de viento sur. La violencia en Euskadi*. Barcelona: Antártida-Empúries.

Aulestia, Kepa (1998) *HB: crónica de un delirio*. Madrid: Temas de Hoy.

Azurmendi, Mikel (2000) *Y se limpie aquella tierra. Limpieza étnica y de sangre en el País Vasco*. Madrid: Taurus.

Baca, Enrique, María M. Pérez-Rodríguez, María M. and María M., Cabanas, María M. (2012) 'Short- and long-term effects of terrorist attacks in Spain'. In *The Trauma of Terrorism. Sharing Knowledge and Shared Care*, eds Yael Danieli, Daniel Brom and Joe Sils, 157–170. New York: Routledge.

Bauman, Zygmunt (1995) *Life in Fragments: Essays on Postmodern Morality*. London: Sage.

Bullain, Iñigo (2011) *Revolucionarismo patriotico. El Movimiento de Liberación Nacional Vasco (MLNV). Origen, Ideología, Estrategia y Organización*. Madrid: Tecnos.

Burleigh, Michael (2008) *Blood and Rage. A Cultural History of Terrorism*. New York: Harper Collins.

Calleja, José María (2006) *Algo habrá hecho. Odio, muerte y miedo en Euskadi.* Madrid: Espasa.

Calleja, Jose María (2009) *La diáspora vasca. Historia de los condenados a irse de Euskadi por culpa del terrorismo de ETA.* Madrid: Aguilar.

Casquete, Jesús (2009a) *En el nombre de Euskal Herria. La religión política del nacionalismo vasco radical.* Madrid: Tecnos.

Casquete, Jesús (ed.) (2009b) *Comunidades de muerte.* Barcelona: Anthropos.

Castells, Luis (2013) 'La historia del terrorismo en Euskadi: ¿entre la necesidad y el apremio?' In *Construyendo memorias. Relatos históricos para Euskadi después del terrorismo*, eds José María Ortiz de Orruño and José Antonio Pérez, 210–244. Madrid: La Catarata.

Castells, Luis and Fernando Molina (2013) 'Bajo la sombra de Vichy: el relato del pasado reciente en la Euskadi actual'. *Ayer* 89: 215–227.

Criado, Henar (2011) 'Bullets and votes: Public opinion and terrorist strategies'. *Journal of Peace Research* 48: 497–508.

De la Calle, Luis (2007) 'Fighting for local control: Street violence in the Basque Country'. *International Studies Quarterly* 51: 431–455.

De la Calle, Luis and Ignacio Sánchez-Cuenca (2004) 'La selección de víctimas de ETA'. *Revista Española de Ciencia Política* 10: 53–79.

De la Calle, Luis and Ignacio Sánchez-Cuenca (2013) 'Killing and voting in the Basque Country: An exploration of the electoral link between ETA and its political branch'. *Terrorism and Political Violence* 25: 94–112.

Domínguez, Florencio (1998) *ETA: estrategia organizativa y actuaciones, 1978–1992.* Bilbao: UPV.

Domínguez, Florencio (2003) *Las raíces del miedo. Euskadi, una sociedad atemorizada.* Madrid: Aguilar.

Elorza, Antonio (2001) 'Vascos guerreros'. In *La historia de ETA*, ed. Antonio Elorza, 13–80. Madrid: Temas de Hoy.

Etxeberria, Xabier (2010) 'Historización de la memoria de las víctimas del terrorismo'. In *Violencia política. Historia, Memoria y Víctimas*, ed. Antonio Rivera and Carlos Carnicero, 287–316. Madrid: Maia.

Fernández, Gaizka (2013) *Héroes, heterodoxos y traidores. Historia de Euskadiko Ezkerra, 1974–1994.* Madrid: Tecnos.

Funes, María J. (1998) *La salida del silencio: movilizaciones por la paz en Euskadi, 1986–1998.* Madrid: Akal.

Garmendia, José María (1979) *Historia de ETA.* San Sebastián: Haramburu.

Hamilton, Carry (2007) *Women and ETA. The Gender Politics of Radical Basque Nationalism.* Manchester: Manchester University Press.

Ibarra, Pedro (1989) *La evolución estratégica de ETA. De la 'guerra revolucionaria' (1963) hasta después de la tregua (1989).* San Sebastián: Kriselu.

Irvin, Cynthia (1999) *Militant Nationalism. Between Movement and Party in Ireland and the Basque Country.* Minneapolis and London: University of Minnesota Press.

Jáuregui, Gurutz (1981) *Ideología y estrategia política de ETA. Análisis de su evolución entre 1959 y 1968.* Madrid: Siglo XXI.

Juaristi, Jon (1997) *El bucle melancólico. Historias de nacionalistas vascos.* Madrid: Espasa.

Juaristi, Jon (1999) *Sacra Némesis. Nuevas historias de nacionalistas vascos.* Madrid: Espasa.

Leonisio, Rafael (2013) 'Las víctimas del terrorismo en el discurso de los partidos políticos vascos: una aproximación cuantitativa (1980–2011)'. *Revista de Estudios Políticos* 161: 13–40.

Llera, Francisco and Rafael Leonisio (2015) 'Los secuestros de ETA y sus organizaciones afines, 1970–1997: una base de datos'. *Revista Española de Ciencia Política* 37: 141–160.

López, Raúl (2013) 'Lo puro frente a lo contaminado. La absolutización política en la Euskadi de la transición'. In *Por surcos y calles. Movilización social e identidades en Galicia y el País Vasco, 1968–1980*, ed. Damián Lanero, 173–211. Madrid: La Catarata.

López, Raúl (2015) *Informe Foronda. Los efectos del terrorismo en la sociedad vasca*. Madrid: La Catarata.

López, Raúl and Gaizka Fernández (2012) *Sangre, votos y manifestaciones. ETA y el nacionalismo vasco radical, 1958–2011*. Madrid: Tecnos.

Mansvelt Beck, Jan (2005) *Territory and Terror. Conflicting Nationalisms in the Basque Country*. New York: Routledge.

Martín-Peña, Javier and Susan Opotow (2011) 'The legitimization of political violence: A case study of ETA in the Basque Country'. *Peace and Conflict* 17: 132–150.

Martín-Peña, Javier, Álvaro Rodríguez-Carballeira and Susan Opotow (2011) 'Amenazados y víctimas del entramado de ETA en Euskadi: un estudio desde la teoría de la exclusión moral'. *Revista de Psicología Social* 26: 177–190.

Martín-Peña, Javier, Álvaro Rodríguez-Carballeira, Ana Varela-Rey, Jordi Escartín and Omar Saldaña (2015) 'Victims of ETA in the Basque Country: Their experience of terrorist threats'. In *International Perspectives on Terrorist Victimisation. An Interdisciplinary Approach*, eds Javier Argomaniz and Orla Lynch, 49–75. Basingstoke: Palgrave.

Martínez de Murguia, Beatriz (2001) *Descifrando cenizas. Persecución e indiferencia*. Barcelona: Paidós.

Martínez-Herrera, Enric (2009) 'Receptividad y extremismo nacionalista en el País Vasco (1977–2007): una evaluación multivariante'. *Revista Española de Investigaciones Sociológicas* 125: 81–113.

Mata, José Manuel (1993) *El nacionalismo vasco radical. Discurso, organización y expresiones*. Bilbao: UPV.

Mate, Reyes (2008) *Justicia de las víctimas. Terrorismo, memoria, reconciliación*. Barcelona: Anthropos.

Mees, Ludger (2001) 'Between votes and bullets.Conflicting ethnic identities in the Basque Country'. *Ethnic and Racial Studies* 24: 798–827.

Mees, Ludger (2003) *Nationalism, Violence and Democracy. The Basque Clash of Identities*. Basingstoke: Palgrave.

Miley, Thomas J. (2007) 'Against the thesis of the "civic nation". The case of Catalonia in contemporary Spain'. *Nationalism and Ethnic Politics* 13: 1–37.

Molina, Fernando (2015) 'El conflicto vasco. Relatos de historia, memoria y nación'. In *El peso de la identidad. Mitos y ritos de la historia vasca*, eds Fernando Molina and José Antonio Pérez, 181–223. Madrid: Marcial Pons.

Molina, Fernando (forthcoming) 'Violencia en comunidad. El terrorismo nacionalista y la política del miedo'. In *Euskadi, 1960–2011. Dictadura, Transición y Democracia*, eds Juan Pablo Fusi and José Antonio Pérez. Madrid: Biblioteca Nueva.

Muro, Diego (2008) *Ethnicity and Violence. The Case of Basque Radical Nationalism*. New York: Routledge.

Muro, Diego (2009) 'The politics of war memory in radical Basque nationalism'. *Ethnic and Racial Studies* 32: 659–678.

Pérez, José Antonio (2010) 'La memoria de las víctimas del terrorismo en el País Vasco. Un proyecto en marcha'. In *Violencia política. Historia, memoria y víctimas*, eds Antonio Rivera and Carlos Carnicero, 317–351. Madrid: Maia.

Pestana, Carlos, José Passos and Luis Gil-Alana (2006) 'The timing of ETA terrorist attacks'. *Journal of Policy Modeling* 28: 335–346.

Prieto, Jesús (2011) *Marcados por el estigma. Terrorismo y víctimas en Euskadi*. San Sebastián: Hiria.

Reinares, Fernando (2001) *Patriotas de la muerte. Quienes han militado en ETA y por qué*. Madrid: Taurus.

Reinares, Fernando (2004) 'Who are the terrorists? Analyzing changes in sociological profile among members of ETA'. *Studies in Conflict and Terrorism* 27: 465–488.

Sáez de la Fuente, Izaskun (2002) *El MLNV: una religión de sustitución*. Bilbao: Desclée de Brower.

Sánchez-Cuenca, Ignacio (2001) *ETA contra el Estado. Las estrategias del terrorismo*. Barcelona: Tusquets.

Sánchez-Cuenca, Ignacio (2007) 'The dynamics of nationalist terrorism: ETA and the IRA'. *Terrorism and Political Violence* 19: 289–306.

Sánchez-Cuenca, Ignacio (2009) 'Explaining temporal variation in the lethality of ETA'. *Revista Internacional de Sociología* 67: 609–629.

Sánchez-Cuenca, Ignacio and José María Calleja (2006) *La derrota de ETA. De la primera a la última víctima*. Madrid: Adhara.

Santos, Doroteo (2009) *El miedo social en el País Vasco en relación con el terrorismo de ETA*. Bilbao: Bakeaz.

Spencer, Anthony T. and Stephen M. Croucher (2008) 'Basque nationalism and the spiral of silence: An analysis of public perceptions of ETA in Spain and France'. *International Communication Gazette* 70: 137–153.

Sullivan, John (1988) *ETA and Basque Nationalism: The Fight for Euskadi, 1895–1986*. New York: Routledge.

Tremlett, Gilles (2008) *Ghosts of Spain. Travels through Spain and its Silent Past*. New York: Walker and Company.

Varela, José (2001) *Contra la violencia. A propósito del nacional-socialismo alemán y del vasco*. Alegría: Hiria.

Varela-Rey, Ana, Álvaro Rodríguez-Carballeira and Javier Martín-Peña (2013) 'Psychosocial analysis of ETA's violence legitimation discourse'. *Revista de Psicología Social* 28: 85–97.

Waldmann, Peter (1997) *Radicalismo étnico. Análisis comparado de las causas y efectos en conflictos étnicos violentos*. Madrid: Akal.

Waldmann, Peter (2008) 'The radical milieu. The under-investigated relationship between terrorists and sympathetic communities'. *Perspectives on Terrorism* 2: 25–27.

Whitfield, Teresa (2014) *Endgame for ETA. Elusive Peace in the Basque Country*. New York: Hurst & Co.

Wieviorka, Michel (1997) 'ETA and Basque political violence'. In *The Legitimation of Violence*, ed. David E. Apter, 293–348. London: Macmillan.

Zulaika, Joseba (1988) *Basque Violence. Metaphor and Sacrament*. Reno: University of Nevada Press.

Index

Page numbers in *italics* denote tables, those in **bold** denote figures.